Rowland Parker was born in 1912 in North Lincolnshire. His father, grandfather and great-grandfather were all farmers and his youth was spent in the country. He was educated at Louth Grammar School, won a scholarship to Nottingham University and then trained as a teacher. In 1935 he joined the staff of what was then the Central School, Cambridge, and, except for the war, remained there until his retirement in 1972. He enlisted in the Royal Artillery in 1940, and served in North Africa, Italy, Egypt, Syria and Palestine, where he began to take an interest in archaeology and history. Since 1946 he has lived in Foxton, increasingly absorbing himself in the raw material of this book. He has also written *Cottage on the Green* and *On the Road*. He is married and has one adopted daughter.

ROWLAND PARKER

The Common Stream

PALADIN
GRAFTON BOOKS
A Division of the Collins Publishing Group

LONDON GLASGOW
TORONTO SYDNEY AUCKLAND

Paladin
Grafton Books
A Division of the Collins Publishing Group
8 Grafton Street, London W1X 3LA

Published in Paladin Books 1976
Reprinted 1976, 1978, 1979, 1982, 1986

First published in Great Britain by
William Collins Sons & Co Ltd 1975

ISBN 0-586-08253-0

Printed and bound in Great Britain by
Hazell Watson & Viney Limited,
Aylesbury, Bucks

Set in Monotype Ehrhardt

Contents

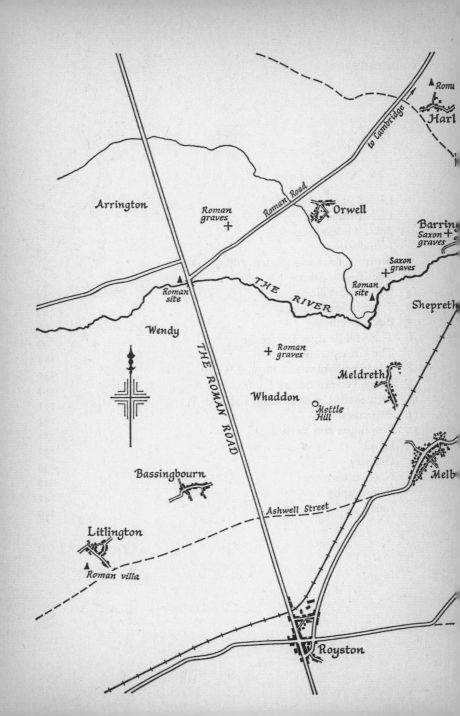

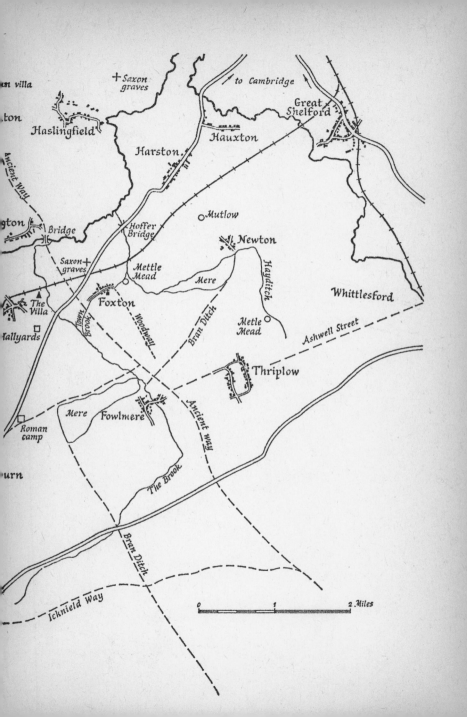

Illustrations

Maps

Acknowledgements

One cannot spend thirteen years on researching and writing a book without becoming indebted to a lot of people for help, advice and encouragement. The hesitation with which I approach the duty of thanking them is caused by doubt as to my ability to do it adequately, certainty that I shall have forgotten some to whom thanks are due, and uncertainty as to the order in which I ought to mention those whom I have remembered. Alphabetical order would seem to be the least invidious method. But that would place Philip Ziegler last on the list, which will not do, for his wise and tactful suggestions have resulted in the revision of large sections of six chapters of the book. Derek Parker, George Ewart Evans and several others have helped in a similar way. Without their help the book would not have reached the stage of publication, and I marvel at the patience shown by those kind people towards an amateur writer so inexpert that he had to write the book three or four times before getting it right.

If time spent and trouble taken on my behalf were the deciding factors in determining precedence, then first place on the list would go to Mr J. M. Farrar, the Cambridgeshire County Archivist, and his staff at the County Record Office. At frequent intervals over a period of ten years they kept me supplied with documents, copies of documents, maps, reference-books, etc., far too numerous to be listed in detail, without which I could not have begun my work, far less finished it.

It would not have been inappropriate to have followed the time-honoured practice of putting ladies first. Miss H. E. Peek, Keeper of the University Archives, kindly made available to me copies of the wills and probate inventories in her custody, and her former assistant, Miss M. E. Raven, performed feats of weight-lifting worthy of much more than this brief mention. Mrs D. Owen, Ely Diocesan Archivist at the University Library, saved me much time and gave herself no little trouble for me. Without her I should not have known of the volume of Overseers and Churchwardens Accounts which provided the material for a whole chapter of the book.

The chapter on the medieval village was made possible by courtesy of the Master and Fellows of Trinity College, Cambridge, through the kind co-operation of Mr J. G. Camps and Philip Gaskell. To them, as to the Trustees of the British Museum, the Principal Probate Registry and the Historical Manuscripts Commission, I tender my warmest thanks.

I have had more good fortune than I deserved both as regards the nature and the timing of much of the help received. Dr Martin Henig, of the Oxford Institute of Archaeology, produced a masterly report on the Shepreth gem just at the moment when such encouragement was badly needed. My good friend Peter Layng supplied me with transcripts of Parish Registers when they were the very thing I wanted.

Then there are all those people in and around the village who tolerated, even encouraged, my prying and questioning. Whilst thanking them all most heartily, I will mention but two: Mr Walter Stock, whose long memory was an invaluable asset, and Joe Cox, from whose photographs most of my sketches were made.

It is inevitable that a book like this, involving so much translation, transcription, deciphering and interpretation, should contain some errors. I hope that they are not too numerous or too noticeable, and accept the sole responsibility for them.

R. P.

Cottage on the Green
Foxton
April 1974

Let not ambition mock their useful toil,
Their homely joys and destiny obscure;
Nor Grandeur hear, with a disdainful smile
The short and simple annals of the poor.

THOMAS GRAY, 1750

Introduction

This is a true story with a triple theme. It tells firstly of a brook or stream, 'common' in the sense that it is but one of a thousand such streams which spring from the folds of hills everywhere, and especially in the chalklands of East Anglia. This particular stream rises a few miles to the south-east of Royston and meanders gently on a mere ten-mile course to join the river Rhee. In order to find it today you would need a large-scale map, and you would need to know exactly where to look for it, because the stream has no name, nor ever had, other than 'Brook'. Even the local inhabitants are for the most part unaware of its existence. And having found it, you also would have some doubts; for in places the stream has been filled in and it flows, if at all, in an underground pipe. In other places it is so overgrown with nettles and reeds and tall grasses that you might well fall into it before you knew that it was there. In yet other places, especially in a dry season, you could walk dryfoot along its bed for long stretches, as do the hares and pheasants. Only the willows mark its course with any real prominence, and even they, stricken by age and neglect, are fast disappearing; for no one, it seems, ever thinks of replanting a willow. How can such a miserable stream, such a symbol of neglect and decay, have significance enough to merit its role as one of the principal threads in my story?

Part of its significance lies in that very fact, that it *is* a symbol of decay. Part lies in the very distant past, long before that story begins, when every spring of water and every stream born of those springs was the object of veneration by groups of primitive men who knew, as surely and instinctively as the birds and beasts still know, though most men have forgotten, that the water of those springs and streams was Life itself. The unfailing flow of that precious commodity, over which man had no control, could only be the bounteous manifestation of a divine power, indeed the very abode of divinity itself. And so the mind of man peopled the springs and streams with spirits, nymphs, goddesses – always female, for the notion of fertility was inevitably linked with the perennial flow of water. Then later, when man ceased to wander, developed the art of living always in one place, that place was determined by one of those springs or streams. Every village, not just in East Anglia but all over the world, owed its original location in part at least to the proximity or availability of water. Nymphs and sprites faded into the background, only vaguely remembered if at all, and considerations of practical common-sense took their place.

As man became more and more settled, and needed to define the area of his settlement, practical considerations found another role for the stream. What better boundary-marker could there be? This aspect of the stream's significance is invisible on the ground today, but clear enough on the map. To the ten miles of our particular stream we must add a further seven miles of contributary streams. Of that total of seventeen miles, well over half constitute either county boundary, between Hertfordshire and Cambridgeshire, or parish boundaries separating the parishes of Reed, Barley, Great Chishill, Melbourn, Thriplow, Fowlmere, Shepreth and Foxton. At about the same time as the stream acquired this secondary role, the word 'common' also acquired a second meaning. It became common in that it belonged to no one in particular, but to everyone in general – everyone, that is, in one particular community. It was in fact the only thing, other than air, sunshine and rain, which was really and truly 'common'.

At least four of the villages listed above owe their existence to this one small stream-complex, and the account of the birth and growth of one of them, Foxton, is the second thread of my story. Rather more than a thread, it is a relatively wide and long expanse of tapestry. Long in that it extends over two thousand years. Wide in the sense that, though I may seem to tell only the story of one small village, I am in reality telling the story of many villages. All over East Anglia, the East Midlands, Central and Southern England – an area extending some eighty miles in all directions with Foxton at its geographical centre – there are hundreds and hundreds of villages. To tell the story of one is, in a way, to tell the story of them all. Of course they had, and still have, their differences and their individual characteristics. But the main stuff of which my tapestry is woven – early settlers, manors, serfdom, freemen, yeomen, buildings, crops, constables, enclosures, etc. – is common to them all. I might have chosen to illustrate my theme from the records of all the villages; had I done so I would have lost in depth and continuity what I gained in width. I might have tried to deal with a hundred villages in the same detailed manner as I have dealt with Foxton and its immediate neighbours; that would have entailed another hundred years or so of research, and I do not think I shall live that long. Moreover, the result would have been not one book but fifty, all very much alike. I chose to write about Foxton because I happen to live there; because, by pure chance, there is a remarkable wealth of documentary material available relating to Foxton; because unique archaeological opportunities in the immediate vicinity have presented themselves, again by pure chance. It so happened that, a few years ago, the river Rhee was properly dredged for the first time in its long history, and the dredger brought to light along with the mud enough relics of the past to fill a small museum. Not every villlage, of course, can boast a Roman villa, and my villa belongs geographically to Shepreth; but, as there were no parish boundaries when Roman villas were built, I have not hesitated to include it in my story. It was not chance which put the villa there; it was that same practical common-sense to which I have already alluded.

The third thread of my discourse which you will find – not always very obviously – interwoven with the others is again 'the common stream'. Here I am using the phrase metaphorically. This is no chronicle of kings and prelates and nobles, though here and there brief mention will perforce be made of some of them. It is the story of the Common Man, of the ordinary men and women who in their countless thousands have trudged through life and then departed from it, leaving little visible trace. That little, multiplied a millionfold, constitutes a large slice of what we call our national heritage. We are all, with few exceptions, descended from those common men. We live in a land which is still largely what they made it – still largely so, despite recent efforts to alter much of it out of all recognition. Those efforts are however succeeding well enough to lend an atmosphere of urgency to a book like this, which seeks to record something of the past before that past wholly disappears. We have inherited the characteristics and temperaments which caused those common men to act as they did. Given the same circumstances, we would have done – would probably still do – what they did. We would almost certainly fail to do what they failed to do, without the knowledge born of their failures. Human nature does not change very much, if at all. You will not be straining imagination far, and I shall have succeeded in my task if, in reading the pages which follow, you sometimes get the impression that you are reading about yourself – or, let us say, about your neighbour.

I said earlier that my story was true. I say it again, with this qualification: there are some parts of my story which cannot be categorically stated to be either true or false. In the early chapters especially there are statements and descriptions which depend upon the accuracy of my interpretation of such evidence as is available. There are instances where the facts may be insufficient to warrant any definite opinion. Where this is the case, I hope I have made it clear. Where I have not written what actually did happen, I have written what I firmly believe, and have good reason to believe, could have happened. I trust that any professional historian who may chance to read this book, and whose opinions are at variance with mine, will forgive me when I plead as excuse that I am not writing 'history', but a story. That is why I have refrained from giving references for every statement which I make, or quoting the views of other writers in order to refute or confirm them. Where it seems desirable I have referred briefly to the sources of my information at the beginning of each chapter, and I had no wish to clutter up the text with notes which the non-historian would probably not trouble to read or verify.

Ask one of the thousands of motorists who travel regularly along the A10 and he will tell you that Foxton is a level-crossing sandwiched between two garages half-way between Royston and Cambridge. Ask one of the residents or intending residents, and you will be told that Foxton is where they have built and are building all those new houses 'just off the A10'. They are right; but ask me, and I will tell you something more. Get away from that traffic roaring along the main road; ignore the barricades of new houses confronting you at the north, east and west approaches – unless you want to buy one – and come with me to the heart of things. Leave your car and walk; otherwise you will be out of the village again in less than two minutes and you will say: 'Yes, I know Foxton – a church and a pub and a few old houses. Very quaint. I love these old villages.'

It isn't 'quaint', you know. It's very ordinary really. Just half a mile of street with houses strung out along it. But take a closer look. Sit for a while on the wooden shelter on the Green and look around; your gaze will take in five centuries of domestic architecture, and do it with pleasure, for this is the prettiest part of the village; one of the prettiest spots in England when the cherry-trees are in blossom. Let your mind wander back over those five centuries, and another five if you can manage it; you will have outstripped human memory, but not human presence. Within a stone's throw of where you sit men have worked and played, bought and sold, drunk and laughed and cursed for those ten centuries and more. Look down the village street, past the conical brick cottage which was once a malthouse, past The Old Black Boy – a pub for two hundred years but a pub no longer – to cottages with whitened walls and roofs of thatch or moss-grown tiles. Then wander along that street. The new bungalows and houses do not clamour for your attention; each seems to know that it is only the latest in a long succession of houses on that self-same spot, and not the last. The south side of the street affords a view of fields on a chalky hill-side. You have only to climb a gate to get into a grass field, though you have a fine view of the huge thatched barn without doing that.[1]

At the road junction you can take in at a glance the school, the chapel, the one and only pub, the Post Office cum shop, and the academic-looking building of the University Tutorial Press; no architectural merit here, just plain workaday utility. But beside you, and beyond along Station Road, are more thatched cottages. Those low broad eaves, leaning walls and squat square chimneys suggest 'Tudor' even to the uninitiated; and Tudor they are, more so even than the plain exterior suggests, for their real attraction is the timber framework visible only on the inside, and not always then. Further on there are more, so obviously restored or in process of restoration that you suspect, rightly, that they are occupied by new-comers to the village, not by families whose forebears have lived here for generations. The church-tower has been visible all the way along the street. The Bury (see illustration on p. 161) is not so easily noticed, and when you do see it you might not guess that an Elizabethan house stands hidden there. You would ask in vain for the 'lord of the manor', but you would see a room once used as court-room of the manor, and cellars once full of manorial ale, on a spot where once stood manorial halls.

Cross the road to the church. Everybody says it is a 'pretty' church, and everybody is right. Most village churches are pretty. This one looks all the prettier for being seen against a background of trees and green fields, and for having as near neighbour the village hall which is just about as plain as any building could be. The tombstones in the church-yard will tell you little beyond the names of several generations of recent Foxtonians. The elevation of the church-yard several feet above the surroundings will tell you that many more generations lie beneath your feet. Be as respectful as you may, you cannot tread one yard of ground outside this church, or inside for that matter, where mortal remains do not lie buried. The door is unlocked and visitors are expected, so do go in. The guide-book will give you all the information you need. Then let your imagination take over. Let it take you back through the centuries. I don't mean the centuries of

1. Unhappily destroyed by fire, 31 May 1974.

Decorated, Perpendicular, Early English and all that. I mean the centuries of people, parsons, priests, pilgrims – right back to pagans. Here around you is epitomized the life, the hope, the folly of a thousand years. No book that I might write could ever do as much for the sensitive mind as twenty minutes quiet contemplation in an ancient village church.

Out in the sunlight, look once more at the street of houses, the farms, the countryside beyond. That is the setting of the story which I am about to tell.

1 British Village and Roman Villa

The sluggish stream, fringed with reeds and decaying trees, creeps unobtrusively between overgrown spinneys, past derelict quarries and low-lying patches which still defy all efforts at cultivation. Apart from these latter, the land on either side bears crops of wheat, barley or sugar-beet which effectively hide all traces of former human habitation. Except in the autumn, when the land has been ploughed and harrowed in readiness for the next crop. Then you may see here and there, if you keep your eyes turned towards the brown pebble-strewn earth, fragments of pottery or red tile, an oyster-shell, a patch of lighter soil strewn with larger flints. It was the discovery of half a Roman roof-tile on the surface in the spring of 1968 which aroused my curiosity and started me on a trail of exploration which led, after much digging in that gravelly soil and much delving into rumours and reports to the discovery of a Roman villa and a British village.

Before beginning the story, I want you to look at the map overleaf (p. 22) which will show you more clearly where we are, what is there now, and what was there two thousand years ago. The shaded area along the course of the Brook indicates that here it was really an elongated mere, a quarter of a mile wide at the widest point, and easily fordable at the narrowest. The black dots indicate the location of hut-sites. There is no point in trying to count them, for the representation is only diagrammatic. There are in fact more than a hundred sites, all of which may not denote huts; some could have been threshing-floors or buildings other than dwellings. It was obviously not possible to excavate them all, and some of them do not show on the surface. It is quite probable that many more sites have been obliterated by the spinney, the quarries and the railway. The spot marked A is where grain-storage pits were found in about 1885. The spot marked B is where the burial-ground was found and partially explored in 1895 and 1903. Grain-pits and burials had all disappeared by 1910, swallowed by the advancing quarries, two huge pits which are now

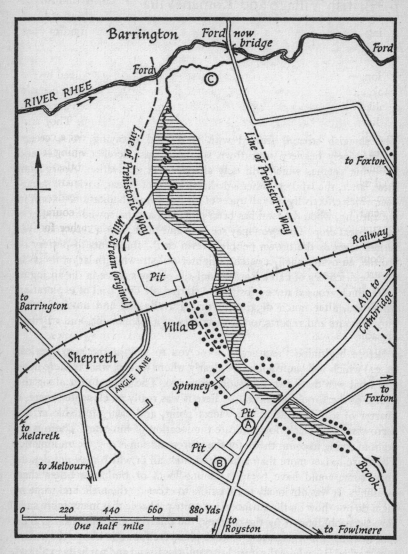

Map showing the British Village and Roman Villa

flooded. The ancient way shown running from the ford southwards through the village was still shown as a road on the Enclosure Map of 1823, leading from nowhere to nowhere. With that in the background of your mind, let us slip back in time two thousand years or so.

For longer than any of them could remember, the People had lived by the Brook, and if you had asked them who they were and whence they came it is unlikely that they could have told you. Many years before, their ancestors had lived in the northern part of what we now call Belgium. They had crossed the narrow sea, not unwillingly, though no doubt under a certain degree of compulsion in the form of stronger tribes and diminishing crops, to find a home in this fertile valley of light rich soil. They doubtless had a tribal name, but it matters as little to us now as, I imagine, it mattered to them then. In the days of migration they must have had a leader, one chosen for his wisdom in planning a move and for his skill and courage in carrying it out. Now their headman was probably chosen rather for his experience in rearing cattle and organizing the growing of crops than for his courage. No more wandering for them. Here was water; here was pasture in plenty for their oxen, sheep and pigs; here they could grow wheat, barley and rye enough to feed themselves and fatten their livestock. The pools and meres were well-stocked with fish and eels, easy to catch with nets in the clear spaces or with traps where the reeds made nets unusable. Those reeds, though a restriction on their fishing activities, were one of the many assets of the site, for they provided a plentiful supply of material with which to build the huts strung out along the brook. Moreover, they harboured many water-fowl, especially in winter. The motionless figure crouching knee-deep in cold mud for hours at a time considered his patient vigil amply rewarded if a lucky shot with sling and stone added a heron or a duck to the family larder, for meat was scarce in winter. They could live here by this brook, these people, for ever – or for as long as others let them live.

Not that there was any real threat to their security of tenure, so far as they could see. Some years ago, when it was rumoured that more peoples had come across the sea and were seeking land on which to settle, it had been suggested that they ought to make a ditch to protect themselves and their animals. The ditch had in fact been started, but was soon abandoned because there seemed to be no real need for it. Their neighbours to east and west were people like themselves, with undefended villages strung out along brooks exactly as was theirs. To the south of them there was ample space as far as the great mere (which, centuries later, was to be called, as they no doubt called it in their language, Fowlmere). To the north of them was the river, beyond which, as far as they were concerned, nothing really mattered. Across the river lived another group of settlers, a clan somewhat larger and therefore more powerful than their own. Although they spoke the same language, worshipped the same gods and lived in precisely the same way as the peoples south of the river, these People-beyond-the-river were so different that the only way to maintain amicable relations with them was to keep at a distance and give in to any demands which they might make. They, the People-beyond-the-river, evidently feared the attack of an enemy, for they lived in a village surrounded by a ditch and palisade. And since no enemy ever appeared from the woodlands on the higher ground behind the village, these people, determined that they should have enemies, chose to vent their spite on the peaceful People of the Brook. Not content with their own side of the river, they laid claim to a stretch of land on the south side, where they pastured their animals and reaped a crop of hay every year.

The Brook People, having no alternative, tolerated this violation of their territory. Likewise they were more curious than resentful when the other people used the south side of the river for their burial-ground. What did come near to rousing them to protest was the discovery that the People-beyond-the-river, instead of burying their dead decently in the chalk like every sensible clan, made a practice of burning their dead on a great fire of wood, and putting the ashes in pots, which they then buried. This wasteful practice, it seemed, only applied to the richer and more important members of the clan; and the richer a man was when alive, the bigger and better the pot in which his remains were buried. The Brook People came to this conclusion after digging up as many of the pots as they could find in the dark. Of course the People-beyond-the-river soon discovered what was going on, and they put an abrupt stop to the pot-stealing by breaking the pots at the time of burial and placing them inside larger pots, likewise rendered unusable. If you will glance again for a moment at the map you will see a spot marked C, not far from the river and the ford. It was here that in 1852 one of these burials was accidentally discovered by a man whilst ploughing. The rare and attractive Arretine[1] bowl, found fragmented inside an amphora, was reconstructed and is now in the Cambridge Museum of Archaeology and Ethnology.

1. This and other terms which may not be familiar to all readers will be found explained in the Glossary on p. 239.

Whether the People belonged to the federation of tribes which we call the Iceni, or to the Trinovantes, or to some other group, I cannot say, not knowing where the tribal boundaries were, if there were any. They themselves were probably equally uncertain on this point, simply paying tribute when it was demanded either in the form of corn or cattle or young men to serve in the army of whichever tribal 'king' happened to be the most aggressive at the moment. There is reason to believe from what little is known of the political situation in England before the coming of the Romans that our People of the Brook lived through a period of anxiety as a result of the aggressive expansion of the group of Belgic tribes called Catuvellauni to the south-west of them. The People-beyond-the-river may well have formed part of one of these hostile tribes.

When the Roman army of Julius Caesar defeated the Belgic chieftain Cassivelaunus and destroyed his stronghold at Wheathampstead our People probably enjoyed about two generations of relative peace and prosperity. There is evidence to show that, after the events of 55 and 54 BC, and perhaps because of those events, their mode of living was markedly influenced by trading contacts with Gaul and the rest of the Roman Empire. One of the principal items of commerce imported into the country seems to have been pottery. This impression may be distorted by the fact that pottery is almost indestructible; broken fragments survive when most other materials perish. It is nevertheless clear that much pottery was imported, and that the pots were bigger and better than those which the British had been making and using.

One effect of this was the abandoning by the People of their age-old practice of storing their grain in pits dug in the chalk, a method of storage which can never have been really satisfactory. Even though the grain was part-roasted to prevent germination, it would still have gone mouldy after the same pit had been in use for a few years, a fact borne out by the large numbers of these grain-pits which have been found. It may be, of course, that partly-germinated, slightly mouldy grain was what was needed to make the kind of drink which best suited British palates. Some such brew will figure in our story for a very long time. But bread was needed as well as beer, and the storage of grain in large earthenware jars was an undoubted improvement on the old method; it was still in use some thirteen hundred years later. The People continued to use their rough locally-made pots, of course, but it would seem that they preferred the better, imported wares when they could get them.

It has been suggested that they were introduced to a heavier and more efficient type of plough at about this time. The evidence for this however is slight, and on these light soils they would have been able to manage well enough with the wooden contraption, little more than a suitable crooked branch fitted with an iron point – perhaps even without an iron point – which they had always used. Hones for sharpening knives and sickles, and circular querns for grinding corn, were certainly imported from across the Channel and used by our People, for numerous fragments of such articles were found on the site of their village.

So well established was the contact with the Roman world that when, in AD 43, a Roman army again invaded Britain, many of the Celtic population in the south-east actually welcomed the invaders, possibly feeling that they had less to fear from them than from their own turbulent neighbours and racial kinsmen. Such opposition as there was, led by Caratacus, one of the sons of old King Cunobelinus, was rapidly overcome, and Colchester became the capital of a Roman province. Within a few months the People of the Brook would be made aware of their new status as subjects of the Emperor. What that meant in effect was that from then on they would pay their tribute of corn, hides and wool to the agents of the Roman Governor, and their young men would be liable for enlistment in the auxiliary units of the Roman Army. It might also have meant that a quota of their womenfolk was demanded for service as slaves; but if that were so, it was not a Roman innovation. Any memory which may have lingered on as to their tribal origin and allegiance could now be allowed to lapse, for tribal hostilities were a thing of the past. Having been conquered, the People ran no risk of being attacked by anybody, and it seems reasonable to suppose that in the early days of the Province the Roman soldiers aroused more admiration than fear in the native inhabitants.

We know of course that there were some who were not content with their new masters, and that many of them fled westwards into regions where resistance presented fewer risks. The others stayed where they were and continued to till their lands. When the Governor Ostorius ordered the disarming of all the natives in the Province it seems that there was a fair measure of compliance with the order. Our People most probably had nothing but sickles and knives in any case, to which the order did not apply. The Iceni however, living in the territory to the north-east, resented the order to disarm. Instead of handing in their weapons they used them in an attempt at revolt, a rash gesture which involved them in a crushing military defeat. The site of the battle, if it could be called a battle, is not known, but it was probably near enough to the People of the Brook for them to hear about it at first hand, perhaps to see some of the wounded who fled the slaughter. They can hardly have known that they were witnessing the opening scene of a tragedy which was to wreck their own lives.

Peace was quickly restored and life went on as before. The People probably saw little of the Romans, though some of them may have participated compulsorily in the construction of the great new road a few miles to the west of the village. This road, straight as a spear, came from the south and led to the north for such distances in both directions as the People had no need or wish to travel. Whether it interested them or not, however, they must have been forced to admit that it was a great improvement on the numerous tracks which traversed their area and had served as roads until that time, and which indeed were to serve as roads for many centuries yet to come.

Soon after this the sight of Roman soldiers must have been even rarer, for the bulk of the army was campaigning in the west, far beyond the boundary of the Province. Before setting out on his campaign Ostorius inaugurated a measure which was to prove of great interest to the People. Many of the soldiers had by this time completed their twenty-five years of service and were due for discharge. Rather than return to their homes – if they had any 'home' after marching all over Europe for the best part of their lives – many of them chose, or were ordered, to stay in Britannia. Some had no doubt taken British wives; others probably intended or hoped to do so.

The Governor, whilst needing every available man in his army, also needed to leave behind in the Province a nucleus of trained men in case further trouble should break out. So he established what was called a *colonia*, based on and administered from Colchester. To each time-expired veteran was allotted a plot of land in the vicinity of the capital, where the old soldiers could become new farmers. The officers naturally expected something on a grander scale, and their gratuity took the form of quite considerable grants of land, which was obtained by the simple expedient of taking it from the British. The size of these officers' holdings meant that they could not be concentrated near the capital, as was the *colonia*, and that they would be widely scattered over the whole province, even in the remotest parts.

That obvious fact, and the evidence brought to light by excavation recently on the site of the village, justifies the use of a certain amount of imagination in reconstructing the events of the year AD 48 (or thereabouts) in one of those remote parts of the province. We cannot know all the facts, and must therefore make some assumptions based on the facts which we do know. We may safely assume, for instance, that the People of the Brook received a visit from a small party of officials, in the course of which visit they learnt that a portion of their land had been granted to an ex-officer of the Roman Army; learnt also, no doubt, the serious consequences which would follow any attempt to thwart or hinder the settlement of that ex-officer. Likewise we may assume, with near certainty in this instance, the arrival soon afterwards of a team of workmen with cart-loads of bricks, tiles and sawn timber, things which the villagers had never seen before.

Any resentment which had been caused by the first visit, or kindled since that visit, would, I feel sure, have given way to an excited curiosity as a result of the second visit. Soon the villagers would have been busy collecting large flints and stones from the surrounding fields, whilst others dug loads of grey clunch from the pits a short distance to the north-west. Whether they were paid for the work or not I cannot say; if so, they must have taken good care of the coins which they received, for not one seems to have been lost – at least, not one has yet been found. Perhaps they were used to make bracelets or necklaces. Payment, if any, may have been made in kind. The villagers may have been conscripted for the work and kept at it with the aid of whips, though I cannot believe that that was so. I cannot imagine a man taking up residence in a spot such as this, at a time like that, without the friendly co-operation of the native populace. Coercion would have entailed the presence of an armed guard. There could not have been sufficient armed men available to watch over the construction of every villa in the province, or to ensure their protection when once built. All the known facts of the circumstances point to a considerable degree of collaboration.

Moreover, I would say that the collaboration was facilitated in no small measure by the novelty of the whole affair. The villagers would be fascinated as they watched the mortar being made, the timbers being cut to shape and fitted together on the solid foundations of flints and cement. The bags of iron nails must have aroused their cupidity, and several must have been stolen to be converted into knives. Before their wondering gaze the walls of the villa rose to a height hitherto unconceived for house walls. Then the rafters were fixed into position with those tantalizing nails, and the tiles laid on them. It was probably at this stage of the operation that wonder and admiration began to give way to doubt in the minds of some of the spectators as to the wisdom of the Roman responsible for all this novelty. To place heavy slabs of baked clay like that in a position from which they might fall on a man's head was surely tempting providence? And, surely, things like that could not keep out the wind and the rain as did branches covered with a thick layer of rushes and turf? They could not know that some sixteen hundred years were to elapse before ever a roof was to be built like that again in this locality – and then not nearly so weather-proof as that roof was when finished.

Some of the villagers, I think, were not content to be mere spectators, but participated to a degree beyond that required by the master's orders, learning how to mix mortar, how to make plaster, perhaps even to handle hammer and saw, tools quite new in their experience. Few, if any, of them can have learnt the art of applying the plaster to the walls, and fewer still the art of mixing the bright colours – red, white, blue, green and yellow – with which the plaster was decorated; though it is fairly certain that at least one of them did do so. As for the making of the floors, I doubt whether even one of them learnt how to set those thousands of one-inch cubes of sandstone in a bed of cement, or saw it done. Much later – some two hundred years later – native craftsmen did learn the art of making mosaic floors, but at this early stage the skilled craftsmen were all imported from overseas.

The villa was at last completed, along with stables, barn and outhouses, including a little shed with a cobbled floor in the garden where the master, once installed, took a bath every day. Perhaps not *every* day, but certainly with considerable frequency. When the villagers learnt of this strange habit, as they no doubt soon did from one of his household staff, it must have confirmed the doubts which had arisen earlier in their minds as to his sanity. True, there was no lack of water in the Brook, but to use it for such a purpose as that was unheard of.

Further evidence of this Roman's eccentricity was provided when, perhaps before the completion of the villa – if not before, then certainly very soon after it – he ordered all the native huts situated west of the villa to be removed and all those east of the villa to be rebuilt in straight lines on a rectangular grid pattern. I can only presume that it was done on Roman orders. No British village such as this, to my knowledge, has ever been discovered which was not closely associated with a Roman villa, and only about four such exist. Others have no doubt yet to be discovered. The rectangular grid layout was a peculiarly Roman and military idea. As for the removal of the huts from the west to the east of the villa – a task of no great difficulty which could be accomplished in a couple of days or so – I think the simple explanation for it is that the prevailing winds blew mainly from west to east, and that the Roman ex-officer was more sensitive to the smell of the peasants' huts than they were themselves.

Apart from that aspect of nicety, it is a fact, which even the most churlish of peasants must have soon admitted, that the novel geometrical arrangement did make movement about the village easier for man and

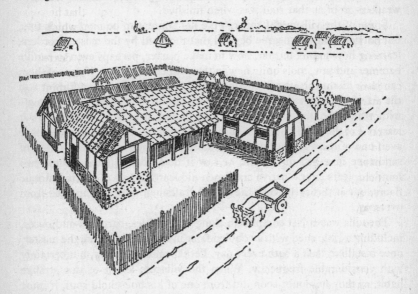

Reconstruction of the Roman Villa

beast, reduced the risk of many huts being burnt down when one caught fire, and gave everyone an equal share of space. Some of the villagers evidently took advantage of the enforced move to build for themselves a new type of hut, rectangular instead of round, with low walls of flints set in mud. A few even tried their hand at making mortar, though not with any lasting success – only one instance was found where the mortar was still recognizably mortar when excavated.

I can only guess as to the basis on which the villa estate was organized, for such matters leave no traces on or in the ground, but I am strongly tempted to see it as the forerunner of what later came to be called the 'manorial' system. It is, I think, fairly certain that the Roman master would have a number of slaves in full-time service, and that he would be able to call upon some, perhaps all, of the villagers for certain seasonal tasks such as ploughing, haymaking and harvesting. His domain of perhaps three or four hundred acres would, I imagine, include several compact blocks of arable land and a large stretch of pasture. Some of the pasture he might share in common with the villagers; some – the best parts, no doubt – he might fence off for the exclusive use of his own stock. All that is speculation. What I do know for certain about his farming is that he kept oxen, pigs, sheep and chickens, and that he grew corn, some of which was ground to make flour, as did the peasants.

About the man himself, little of course can be said with any degree of certainty except that he was an ex-officer. That, I think, is quite certain. That being so, he would be past middle age and fairly well-off. I think he was married – there was certainly a woman on the premises, for many of the pots found were clearly part of a lady's toiletry outfit. It would be only natural and in accord with common-sense that a man in that situation should have a wife, though whether she was British or Roman of course I cannot say. There would be no social degradation for the Roman in having a British wife, but it would undoubtedly be something of an honour for her to have a Roman husband of such status. Although the wife of a farmer, and as such far removed from a life of luxury and idleness, she would have slaves to command and would enjoy comforts unknown in a normal British household, such as a well-equipped kitchen and a good supply of table-ware, including some fine glass. To live and work in a house with tiled floor, glass windows and locks on the doors must have been ample compensation for any disadvantages there may have been.

I do not think that they had any children. Children have playthings which get broken and left lying about; none were found. I think that the ex-officer wanted children, or at least a son. That may seem like a wild supposition. It may be; but, if well founded, it would explain the extraordinary number of oyster-shells found on the site. All Romans, it seems, ate oysters, partly no doubt because they liked them, but also because they believed that oysters promoted virility and fertility. Any Roman site provides a fair yield of oyster-shells; few sites can rival this both for the quantity and quality of its shells. If my calculations are correct, an average of two dozen oysters were consumed here each week for about eleven successive seasons, and there was at least one occasion when three dozen were eaten at one session. Seventy-two shells were found all together in the remains of a wooden pail which had been thrown or left standing just outside the kitchen-door. Amongst them was a small unopened oyster and a broken bronze lock-bolt which had clearly been used as an oyster-opener.

These oysters would almost certainly have been brought from Colchester by an itinerant trader who did the round of all the villas in a particular area, carrying his wares in large vessels or skins filled with brine. They might have been specially sent from Colchester by a former colleague of the officer. The only other thing we know, or can safely assume, about that officer is that, in common with most military men, he had a hearty thirst. Whether his taste was for wine or for home-brewed ale is not certain. Wine, I should say, for many fragments of amphorae were found, and a dozen flagons. One of these latter was almost intact when found, one other was capable of complete reconstruction and is a beautiful object, whilst two others, with a capacity of nearly two and a half gallons, are the largest I have ever seen.

Of all the clues unearthed from the villa area and rubbish-pits to throw light on this Roman and his way of life, none can compete in interest and fascination with one small object found in the final stages of excavation at the bottom of a pit in a layer of black slime four feet below the surface. This is an oval seal-stone of sardonyx, with an intaglio image of Eros on its convex surface. Dr Martin Henig, of the Oxford Institute of Archaeology, who reported on it officially, has said of it: 'it is one of the best gems, if not the best, ever to have been found in Britain'. It certainly is of rare beauty and exquisite craftsmanship, and must at one time have belonged to a very wealthy man, possibly even to the Emperor himself. Tiberius, according to the historian Seneca, was wearing such a gem on his finger at the moment of his death. Seneca presumably had some reason for noticing and recording such a detail; he also had a financial stake in the exploitation of Britain. The symbolic significance of the intaglio image – Eros was the personification of the loveliness of young men and boys – accords well with the known tastes and character of Tiberius and other eminent Romans. One can only speculate as to the origin and history of this gem. The discovery of it is clear enough; how it came to be where it was found is also reasonably clear; the rest is intriguing obscurity.[1]

The months lengthened into years. Each year brought its round of ploughing, harrowing, sowing, reaping, threshing. Each year brought its crop of

1. The gem and some of the pottery are now in the Cambridge Museum of Archaeology and Ethnology.

lambs, calves, piglets, chicks. Life was normal, therefore good. The villagers, we may suppose, had adapted themselves to their foreign master and his ways, and found some advantage in his presence. The Province was peaceful. Or so it seemed.

Then one day in early spring, in the seventh year of the Emperor Nero's reign, the trouble which for years had been smouldering beneath the surface of affairs broke out into the open. Once again the point of eruption was in the land of the Iceni. Their king, Prasutagus, who had recently died, had been a loyal ally of Rome. As a reward for this loyalty, despite the unfortunate incident of the revolt over banned weapons some ten years before, or perhaps because of his role in that affair, he had been allowed to retain his independent status, nominally at least. Now the imperial policy had changed, and it was decreed that there should be no more client kingdoms within the Empire. The so-called kingdom of the Iceni was to be henceforth part of the province of Britannia. The emissaries of the Roman Procurator, sent from Colchester to put the imperial edict into effect, carried out their orders in an unwarrantably high-handed fashion which provoked Queen Boudicca to indignant protest at the confiscation of the royal property and estates. Roman arrogance was followed by outrage. The queen was flogged and her daughters violated. Protesting Icenian nobles received similarly harsh treatment. Indignation rapidly flared into revolt.

Weapons which were supposedly handed in ten years previously were brought out from concealment. Boudicca rallied her forces, placed herself at the head of a rebel army – 'army of liberation' would be the term today, and might have been then – and marched on Colchester. The city, undefended save for the veteran colonists, was an easy prey. Within a day it was reduced to a blackened smoking ruin. The magnificent new temple built in honour of Claudius, wherein those Romans who escaped the first onslaught took refuge, lasted for two days longer, then it too was destroyed. The Trinovantes, in whose one-time territory Colchester lay, far from resisting the revolt in any way, readily joined it. They had suffered more than hurt pride at the hands of the Romans. Their land had been confiscated, and many of the wealthier amongst them were heavily in debt as a result of the activity of the Roman financiers, prominent amongst whom was the philosopher-historian Seneca. The poorer people no doubt felt that they had nothing to lose and much to gain by joining in the uprising. We have only the Roman account of the affair to guide us, and cannot know what the British views were, but it seems fairly evident that the

British aim was the total destruction of every Roman and everything Roman in the land.

Where was the Roman Army? That question must have been uppermost in the thoughts of our villa-owner when news of the revolt reached him. The answer is that the Roman Army, commanded by Paulinus and consisting of perhaps two thirds of all the Roman forces in Britain, was in Anglesey, engaged in wiping out, it was hoped, the last of the Celtic opposition. Two weeks of forced marching separated that army from the scene of the revolt. One wonders how much that fact, of which Queen Boudicca cannot have been wholly ignorant, contributed to the timing of the revolt. On the whole, though, it would seem that passions played a bigger part than planning.

Garrisons, much depleted in strength, had been left by Paulinus to keep vigil from their widely-separated fortress-camps. The nearest to Colchester was stationed either at Lincoln or, more probably, near Peterborough. A force of some two thousand was already hastening from there towards the land of the Iceni. The rebels sallied boldly forth to engage this force, which they met and routed somewhere east of Peterborough and north of Cambridge, killing all but the commander and a small force of cavalry who fled to the safety of their fortress-camp pursued by the rebels.

The villa-owner can have had no clear knowledge of this, though rumours were probably spreading far and wide. Nor can he have known that the rebels, intoxicated with their military success, had turned back and were advancing on London, pouring down that straight new road in an ever-swelling tide of fury. For a week or so he must have lived in an agony of uncertainty. The first sight of columns of smoke or a ruddy glow in the sky to the north must have told him that disaster was imminent, but even had he known for certain that bearing down on him was a horde of wild Britons intent on loot and destruction there was little he could have done about it, no refuge to which he could have escaped.

The end, when it came, must have been brutal and sudden. It is perhaps as well that I cannot say in what manner the villa-owner and his wife were killed. That they were killed there can be little doubt. That the villa was burnt and ransacked is quite certain. The evidence of this was all too clear when the remains were excavated. There was charred wood all round the walls. In one of the pits was found the charred remains of a stout oak door with iron hinges and handle still attached, and two lock-bolts which, though little worn by use, had been shattered by violence. I should like to think that the villagers took no part in a crime which they were powerless to prevent, and I am prompted to do so by the fact that one of the huts was burnt down at the same time as the villa, suggesting some attempt at resistance or at least a reluctance to participate.

Every article of value in and around the villa, not counting burnt nails and lumps of molten lead, was taken – every article but one. The man who stole the beautiful seal-stone – either wrenched from the finger of its murdered owner or ferreted out from its secret hiding-place – saw value only in the gold ring in which it was set. The stone was to him nothing but a worthless trinket which might also be dangerous, bringing retribution upon him at the hands of the Romans or, more likely, since there would be no more Romans, at the hands of one of their gods whose image it bore. So he prised the stone from its setting with the point of his dagger – an act which could only have been committed in daylight – and threw it into the near-by cess-pit. It sank to the bottom of the slime and lay there undisturbed for nineteen hundred years.

The rebel horde passed on its way towards the next objective, Londinium. Paulinus, in answer to the urgent summons which had reached him, had already arrived there with a small section of his army. He realized the hopelessness of trying to defend the city and left it to its inevitable fate. Verulamium (St Albans) was likewise sacked and burnt. At all three towns, Colchester, London and St Albans, the story of those days of terror can still be read in the layer of ashes and reddened earth revealed by excavation. The final act in the drama took place somewhere along the Watling Street, at a spot carefully chosen by Paulinus but never identified. The Roman army was now ten thousand strong, the remainder having arrived from Anglesey. Boudicca's force was said to number 250,000. It would seem highly probable that many of the British warriors were intoxicated, and many more severely hampered by the loot which they were carrying, for, due allowance having been made for the exaggeration and bias of the Roman historian whose account is the only one we have, the outcome of the battle was an overwhelming defeat for the rebels. Tacitus put the British dead at 80,000, the Roman losses at 400 killed and a similar number wounded. Whatever the statistical truth of the matter, one thing was clear: the revolt was ended. Another thing soon became clear: Paulinus was determined that there should never be another revolt in this part of the province.

Back at the village by the Brook, as at numerous other villages in the province, a novel situation must have confronted the villagers. Recorded history does not help us much here; we must rely largely on reasoned guesswork and such evidence as the spade has provided. It is to be assumed that the former headman of the village, or a replacement for him, took command once more. There was a clearing-up operation to be done and someone must have taken charge of it. The bodies of the villa-owner and his wife were recovered from the ruins of the villa, or taken down from the rude frames on which they had been crucified, or picked up from wherever they were thrown, and bundled without ceremony into two hastily-dug graves on the edge of the burial-ground. Now that sentence, I am sure, will strike the reader as pure speculation on my part. And so it might have been, were it not that other spades and eyes than mine have been active in this vicinity.

In 1885 Professor T. McKenny Hughes noted the existence of a burial-ground on what was then a low chalk hill on the south side of the field in which the villa was located. In 1906 he explored the site more fully, for it was then rapidly disappearing as the quarries were being enlarged. Speaking of this same burial-ground he said: 'All graves but two had clean-cut vertical sides. The two exceptions were in shallow pan-like depressions scraped out of the surface of the chalk, and into these bodies seem to have been hurriedly thrown, or to have been subsequently disturbed.' The sketch which accompanies his report makes it clear that these two burials were the last to be made in that cemetery. Professor Hughes knew nothing about the villa, though he did deduce that a village community had lived there. Of course, that proves nothing. But it fits my story remarkably well.

I am relying once more on the evidence of my own hands and eyes when I say that the remains of the villa, which had not been entirely destroyed by the fire, were dismantled right down to the foundations. Every bit of usable material, flints, bricks, tiles, timber, was salvaged. The dismantling of the wrecked villa probably provided as much entertainment as its construction had done. There are signs that even the children took part in their own way, salvaging pretty bits of broken crockery and window glass which they carried off to their own huts, only to throw them away when the novelty had worn off. Glass in particular was found near several hut-sites; it certainly did not belong there.

Someone – let us suppose that it was the headman of the village, and that it was his hut which had been burnt when the villa was attacked – built for himself a new house only thirty yards from the site of the villa, using the best of the salvaged material. The foundations of his house were not very solid, the walls were not as high as those of the villa had been, and he could not manage a proper roof; presumably he had no nails, not enough straight rafters and not enough tiles. Or he may have had no intention of using tiles on his roof. The roof-tiles which were salvaged were not however wasted. He knocked off all the projecting flanges and used the tiles to make two of his floors, setting them in a layer of pink cement, and making such a good job of it that they are still there today. The inside walls of one of his rooms were plastered, and painted red and white. He also had a kitchen. The new house was perhaps not quite up to villa standard, but it was a fair imitation, and must have conferred on the owner a status such as few village headmen had ever known.

For a time, perhaps several months or even a year, the villagers would be able to persuade themselves that they were living in the good old days again; better than the old days, for to all appearances there was no government, no taxes, no laws except those which they made for themselves, and their land was their own again.

Then the truth would begin to filter through to this secluded paradise. The Romans had not disappeared. They were still in control. They were going systematically through the province, district by district, pursuing a policy of strict 'justice'. The massacre of some seventy thousand Romans had to be paid for. All those who had taken any part in the revolt – and many who had not – were to be punished. We do not know the dreadful details; we can only guess at the killing, flogging, enslavement, burning of homes, confiscation of land. We do know that, if there was any difference between British brutality and Roman brutality, it was that the latter was more efficient and persistent. We know that Paulinus carried out his policy of vengeance with such ruthless ferocity that he earned a rebuke from his own compatriots and was eventually removed from office by the Emperor Nero – an indication perhaps not so much of compassion as of concern for the fiscal revenue. We know that the Iceni, as a people, disappeared for ever.

The fear which must have entered into the minds of the headman and his villagers has left its trace upon the site of their village to this day – had left it, until excavation destroyed it. In an attempt to hide all trace of the former villa's existence, the site was thoroughly cleaned up and levelled. The remaining debris still lying around, fragments of brick and tile, plaster, charred wood, ash, pottery, was all shovelled into the rubbish pits. The tell-tale holes still left were filled in with clay, brought from some distance away and tipped in by the cart-load, and topped with a layer of hard-packed coarse gravel. Finally a thin layer of fine gravel was spread over the whole site. No one would have guessed that a villa had once stood there.

Even so, it would seem, the headman's mind was not at rest. He made for himself, in one corner of his living-room, a small sleeping-chamber, using bricks which might have been intended for the floor of one of his still unfinished rooms. That gave him two walls and two doors between him and the outside world at night, when fear was strongest.

Retribution, however slow, was inevitable. It took time to organize the combing-out, village by village, of the entire population. It took time to summon and deploy the military reinforcements from Germany; time to make good the total loss of the official records which had been in the Colonial Office at Colchester. But it was certain that enquiries would eventually be made as to the fate of a particular ex-officer to whom had been granted an estate by a brook near the north-western edge of the province.

One day, I am confident, a troop of horsemen arrived in the village. I doubt whether many questions were asked. One glance inside the new house would tell the Roman soldiers all they needed to know, though it took me several years to unravel the story told by those bricks and tiles in the wrong place. The headman and his family and most of the villagers might already have fled. I do not know. Nor do I know what happened to them if they were still there; but I can guess. Several of the huts were burnt, in particular one in which there was a sleeping-platform made of Roman bricks, the one which had been burnt down once already when the villa was burnt. The new house was not burnt.

The village, it would seem, remained deserted for a time. Then it was reoccupied once more; not all of the huts, about a quarter of them, as though a band of stragglers had returned. For maybe two generations there were people living on the site; not a community, not the People, just some people. When those few died out, or moved elsewhere, the site became derelict. Plaster crumbled from the house walls as the roof decayed, then the walls too crumbled, soon to be no more than grass-grown mounds and ridges. The rushes slowly invaded the one-time village streets, and wild-fowl bred unmolested where once children had played. The Brook flowed on, placid and unconcerned.

Life, too, flowed on. The Romans restored the situation to their own liking and reorganized a bigger and better Province on a new structure, the framework of which was a system of roads and towns, a system adapted to military control and commercial exploitation. More villas were built, and rebuilt, both by Romans and by Britons who fitted into the Roman pattern of life. These villas and towns provide the only remaining evidence we have of life in Roman Britain, and have furnished our modern museums with much that is interesting and enlightening. But it does not tell us the whole story. Within the framework of that structure there were innumerable dark areas into which the remnants of the native population, those not subjected to slavery, were allowed to retreat and survive if they could. They did undoubtedly survive, sometimes in quite considerable numbers, yet of their existence hardly any trace at all is to be found. They were utterly cowed, without identity, without organization, without spirit. There never was another revolt; nor the slightest likelihood of it in eastern Britain. That is why, when the Roman shield, the upper crust, was removed, the land was an easy prey for whoever felt inclined to take it.

2   The Brook-Makers

The Land was still there – always there – land capable of producing far more corn, beef, wool and hides than even the Romans needed. And just across the narrow seas was an expanding population of tribes hungry for land, desperate for living-space, bold enough to take it by force if need be. These Angles, Saxons and Jutes began their piratical raiding and exploration whilst the Roman legions were still in control. There is rather more than a hint that their presence on this side of the sea was welcomed by some, just as that of the Romans had been welcomed. Certainly the surviving Britons, those peasants lingering on in the dark areas of the countryside, offered no resistance when, in the early years of the fifth century, the legions having been withdrawn, the Teutonic invasion began in real earnest. Resistance would in any case have been both impossible and futile, for the invaders had spears, swords, axes, strong arms and quick tempers to enforce their claims. The towns they either looted, destroyed or simply ignored. The roads they avoided as much as possible. They had no use whatever for mosaic floors, heating systems, painted walls, paved streets, mains drainage and all that nonsense. They were countrymen, not townsmen. They wanted land. They wanted it, not to enhance their prestige by the possession of it, not to exploit it for political reasons, but to use it as it should be used, to provide a living for themselves and their descendants. And here, in Britannia, abandoned Roman province, was land, asking to be taken.

No vast fleet of ships, no armies, no generals, no campaigns figure in this 'invasion'. No historians have recorded it, though some made vague references to it. Historically, we might well wonder whether in fact it ever happened, were it not that every square mile of our land, every village, four-fifths of our language, many of our customs and most of our character presents us with irrefutable evidence that it did. The actual details are shrouded in an almost impenetrable obscurity. Which is why I do not hesitate to allow my imagination full play, guided by a handful of faint clues, mostly archaeological.

The invaders would seem to have come in numerous small parties, perhaps clans or families. They sailed into the estuaries and creeks of southern and eastern Britain. They rowed up the rivers. Several boat-loads, having followed the course of Ouse, Cam and Rhee – and bestowed on those rivers names which they still bear – finally shipped their oars at Barrington. Whether they were 'Angles' or 'Saxons' I do not know; nor do I think it matters. They belonged to no king or kingdom. If they owed allegiance to anyone, it was to the chief of their clan, who might – or might not – have been called Bara. These people laid claim to a site on the north bank of the Rhee, and called it Barentun, or something very much like that.

The next batch of migrants to reach the same spot, perhaps a few days later, perhaps a few years later, were told politely but firmly that there was plenty of room for them on the other side of the river. Since the truth of this was self-evident, and they had no wish to get involved in a dispute which might turn out to their disadvantage, the newcomers disembarked on the south bank, with a mental reservation that Bara's clan were not likely to prove the best of neighbours. As they wandered along by the Brook they saw no signs of habitation, only rough pasture, pools choked with reeds, and an unusual number of foxes slinking into the thickets. It was probably this latter feature which prompted the half jocular, half ironical suggestion at the camp-fire conference that night, that 'Foxe-tun' be the name of the settlement which they were about to establish. Jocular or no, the suggestion was adopted, and the joke – if it was one – is now fifteen hundred years old.[1]

So the newcomers settled in, between the Brook and the river, but not too near the latter. Within a week they had felled small trees to build their huts, begun to clear the ground for tillage, and taken good stock of their surroundings. To the west of them was the muddy lake which, with

1. To be perfectly honest, I do not know the true origin of the name Foxton. Nor does anyone else. With all due respect to the late Professors Reaney, Ekwall and others, I believe this to be the case with a great number, in some areas as many as three-quarters of our village names. Some, such as Newton, Newmarket and Fowlmere, are so obvious as to need no explanation. Others, such as Shepreth – 'sheep brook' – Orwell – 'spring by the hill-spur' – and Stapleford – 'ford marked by posts', have yielded their secrets to etymological study. Most of the others are almost certainly based on personal names, but what those names were is anybody's guess. Before the name of Foxton was ever written, it was in use orally for five hundred years, in the course of which it could have changed, not drastically, but enough to hide the original significance, which could have been a personal name or a nickname. The only certainty is that the ending '-ton' stamps it as Anglo-Saxon.

characteristic realism, they called Oslac ('muddy lake' – the name was still in use fourteen hundred years later, four hundred years after the lake had been drained). To the south was the first stretch of land which they cultivated and called Hamm Field (which could be 'brook field' or 'home field'). Beside their village was a meadow called Gannock – that is what it was called in the thirteenth century and right up to the nineteenth, so presumably they called it that; but it could have had that name before Anglo-Saxons came, for there is a Celtic air about it; it is one of the few wholly inexplicable names. In front of them, that is between the village and the river, was a meadow which they called Gossham and which suggests that they had brought with them some geese and that the geese, until they went into the pot, lived in the brook. It also suggests that the owners of the geese were not so particular about drinking muddy water as their descendants were to be many years later; though the Brook at this point was such a strong clear stream that any mud stirred up by the geese would quickly disperse. So strong was it in fact that, in the early days of the settlement, a water-mill was set up by the ford, where the Brook joined the river. (Where the present road bridge is.) No sooner was the mill established and working than the Barrington people declared that it was in *their* territory. A compromise was arrived at in the form of joint usage of the mill, but only, I suspect, because the Barrington people were more numerous. The dispute, which sounds strangely like an echo of the dispute which had marred relations between the People of the Brook and the People-beyond-the-river nearly five hundred years previously, was to last for a long long time. It was still alive twelve hundred years later, long after the mill had disappeared. Such feuds and animosities between neighbouring villages are a commonplace, often continuing when the original cause – if there ever was a real cause other than human perversity – has long since been forgotten.

Apart from the almost dried-up course of the Brook, or Mill Ditch as it was later called, there is now nothing to be seen to indicate that the early settlers were here. The land has been cultivated for centuries, and most of it turned upside-down in the coprolite-digging of the nineteenth century, so that all trace of habitation has disappeared. The only clues to its existence are the names mentioned above, some graves discovered along the Barrington Road, half a millstone dredged from the river, and a few pits, now obliterated. The map on p. 44 will help to clarify the location. Such is the effect of a hundred years of human habitation on the face of the earth.

The boats which brought the first-comers must have plied back and forth between their new land and their former homeland many times, bringing more settlers, wives, children, livestock, seeds, tools, etc. Other clans or families must have pulled in to that same spot on the bank of the Rhee, to be told by the Foxton people that there was 'plenty of room further on', and directed along the already ancient way which led to the south and east. Soon the whole area would be dotted with settlements, wherever there was water, workable land and pasture. The same sort of thing had been happening, on and off, for perhaps five thousand years, but never before on this scale, and never before with this effect. It is, I believe, the most momentous thing that ever happened to England – the common man's England. It *made* the common man's England, and nothing that has happened since has succeeded in wholly undoing what was then done. Be it noted, moreover, that it was done, so far as we can judge, without the slightest aid or intervention of either politics or religion. That is not to say that these people had no politics; but if they had, we know nothing at all about them. We know that they had a religion of sorts, which we have been taught to dismiss contemptuously as 'pagan' – rustic superstition. We know that Christianity, when it came back to eastern Britain, was grafted on to the rites and celebrations connected with those pagan beliefs. The names of some of their gods have survived in the names of the days of the week. Their mode of burial indicates belief in some form of life after death. We know of nothing to indicate that their beliefs were a potent factor in life before death.

Of course, not all the parties of settlers made their whole journey by boat. Many would have a longish trek by land from the point of disembarkation to a place where they finally settled, a trek which might last for several years. Parties which had set out in one direction would often clash with those travelling in the opposite direction; then the smaller and weaker party would give way. Where groups of native Celts were encountered, they would be given the simple choice of either accepting the newcomers and living with them – possibly as slaves – or going elsewhere. Just how much amalgamation of the two races there was has never been determined, but I am inclined to think that it was quite considerable, wherever the Celts were in the minority. Persecution and enslavement, slaughter even, of minorities must have occurred; but it would be erroneous, I believe, to think of the Anglo-Saxons as wishing or trying to wipe out the population already existing in the land. There was room for all. Where the Celts were in the majority, over in the west of Britain, it was a different

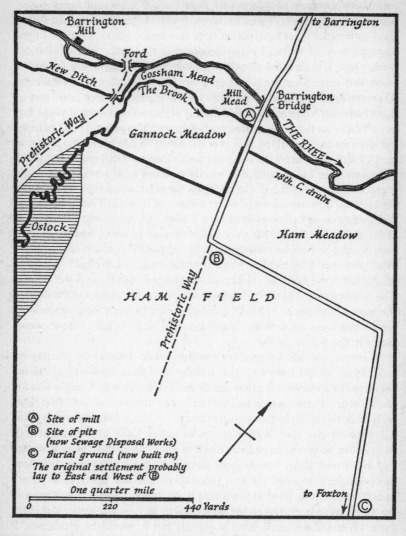

Barrington Mill

Ford

New Ditch

Gossham Mead

The Brook

Mill Mead

Barrington Bridge

to Barrington

Prehistoric Way

Gannock Meadow

THE RHEE

18th. C. drain

Oslock

Ham Meadow

H A M   F I E L D

Prehistoric Way

Ⓐ Site of mill
Ⓑ Site of pits
   (now Sewage Disposal Works)
Ⓒ Burial ground (now built on)
   The original settlement probably
   lay to East and West of Ⓑ

One quarter mile

0   220   440 Yards

to Foxton

Map showing the area of the early Saxon settlement

44

story. The Saxon invaders suffered at least one serious repulse, and their penetration was permanently halted. How much this was due to organized racial resistance, how much to the geographical limits of good agricultural land, none can say for certain.

After two or three generations, the time would come when saturation-point was reached, or would seem to have been reached in many areas. There were still vast tracts of uncleared woodland which could be and later had to be exploited. But once the open land was fully occupied, and when, as was inevitable, politics began to play a part after all, with or without the assent of the common man, then the question of boundaries arose. Especially the boundaries of the 'kingdoms' which, it seems, began to form towards the end of the fifth century. Then once more a situation arose which bears a striking resemblance to that which had existed six centuries earlier in our part of the country. The Foxton people, like the People of the Brook, found that they had chosen an embarrassingly situated plot. They too were claimed as subjects first by one 'king' then another. It was, I feel sure, a matter of complete indifference to them whose kingdom they were in; but as each conflicting claim of sovereignty involved them in the loss of livestock or lives, they were gradually forced into caring. One could not remain indifferent to the loss of one's best or only ox.

Furthermore, the settlement by the Brook, so eminently suitable in the conditions prevailing when they first came, was found to have serious disadvantages as conditions changed. With an important main road running through the middle of their village, access to unwelcome visitors was all too easy. When danger threatened, as it constantly did, especially from the far bank of the river, there was no means of affording protection for their cattle and womenfolk, such as the Barrington and Fowlmere people had. What they needed was a moated enclosure, or a hill which could be fortified with stockaded terraces, or both. In any case, their low-lying site was subject to flooding. So they decided to move.

The decision would have been much easier to put into practice if it had been made a hundred years earlier. There was now no site available within easy reach to which they could move, unless they went up into the forest and cleared a site. That was too drastic a step to be contemplated seriously. Besides, they had no wish to abandon their Brook. There must have been many a long and serious discussion, and many a re-examination of the site on the other side of the Brook – where strange red bricks, objects of suspicion, were sometimes found – before a plan was at last evolved, the boldness of which must have frightened some whilst it excited others.

They would not abandon their Brook; they would make it flow where they wanted it to flow. And they would still keep their old site, both during and after the move. This is one of my reasons for asserting that religion was a non-active factor in their actions; six hundred years previously, if anyone had suggested that man should interfere with the course of the Brook, I am sure that the idea would have been rejected as sacrilege. Now, it was hailed as salvation.

The map on p. 47 shows more clearly what they did than would an attempt at a detailed verbal description. In short, they dug a new channel and diverted some of the water of the Brook round the base of West Hill to flow steadily to the other brook, filling the moat en route, thereby creating the perfect village site. Well, nearly perfect. One thing the new brook could not do, and never did do, was drive a mill. But that did not matter all that much, as they already had one mill, and eventually got access to two others. Whoever devised and organized the operation must have been a genius, or so it seems to us today. And yet, I wonder. Such an undertaking nowadays would involve surveys, plans, estimates, contracts, machinery and the services of expert specialists, to say nothing of red tape. Was it, for those sixth-century Saxons, those common men, all just a matter of common-sense and hard work? A matter so ordinary that even the dimmest of them could see what had to be done and how to do it? Did they have an instinctive eye for landscape, a quality which we have utterly lost? If that were so, the feat still deserves our admiration. Somebody must have been in charge, and every man, woman and child in the community must have taken part, wielding a mattock or spade, or carrying a basket. They had no other tools with which to do the work. I doubt whether there was ever again such a truly communal achievement in Foxton. I wonder how many other villages were born of such an effort. On reflection, hundreds must have been; all those forest clearings, for instance, and many villages whose location makes little sense judged by modern considerations. And, be it noted, it was all done without paper, plan or pay.

The new brook, which will be referred to henceforth as the Town Brook, had a mean depth of about four feet and was two feet wide at the bottom. (Its profile was clearly revealed a few years ago when the trenches for mains drainage were excavated.) It was about 2250 yards long, not including the moat. I have not troubled to estimate how many tons of earth and chalk had to be moved. That splendid spade-work fixed the position of Foxton for ever, and determined its shape for the next twelve hundred years. It was not until well after the year 1800 that any house in

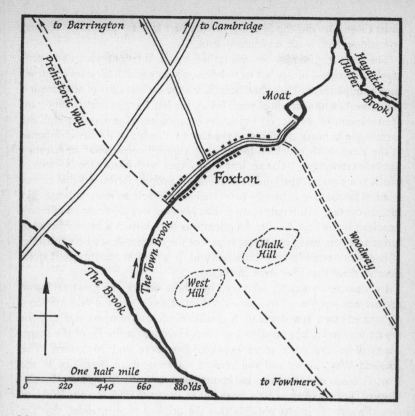

Map showing the course of the Town Brook, which determined the position and shape of the village

the village was built further than about eighty yards from the Town Brook, and most of them were within a few yards of it.

Fairly soon after this, the political situation seems to have become more involved. Little kingdoms merged into bigger kingdoms or federations. The territorial rivalries and ambitions of 'kings' began to make life unnecessarily difficult for the common man. Left to his own devices, he would, I am sure, have been content to get on with the real business of life, which was cultivating the land and rearing stock. Instead, he constantly found himself compelled to join the army of the local king and fight, or assist those who did the fighting, or take part in some mammoth digging operation which made no sense to him.

The East Angles had become united into a kingdom which was geographically suited to a policy of isolation, a policy which their leaders tried hard to implement. There had been, since the earliest days of settlement – and indeed for thousands of years before the last wave of settlement – a lot of movement of people, on legitimate business or otherwise, through the narrow gap between the forest of the Essex uplands and the broad expanse of the Fens, both of which in the sixth century constituted an effective barrier to movement. The ancient ways – they were hardly roads – two of which ran through the land of the Foxton people, facilitated this movement. The numerous brooks presented no obstacle to man or beast, but the meres were a different matter. The obvious way to create an effective frontier for the East Anglian kingdom was to construct a barrier between forest and Fen, using the meres as part of the defence-line where possible. If it did not entirely keep intruders out, it would at least make it quite clear to them that they were intruding.

I do not know exactly when, or by whose orders, the great exclusion project was put into effect. I should think it was about the year AD 600 – plus or minus a few decades. A double ditch and rampart was dug for nearly four miles in a straight line from Heydon, on the lip of the scarp, downhill to the great mere between Fowlmere and Melbourn. The Icknield Way, as we call the ancient trackway from Berkshire to the Norfolk coast, and its romanized counterpart, now the A505, were thereby blocked, but a gap must have been left in the earthwork for our Brook to flow through. It is just possible that the original plan intended that the Brook should fill the ditch and convert it into a moat, but such an idea would not last for long. The mere took care of the next one and a half miles, then came a further two miles of ditch to the other mere. It would, I imagine, be on this latter stretch that the Foxton men, together with those of several other villages, were employed, much against their will. They had had a real incentive to dig their own Town Brook, but this ditch was a foolish idea, of no benefit to them or to anybody else so far as they could see. Admittedly, it would make cattle-raiding more difficult, but even that was a dubious asset. If the Bran Ditch (or whatever they called it) prevented Middle Angles or Mercians from stealing East Anglian cattle, would it not equally prevent East Anglians from stealing Mid-Anglian cattle? Anyway, the Foxton men argued – amongst themselves, of course – they, the Foxton men, were going to be on the wrong side of the

Ditch, and in the very front line of attack, from whichever direction it came.

I think that that is what they thought, and I think that it was in all probability the Foxton men who hit on an idea for ensuring that the plan would not work. It was quite a simple matter, really, to make sure that the Ditch would be ineffective soon after its completion. Simple, that is, for men who could handle spades and had an eye for landscape – both of which attributes we know the Foxton men possessed. All they had to do was dig out the Hayditch (meaning 'boundary ditch' – we now call it Hoffer Brook) to a depth of another two feet, and keep it well scoured for a time, then the mere which formed the northern bastion of the Bran Ditch would be drained dry, and the way into East Anglia wide open. I may of course be crediting the Foxton men with an astuteness and perspicacity beyond their powers. It could have been the chief tactician of the Mercians who devised the plan to drain the mere. In which case it was still most probably the Foxton men who did the digging.

Whoever planned and did it, it was done. The northern mere was drained, and the area which it once occupied is called Draymer to this day. The land thus reclaimed provided space for another settlement, and the village of Newton came into being – not immediately, but some time after the draining of the mere. The East Angles, however, did not lightly abandon their plan. They tried again, six miles further back into their own territory, beyond Pampisford. That attempt likewise proved a failure and never reached completion. So they moved six miles further back still, and built the Fleam Dyke from Balsham to Fen Ditton ('ditch town') with Fulbourn Fen in the middle. As a superb country walk for future generations it was a great success, but it does not seem to have fulfilled its immediate purpose, for they went still further back and finally built what we call Devil's Ditch (I doubt whether they called it that) from Woodditton to Reach. Whether that really worked or not we shall never know, but it certainly is a fine monument to human endeavour.[1]

*

1. In view of the long-standing controversy and speculation about the Cambridgeshire Dykes, and as the extension of the Bran Ditch from Fowlmere to Newton has never before, to my knowledge, been mentioned, perhaps I ought to make a brief statement of evidence. There is firstly the visual evidence at the southern end of the Foxton–Fowlmere road; you can still see the line of the ditches, despite the ploughing-out and filling-in of the last hundred and fifty years. Then there are documentary references in plenty: (i) Chatteris Cartulary, f. 125 v., c. 1250, 'Apud dik duas acras', two acres at the ditch. (ii) Foxton Bury manor-court rolls, 1320, refer to land in Thriplow as 'one rood at Grimmisditch'. (iii) Court rolls, 1583, refer to land known to be on the Foxton–Thrip-

The Foxton men, I imagine, were still having the occasional hearty chuckle at having got that unwanted boundary well away from their back door when they discovered to their dismay that they had acquired another boundary at the front door. The Mercians had overrun the Middle Anglian kingdom, and established their boundary at the river Rhee. Foxton was now in a sort of No Man's Land. I do not think that they minded that very much. Their dismay was occasioned by the realization that they were more likely to find themselves once more in the path of an army surging across the river and rampaging along the road which went past the west end of the village (Cynig-gata, 'the king's road', part of which still existed as 'Coneygate' until recently) and over the hill towards the Dykes. If they had kept to the road it would not have been too bad, but since it was only a few feet wide and barely distinguishable from the surrounding land anyway, the passage of an army meant the flattening of much of their corn. They had further cause for alarm in that, the frontier being so near, they were likely to get less warning of the need to hustle their cattle and women inside the moated enclosure at the east end of the village. Had it not been for these frequent incursions they would perhaps never have known of the political developments of this period. The arbiter of early Saxon politics was the sword; the basis of Saxon life was the plough. For every thousand who lived by the sword, there were a hundred thousand who lived by the plough. If the political situation roused any passion at all in the breasts of Foxton men, other than anger at their trampled crops and stolen cattle, it was perhaps a sort of savage joy at the thought that they could now regard those 'foreigners' of Barrington, nearly a mile and a half distant, with a legitimate hatred. Life was somehow more exciting when one had someone to detest, when humanity divided itself neatly into 'we' and 'they'.

Life was also hard and brutal. Only the toughest survived, and few of those died peacefully on the straw or rushes which were their beds. There must have been some compensations in this endless struggle for existence; some sustaining force other than the instinctive will to live. I wish I knew what it was. Was it, perhaps, their constant contact with the miracles of

low boundary as 'at Bronnesdyche'. (iv) Numerous references to 'the Bank', 'Chadwell Bank', 'Thriplow Bank', 'Bank Shott', etc. (v) Enclosure Act, 1830, defines Foxton boundary as running 'along the centre of the Turnpike Road to a point opposite Thriplow Bank then N.E. to the said bank and S.W. along the centre thereof'. (vi) Finally, and most intriguing of all in my view, the field in which the earthworks are still just visible is to this day called 'Bunny's Mountains' which I take to be a popular corruption of 'Bronnes' and not to refer to rabbits.

nature; the young corn thrusting from the brown earth, the ripe berries plucked from the hedgerow, ewes suckling their greedy lambs, the dawn chorus of the birds? Was life made bearable by the simple fact of always having something to do? The advent of Christianity must have wrought some mitigation of the barbarity which characterized inter-communal relations, and, when its message finally penetrated to the level of village life, it must have afforded spiritual comfort to many who had never known and never would know bodily comfort. I say, hopefully, it must have done so. We have not, alas, one scrap of evidence that it did. Christianity could do little to alleviate the fear and suffering caused by famine and pestilence, beyond providing the victims with a grave in the hallowed ground of the church-yard instead of out on the bleak hillside. Just when those village church-yards came into existence we can only guess, and – unless it happens to be a church which formed part of a monastery – our guess could be anything up to three hundred years wide of the mark.

Slowly, as the centuries dragged on, conditions improved. Law and order, of a kind, replaced fear and chaos. Security for all could only be achieved by the sacrifice of individual freedom. Responsibility was a concept which, if not accepted willingly, had to be imposed, either by force or by the common will. Out of the chaos of barbarism there emerged, thanks to the deliberate and persistent efforts of many men, not common men but in particular kings such as Ine and Alfred, an organized social and political System. To trace its emergence step by step would tax the skill of better scholars than me. I propose to leap across the remaining dark centuries to the year AD 1000; a largely arbitrary choice, but influenced by the fact that there is by then enough historical light to enable one to see fairly clearly, and tell what the System had done for the common men of the village by that date.

The 'vill' had clearly defined boundaries. It always had, in the opinion of those who lived there, but there was now no longer the need to back that opinion by force or guile; it was set down in writing. Most of these charters defining the villages have long since vanished. The ones which survived are those which supported the claim of some nobleman or churchman or religious foundation to ownership of the village or part of it. They were carefully copied and re-copied; sometimes carefully forged; in many of them, indeed in most of them, streams and brooks feature prominently as boundary-markers. The vills, usually in groups of ten, were organized into Hundreds. The Hundred – it has never been satisfactorily determined whether its basis was a hundred families, a hundred hides of land, a hundred fighting men, a hundred monetary units, or whatever else it could have been – was an administrative area created for purposes of justice, taxation and defence of the whole realm. Eighteen hundreds made up the county of Grantebriggeshire; Foxton was in the Hundred of Thriplow. Our Brook was now serving as boundary to county, hundred and parish. Barrington, incidentally, was in a different hundred from Foxton, so the old animosity could continue undiminished.

The land of Foxton and of every other village, once proudly owned by those who had won it, no longer belonged to the men of the village. It belonged nominally to the King, who had granted it, or some of it, in consideration for various dues and services, to various lords. The men of Foxton still cultivated the land, partly for themselves, in return for various dues and services, and partly for their lord, to whom they now owed the traditional allegiance even though he was not of their clan. Much of their independent spirit had gone, crushed out of them not by foreign invaders – as was the case with the People of the Brook – but by the exigencies of the System.

Foreign invaders there had been and still were. For the past hundred and fifty years they had never been long without some form of contact with the Danes who, like themselves, had come first as piratical raiders, then later as settlers. It was in fact the presence of these fearsome newcomers which hastened the adoption of the System. Without organized resistance, it is quite possible that the Anglo-Saxons would have suffered the fate which they themselves had inflicted on the Celts. Indeed, in some areas, they did. But over most of East Anglia the Danish settlers were absorbed into the native population, and even though Danish law was for a time paramount, Danish influence on the language, customs and landscape was relatively slight (in contrast with Lincolnshire, where it was very marked).

In the management of the village the System left the villagers a good deal of independence and responsibility, not as individuals but as a community, and subject of course to the overriding authority of king, sheriff and lord. They elected from amongst their number a leader with the title of Reeve, who held office for one year. He was chairman, spokesman, foreman and scapegoat in turn. One of his many duties was to attend the monthly meeting of the hundred, along with four of his fellow villagers, and there vouch for the good conduct of the whole community. Another was to preside at village meetings, now a routine feature of village life. For all we know, village meetings always had been a feature of village life; we know far too little about them; but it seems certain that they differed somewhat from their modern counterpart, the Parish Meeting or Parish Council Meeting. The only evidence for their existence lies in a few oblique references and a few place-names, now mostly vanished. From these it can be deduced that the meetings always took place in the open air, usually in a meadow, often on a hill or beside a brook, and always well away from the village itself. I should imagine that knives and cudgels were frequently used to reinforce an otherwise unconvincing argument, and I am sure that the debates were punctuated with copious draughts of home-brewed ale or mead. But why the proximity of the brook, I wonder? Could it be that the early meetings were associated with some religious rite? The name which provides the clue to the location of the meeting-place, whether of village or hundred or both, is a variant of the Saxon word meaning 'meeting-hill' – Mettle, Metil, Mutlow, Mutloe, Mutler, etc. Only two instances still survive in the county, but I can vouch for the existence of five in an area of fifteen square miles. The site of the village deserted by the People of the Brook of my first chapter had, by the year AD 1000, become the Mettle Mead of the village of Shepreth, and was still so called five hundred years later.

3   Lords and Villeins

My theme is the story of the common men, nine-tenths of the population of England, but that story will make little sense over the next two or three centuries if I do not say something about the remaining tenth, which the System had by this time placed firmly on top of the other nine. I have already said that the King 'owned' all the land, and that, in return for certain services, he granted some of it to nobles. They in turn granted some of it to knights, who thereby incurred the obligation of military service, and the knights likewise granted some of it to peasants, who thereby pledged their labour and freedom. What the peasant got in return was a very dubious measure of protection and the right to hold just about sufficient land to feed himself and his family. Exactly when the manor, as we later know it, was established, we do not know; but it seems evident that something very like the manorial system was already in being by the beginning of the eleventh century, and perhaps a good deal earlier.

By no means all the land which the King chose to give away went to nobles and knights. Even as early as the seventh century a practice began which was to result in the material and political enrichment of the Church to the point where Church and Crown became rivals for the domination of the land and its people. As I see it, it arose from a misunderstanding or a deliberate misinterpretation of the Gospel message. The king who was buried at Sutton Hoo was provided with fabulous treasures to ensure that he should enjoy in the after-life the same status and prestige as he had enjoyed in his earthly life. Christianity put an end to such burials, but it did not wholly succeed in eradicating the idea which lay behind them. Perhaps the teachers of Christianity did not wish to eradicate that idea, but rather to put it to their own advantage. Material wealth and prestige were clearly not to be considered in the next world; spiritual wealth and security took their place, and had the added attraction that they could be assured before the death of the person whose soul was at risk. Salvation of the soul was treated as a commodity which could be bought by the simple expedient of bestowing gifts on the Church, mostly in the form of grants of land. It may have started as an act of piety or charity. The Church may have sincerely intended to use the gifts for the relief of the poor and the furtherance of true religion. But certainly by the beginning of the eleventh century God was steadily losing to Mammon, and the principle was firmly established that the Privileged on earth should also be the Privileged in Heaven.

And that brings me to the Abbess of Chatteris, who will figure so prominently in the pages which follow that you will almost certainly be prompted to ask how it came about that the head of a small nunnery, isolated amid the watery wastes of the Fens, became the virtual ruler of a village thirty miles away. Her case is typical of many. All over England, abbots, priors and abbesses were acquiring estates, sometimes vast estates, made up entirely of gifts 'for the good of my soul and the souls of my ancestors'.

Here are the facts about the Chatteris nunnery as near as I can ascertain them. Edgar, King of Wessex, Mercia and Northumbria from 957 to 975, encouraged the foundation of monastic houses. His second wife was Aelfthryth (or Alfwen or Ailwen), widow of Aethelwold (or Aethelstan or Aethelwine), earl of East Anglia. She was also the sister of Ednoth (or however else he was called) the first Abbot of Ramsey. And it was she who – for reasons of pure piety, or as an insurance policy for the salvation of her soul, or because it was the fashionable thing to do – founded the Benedictine nunnery at Chatteris at some date between AD 970 and AD 980. The site was probably chosen for its isolation, or because of the proximity of the other foundations at Ely, Thorney and Ramsey. Isolation afforded no real protection, as the Danes had demonstrated all too drastically on several occasions, but in theory at least it encouraged a life of contemplation and detachment from the world, the flesh and the devil.

Detachment from the world did not preclude the Abbess from ownership of land. The nunnery could not very well be endowed with much land in its immediate neighbourhood. That which the royal foundress granted to it was nearly all situated in southern Cambridgeshire – 640 acres in Foxton, 240 in Barrington, 165 in Shepreth, 420 in Barley, 120 in Over. Enough to guarantee an income in rents sufficient to maintain a household of a dozen nuns – the number never rose above fifteen – at a standard of living not wholly in accord with the vow of poverty. This land must previously have been held by the King, or the Queen, or the Earl of East Anglia. Now it was held by the Abbess – for ever. Once bestowed, it was never taken away – not for the next five hundred and fifty years, anyway – though parcels of it were sometimes in dispute, for there were some people who rated the possession of land above the salvation of their souls.

So much for the establishment of the Abbess as landlady, but how did she come to have the authority which she later wielded so effectively? That question is one which I cannot answer satisfactorily, not within the scope of this book. For a hundred and fifty years after the foundation of the nunnery nothing at all is known about it, except that it held the lands listed above and, presumably, collected the revenue. When it does emerge into the light once more, it is clear that the Abbess has acquired certain judicial powers: the right to hold a court, to collect fines, etc. – all of which added to her income. How or when she acquired them I do not know. It is not enough to say that the holding of land meant automatic conferment of rights; two other lords held other land in Foxton; a dozen lords held land in villages where the Abbess held lands; in Orwell, for instance, there were parts of no less than five manors; they could not *all* have exercised jurisdiction. It may be that the original charter of foundation granted the Abbess her authority. It may be that sheer negligence or magnanimity on the part of the other lords left the Abbess with a clear field – a most unlikely supposition, but not to be ruled out. It is even possible that the Abbess owed her authority to a forged charter – many monastic charters were forged, sometimes because the original had worn out and, in copying a new one, it was found expedient to legalize a situation which already existed *de facto*. Be that as it may, the fact is that by 1200 at the latest the Abbess held 'View of Frankpledge' in Foxton, Barrington and Shepreth, which meant that for almost everything short of murder and treason her word was law.

The best-remembered event in English history, which occurred at Hastings in 1066, had, I suspect, remarkably little immediate effect upon Foxton and a thousand other villages remote from the actual battle. It could well be that one Foxton family at least waited anxiously for the return of the sturdy young man who, axe in hand and shield on shoulder, had set out with the Lord Sigar's contingent to answer the urgent summons of King Harold in his hurried march down the Earningastreet to London and beyond. Sigar was the 'man' of Lord Asgar who, we are told, was killed at Hastings. Sigar came back from the battle – that is, assuming that he ever got there – so presumably many of his men did also. The axe carried by that Foxton youth might have been wielded in the famous battle – or it might have been thrown into the river at Barrington in order to furnish an excuse or an alibi. The intention to take no part in the conflict – which was, when all is said and done, a very personal top-level political wrangle – might have originated with Sigar himself. I do not know. But I have the axe, dredged from the river, and I do know that Sigar was left in possession of his manors of Foxton, Thriplow, Shepreth and Orwell, whereas the vast majority of Saxon landholders were dispossessed overnight, so to speak. He, Sigar, had a new overlord, of course. Everybody had a new overlord, except the underlings of Queen Edith.

Every acre which King William did not want for himself he granted to his French friends and supporters – which is precisely why they supported him – prominent amongst whom was Geoffrey de Mandeville, who became overlord of half the Foxton acres. King William had no quarrel with the Church, far from it, and the Abbess of Chatteris was undisturbed in her possessions. Since one overlord was much the same as any other overlord and since none of them ever came near the village anyway, so far as the villagers of Foxton were concerned, the battle of Hastings made little difference. But there was a difference. It became clearer as the years went by. The System which was already in existence was, as a result of 1066, hardened, sharpened, hammered into shape, then riveted upon the countryside in such a way that it remained rigidly fixed for three centuries, and was not finally cast off until the early years of the present century.

If 1066 is the best remembered, 1086 is the date to which historians are most indebted, for the Domesday Book, as it is usually called, gives us the first real glimpse of the villages and villagers of Feudal England. It provides the first written evidence of the existence of many villages. The picture is not as clear as we would wish – scholars are still arguing about the precise meaning of much of it – and its real purpose was not to tell us, or King William, about the people, but about the land; who held what land, and how much tax could be squeezed from it. One thing it does make clear is that England was then, and was to remain, a land of two peoples. Not just French and English, though it began roughly on that basis, but Rich and Poor, Free and Bond, Powerful and Helpless, Those who Mattered and Those who Did Not Matter. The former in each case constituted well under ten per cent of the population; they had names; the latter were nameless; the former owned land, or held it on a basis firm enough to call ownership; the latter owned nothing.

Since this is our very first documentary evidence, let us take a look at all of it. It is brief enough.

The Abbess of Chatteris holds 5 hides and 40 acres[1] in Foxetune of the King. There is land for 8 ploughs. One hide and 40 acres in demesne and there are 2 ploughs. There are 16 villeins and 11 bordars with 6 ploughs. Half a mill worth 10s 8d[2] and meadow for all the ploughs. It is worth £6 and in the time of King Edward was worth £7. This land is and always was of the Church.

Geoffrey de Mandeville. In Foxetune Sigar holds 3½ hides and 20 acres of Geoffrey. There is land for 5 ploughs, one on the demesne, and 5 villeins with 10 bordars have 3 ploughs. There is one slave here and meadow for 5 ploughs. It is and was worth £4. Sigar himself held it under Asgar and could sell and give it, but the judicial powers remained to the lord. In the same vill there is half a mill worth 10s 8d which Robert Gernon annexed in defiance of Geoffrey, as the men of the hundred testify.

Count Alan. In Fugelesmara (Fowlmere) 2 knights hold one hide from Count Alan. There is land for one plough and two oxen, and meadow for one plough. It is worth 20s, at the time of King Edward 25s. Edeva held this land, and it provided 2 watchmen for the Sheriff.

When a copy of all this was made at a slightly later date, with the title of *Inquisitio Comitatus Cantabrigiensis*, the error was corrected, and a further detail added concerning the Chatteris manor: '126 sheep, 32 pigs and 1 horse'.

We may now, I think, dismiss from our minds for the time being the Abbess, Earl Geoffrey, Count Alan and his knights, and Robert Gernon – noting that the latter had thrown his weight into the ancient inter-village feud by claiming half the income of the Foxton mill as a perquisite of his Barrington manor. These lords, having consumed the produce or pocketed the revenue from their manors, had, I believe, no further interest in Foxton, even supposing they knew where Foxton was. Our interest lies with the nameless ones, those twenty-one villeins, twenty-one bordars, two watchmen and one slave. Forty-five men. Double the number, assuming as many women as men; then double the total, assuming as many children as adults; add a few more for luck, and we arrive at an estimated population of about two hundred. This, it is generally agreed, would be an average village population at that time; the same as it had been for centuries; the same as it was to be for quite some time to come.

Life for those two hundred was in a sense much easier than it had been, say, three centuries earlier; they knew exactly where they stood. No poli-

1. Not acres as we know them but rectangular strips measured roughly with a pole of variable length; the basis of calculation was probably what a team of oxen could plough, or what a man could mow, in a day.
2. A note on the changing value of money will be found at p. 245.

tics for them; they were outside politics. No preoccupation with money; they scarcely had any. They had no rights beyond the protection afforded by the law in a dispute with one of their equals; that was slight enough, but heaven help them if they got involved in a dispute with one of their superiors! Their responsibilities were limited to obeying orders transmitted to them by Sheriff or Steward. Their prerogatives were minimal; a few faggots for their firing, a few branches for their roof, a meagre pannage for their pigs – all obtainable from the wooded waste over the hill, approached by Woodway. They did not have to plan; the Reeve did that for them, and most of his problems were solved by simply following routine. They did not have to think. All they had to do was work; start their working life at about the age of six and go on working until they dropped dead from fatigue, illness, hunger or old age, which set in at about the age of forty and did not usually last very long. They may have dreamed of something better; they can have had little hope of ever achieving it.

Their houses or 'cots' – hovels would be a more appropriate word – were strung out along both sides of the Town Brook; single-roomed structures of timber, wattle and daub, roofed with straw or reeds laid over branches; no windows, no chimneys, no floor other than the earth. In fact there was precious little difference between these huts and those which had stood by another part of the Brook a thousand years before. The walls were rather higher. The smells were much the same, for the sheep, pigs and chickens in most cases and for much of the year shared the accommodation with their owners. When I said that they 'owned nothing', that was not quite true, for they did own the contents of their hovels. Their furniture consisted of stools, benches and tables ('boards' to be exact) which they made for themselves. They likewise made their clothes and footwear, from home-spun wool and home-tanned skins. They made their wooden platters, bowls and cups, their tools and implements, the latter with a little help from the smith and the carpenter in the village. It is a fact of some significance that not one single item mentioned in this paragraph has survived to posterity – with one possible exception: spindle-whorls. These are hemispherical objects with a half-inch hole drilled through the centre, to fit on the end of a smooth stick in such a way as to hold a twist of wool and facilitate the twirling of the stick. I have three of them, one made of chalk, one of bone and one of baked clay.

Cooking was done in rough but admirably tough earthenware vessels on open wood fires. The hearth consisted of two or three large stones, out of doors for most of the year, and only brought indoors in the worst weather owing to the obvious risk of setting fire to the hut, an event which even so must have been of frequent occurrence. Large earthenware jars were used for the storage of grain and meal. They were so big and heavy, even when empty, that, once placed in the hut they must have stayed there until broken, and many of them probably outlived several owners. I have a large quantity of fragments of these jars and still hope, one day, to be able to reconstruct at least one.

They ate coarse bread, gruel, cheese, vegetables, pease, boiled mutton and boiled bacon whilst it lasted, with occasionally a chicken, eggs, perhaps a rabbit now and then, though it is not at all certain that they were widespread in England at this date – roast beef never. They ate, that is to say, what they grew and produced. All of them – all except the one slave – held some land, and it is surprising what can be grown on one acre, or even half an acre, when faced with the alternatives of working or starving. Not that starvation was the sole prerogative of the poor; even those who held as much as thirty acres, and had perhaps two oxen to feed as well as their family, would know the pangs of hunger when the harvest failed. The best of harvests did not provide a lot of corn, judged by modern standards. The worst, due to drought or an exceptionally wet season, produced none.

Their basic drink, for young and old, was almost certainly ale, a weak brew made with fermented barley and the water of the Town Brook which flowed past their door. Since the main street was little better than an elongated dunghill, there must have been long periods when the water of the Brook was unpleasant to the taste, to put it mildly. Perhaps the villagers became so accustomed to this that it was hardly noticed, and they developed unconsciously a resistance to germs whose existence they did not even suspect. Contaminated water cannot have constituted the health hazard which it would be considered today, otherwise the whole population would have been wiped out.

Apart from the hovels there were only two other buildings in the village. One was the 'hall' of the Chatteris manor, a building larger than the others but built in much the same fashion, where the bailiff lived and where the Steward came to preside at the court. At what date it came to be called 'Bury' I cannot say. The term ought, strictly speaking, to have been applied to the house – if there was one – within the moated enclosure. I am inclined to think that the greater part of the Foxton land was originally held by Queen Ailwen and that, when she founded the Chatteris nunnery, she intended that the rest of her land in Foxton should provide the endowment of a church in the village. There is no direct evidence of this, but it is suggested by what is known to have been the situation later. As is the case with hundreds of village churches, there is no direct evidence of a church existing in Foxton at this date. It is not mentioned in the Domesday survey because it paid no tax. Yet I am sure that it did exist, and that it stood where the church still stands, opposite the manorial hall. This building also would be of timber, wattle and daub, and thatch. There is one mute but very tangible piece of evidence in the form of the font-bowl; to date it is absolutely impossible, but its massive crudity says assuredly 'Saxon'.

Then of course there was the mill. Though no longer the mill of the villagers, they were compelled to use it, and forbidden to grind their corn at home with hand-operated querns, for the tolls paid to the miller were now a part of manorial revenue. The manorial appropriation of mills was justified to some extent in that the repair and maintenance and frequent replacement of the machinery was a costly matter, as also was the constant work needed to protect the mill against floods and ensure a regulated flow of water. The villagers might or might not have been capable of the sustained communal spirit needed to keep a mill constantly working, owned by all, used by all, paid for by all. My own view is that they *were* capable, and had in fact done it for several centuries; but they could not resist the rapacity of lords who saw in the mill a further potential profit-making concern.

This is just one of many instances in the history of the common man where his own temperament and character, or lack of it, has proved to be his worst enemy. The common men had developed a state of communal apathy and helplessness which was to cripple them for centuries – indeed its effect is still to be seen today. Any revolt against the System in the eleventh century would, I think, have been individual and secretive. Some of the villagers would wish to defy the manorial ban, and use their own quern to grind their own corn; but querns were not easy to acquire or make in this part of the country. It would be easier to put up with the nuisance of carting the corn all the way to the mill and pay the toll, even with the conviction that one was being cheated by the miller. There really did not seem to be any point in fighting against the System, and no hope whatever of winning. And it was no use – it was in fact dangerous – to complain against the lord of the manor, so the miller got all the blame and a reputation for dishonesty thrown in for good measure.

Animals, which figure so prominently in the survey, were no less prominent a feature in the life of the village. Especially the oxen, which pulled the ploughs and carts, and provided meat (for some people), tallow and hides. Without them, the cultivated area could never have extended far beyond the original Ham Field. With their aid, new fields had come or were coming into being: Hayditch Field, Chardwell Field, Downe Field. Each field, as it was developed, was divided into 'shotts' of about twenty acres; each shott into twenty or thirty strips or 'lands'. This still left large areas of pasture, meadow and waste or 'more', mostly alongside the river and the brooks. About a third of the arable land – not necessarily all one field – was left fallow (uncultivated) in any one year to provide a crop of weeds and grass on which some of the sheep and most of the cattle could survive the winter. Those animals – the proportion would vary from year to year – which did not look like surviving a hard winter would be slaughtered and salted down in the autumn. The meadows, as the Domesday survey indicates, were kept specially for the oxen, except during the three months in spring when the grass was allowed to grow for a hay crop, on which those same oxen largely fed in winter. Without the oxen, the agricultural system would have collapsed. Without the meadows, the oxen could not have lived. Without the brooks and the river, there would have been no meadows. Appropriately enough, the only surving memorial of those vital oxen is on the river bank, at the edge of the meadows. There, if one cares to delve in the mud dredged from the river, may be found countless bones – huge shin-bones, skulls, horns, ribs and hooves, sometimes with an iron shoe still attached.

4 The Medieval Village

It is perhaps not surprising that what little documentary evidence there is over the next two hundred years relates almost entirely to the lords and their manors. I have already referred to the villagers as those who Did Not Matter. To the lords, only the land mattered, and the money which it meant to them. Most of the documents between 1086 and 1286 deal with the transfer of land, the right to hold land or to hunt on it, the conditions on which land was held, etc., and the only names contained in them are those of nobles, knights and churchmen. They do however enable us to fill in the manorial background, which, very briefly, I will now do.

The Chatteris manor remained unchanged except that for administrative convenience it tended to merge with the Abbess's other holdings in Shepreth, Barrington, Barley, Madingley and Over; the same Steward supervised them all. The court of the Abbess was held at Foxton, usually twice a year, and through it she exercised a somewhat remote control over Foxton, Barrington and Shepreth. The neighbouring lords only seem to have asserted their rights when it was a question of getting more money, more land, or hunting. Whilst ecclesiastical and monastic estates everywhere were getting larger and richer, the Abbess and her small family remained content with what they had – without, needless to say, refusing the occasional odd gift of a few acres which came their way.

The Mandeville manor in Foxton and Shepreth remained in the same family for a further hundred years or so. Geoffrey, grandson of the original Geoffrey, went on the rampage, terrorizing and plundering the district until he was killed by a chance arrow at the siege of Burwell Castle in 1142. His brother William made some amends by giving £5 annually from the Foxton-Shepreth manor to the Knights of St John at the Preceptory of Shingay. Then the manor was sold – along with the obligation to continue the above gift – to Alan de Shepreth. His daughter Petronilla married William de la Haye, and the De la Haye family held the manor, and everything else on which they could lay hands, for the next hundred and fifty years.

The two knights who held the third manor 'of the Honour of Richmond', were not named, but there is good reason to suppose that one of them – perhaps both – was of the Bancs family. (De Banns, Bancis, Bannis, Scannis – even those who had names seem often to have had little idea as to how to spell them; but of course they could not write.) From an early date the small Foxton manor, or 'lordship', was tied up with other manors at Orwell, Barton, Pampisford and Kingston.

It seems highly probable that the first stone (i.e. chalk) church to be built in Foxton about 1140 was the outcome of Bancs munificence. It is almost certain that Bancs money largely paid for the enlargement of the church about a hundred years later, when the nave of the earlier church became the chancel of the new one. The link between this manor and the church, always vague, is nevertheless constant over a period of nine hundred years.

One of the Bancs family, Mabel, became Abbess of Chatteris, and so much of their land and money was given away that, from being owners of the manor, they became its tenants – a somewhat rare instance of social retrogression in an age when all around them were climbing over each other to get higher in the scale. In about 1260 the manor passed by marriage to the Mortimer family (of Attleborough in Norfolk), at a time when the political situation was again acute, and it was not only the villagers who felt the sharp end of it. The local barons waged their own private wars. Roving bands of armed retainers exploited the general confusion to rob and pillage. If it were needed, there was always the long-standing rivalry between neighbouring villages to serve as excuse. The Kingston manor having been burnt and laid waste in 1263, William de Mortimer built a new manor-house at Foxton inside the defensive ring of the old moat, which was no doubt deepened and widened for the purpose. The name of Mortimer has clung to the site ever since, though it is most unlikely that any Mortimer ever lived there, or stayed there for long. The manor had so few villeins in Foxton that at harvest-time labour had to be brought from Kingston. To be precise, it was not brought – it walked! Throughout the centuries, right up to a time well within living memory, there are countless instances of men and women walking ten miles or more to do a day's work and walking back home again when it was done.

If I appear to be devoting too much attention to lords and manors, it is for what I consider to be good reasons. I have already said that the history of the common man would make little sense without a knowledge of manorial history. I will go further, and say that, without manorial history, manorial documents and records, there would be no history of the common man. If that is not sufficient reason, let me make one further point. So many people today speak of the 'manor' in a tone of awe – or contempt, according to their views – as though it symbolized respectability, good breeding, established tradition and so on. Let us not belittle its antiquity and its importance, but let us be quite clear that the manor played much the same role in medieval society as does the car-factory, the textile-mill, the iron-foundry or the pig-farm in the modern economy. Vitally important the social implications of the manor may have been, but its real basis was economic. It was a 'commodity' which was bought and sold, stolen, bartered, used as a bribe, given away. Its possession carried with it the right to dispense justice, the right to arbitrate in many aspects of life which we now consider matters of individual conscience and will – but these things, too, as we shall presently see, were commodities which each had their price.

The latter end of the thirteenth century brings a flood of light on the scene for the first time. The Hundred Rolls of 1280 (printed and published, but not translated, they are available in most County Record Offices, University Libraries and some Public Reference Libraries) give a complete list of the tenants of the various manors, telling who held what land and on what terms. The Court Rolls of the Chatteris manor, which have miraculously survived in good condition (now in the keeping of Trinity College, Cambridge) tell in great detail the doings of those tenants from 1292 to 1326. Very few manorial rolls of this antiquity have survived; those which have are mostly in college or cathedral libraries or in the British Museum; some have been published. Almost everything which I am going to say in this chapter is based on those documents, with a few further details gathered from the Chatteris Cartulary (British Museum), Assize Rolls (Public Record Office), the 'Vetus Liber' of the Archdeacon of Ely (Cambridge University Library), the notes of John Layer and the writings of the late Dr W. M. Palmer (County Record Office, Cambridge).

It would be wrong to say that anything like a minor revolution has occurred, or is in progress, since the time written about in the last chapter. The System is still in being – very much so – but the structure within the system has changed and is changing. There are now visible quite marked distinctions within the mass of the peasantry. Some are free and some are not. Some are relatively well-off, and some are wretchedly poor. To what extent this is due to a change of heart on the part of the People who Mattered; how much it is due to the influence of the Church; how much to the increasing importance of the role of money in the economy; how much, if at all, to a resurgence of effort and ambition on the part of some of the peasantry – I do not know, or pretend to know. Perhaps it is all of those factors, and many more, combining together to form what we call Progress. Man is marching forward. By the year 1300 he has come a long way, but he still has an awful long way to go. He is marching forward – to what? We are by no means sure of our aims today. We are, I venture to suggest, not at all sure that we have any aims. How much less sure, then, must the medieval peasant have been, assuming that he was capable of thinking about a goal? If he were, what would it have been? Equality? Brotherhood? Liberty?

As I have already hinted, equality hardly seems a likely target. The differences already existing two centuries before as between peasant and peasant in the same community, measured in terms of acres, have widened. For instance, Ralph Kersey holds land of all three manors, to a total of 42 acres, and owns two houses. Reginald Andrews holds 72 acres; Reginald Totington holds 27 acres – at an annual rent of one penny – and neither of them lives in the village. John Dikeman holds 37 acres and a house. William Bancs has 27 acres and three houses. John Harston has 27 acres and a house. These men seem to be in a class of their own. Then comes the common herd, but still with wide variety. Twenty-two men each hold 18 acres; 19 men and one woman each hold 9 acres; 15 men and two women each having holdings of between half an acre and two acres, which are evidently the 'closes' or 'crofts' attached to their houses. The existence of a further score of families becomes evident from the court minutes of the next few years, making it clear that the 69 houses listed and the 69 tenants named were not the whole population, which must have increased considerably in the previous century. It continued to increase steadily for the next forty years until it reached the level of three hundred and fifty or thereabouts, a figure which was not exceeded for another five hundred years.

Yet another distinction which emerges from the records to dispel any notions of equality is that some of the land is held by men who are free; there are 22 of them, holding 340 acres between them. The rest of the land, some five hundred acres, is held by villeins, and it is clear that 'villein' no longer means 'villager', but 'bondman', i.e. one who is bound. He is frequently referred to as 'native', i.e. one who is born to that status. All the free men pay cash rents for their holdings, but three of them still owe certain services to the lord. All the bondmen pay for their holdings by working for the lord, the work being assessed at a cash value of about ten shillings a year, but 15 of them pay cash rents as well, mostly three pence a year, which would seem to be the rent for the land on which their houses stand. Generally speaking, the more land a man held, the lower the rent per acre. There is no uniformity as between manor and manor, between man and man, or between the same jobs done by different men. A few typical examples will illustrate this:

John Aubrey holds 18 acres of land with a house, and he must do 52 days work a year, must plough for 2 days, do 2 boon-works at harvest, mow in the meadow for 2 days, cart the hay, repair the roof of the hall, harrow the oat-land along with his fellows, and he shall receive one hen and 16 eggs. His services are valued at 9s 8d and he pays a rent of 2s 6d.

Thomas Vaccarius (cowherd) holds 9 acres of land with a house, and he must do each year 100 days work, plough one acre and do carting service when required. He shall receive one hen, and shall mow and stack. His services are valued at 10s a year, and he pays a rent of 3d.

Henry Dalibron holds 4 acres with a house and must do 96 days work and shall receive one hen. His services are worth 3s 9d.

William Kitte holds 9 acres with a house in villeinage and must do 102 days work in a year, and must do four quarterly brewings, and two boon-works at harvest, and reap one acre of corn, food being supplied by the lord, and must mow in the meadow for two days, food being supplied, and he shall be given two hens and 20 eggs. The above services are worth 7s a year, at the lord's discretion.

How such a jumble of an economic system had come into being it seems pointless to enquire. I rather think that the clue to the situation lies in the phrase 'at the lord's discretion'. What I fail completely to understand or imagine is how the Bailiff and the Reeve, neither of whom could read or write, ever kept track of what every man was supposed to do, to pay and to receive. Cutting notches on tally-sticks was all very well, but there must have been many aspects which could not be thus recorded. The weather was one of them. There must have been some years when it was just not possible for William Kitte to do 102 days' work on the lord's land, even if he completely neglected the cultivation of his own nine acres. What happened then? Was the deficiency added to the next year's quota? I am inclined to the opinion that the nice precision of the tenancy-charter dissolved into wild approximation when it came up against intractable soil, inclement weather, recalcitrant oxen and unwilling peasants. And yet, the system seems to have worked. We do not know how well or how badly it worked, but it was in operation for a very long time. Perhaps all these simple people were endowed with prodigious memories. Even so, there must have been endless disputes, and a certain amount of sharp practice on both sides. I should think that the daily conversation of those tenants in their non-working time – and in their working-time, too, for that matter – was largely about what they had done, what they still had to do, what they had received and what they ought to have received.

There was one respect in which all the peasants had gained equally. By the year 1250 or thereabouts they had all acquired surnames. Of course they had always had names. They had always known each other as John, Robert, Henry, Peter, Osbert, etc., and even their superiors must sometimes have deigned to address them, if at all, other than as 'churl' or 'fellow'. Some of the women had very pretty names – Isolda, Christina, Lucilda, Katerina, Mariota, Elewisia. Indeed, all the women had pretty names. Who would wish to find fault with Mary, Joan, Alice, Agnes, Maud or Matilda? By the middle of the thirteenth century the increasing amount of documentation for legal and fiscal purposes made it necessary to distinguish one John or Matilda from another, clearly and permanently. So surnames became universal. They are of interest to us, not merely because we still have them, but because in their origin they tell us something about the persons who bore them. They tell, for instance, where a person came from, and thereby indicate more mobility amongst the peasantry than one would have expected – Harston, Kersey, Totington, Barley, Teversham, Luton, Cornwallis, Cambridge (mostly, be it noted, names of free men). They tell of a man's occupation – Smith, Woodward, Vaccar (cowherd), Brewer, Barcar (shepherd), Capellan (chaplain), Husewif, Dikeman, Nutrex (food-seller), Miller, Peyntour, Reckener, Beggar, Reeve, Palmer, Carter, etc. They tell whereabouts in the village he lived – Attegate, Attehill, Attewell, Headwell, West, Hurway, Hille, etc. They tell who his father was, or whose 'man' he was – Andrews, King, Legat, Eustace, Knyt, Marshall, etc. They all tell something about a man or his origin, though it is no longer always possible to decipher it. Some names were, at the time, complimentary – Wiseman, Gudlock, Felice, Godemoder – and some were not – Hoverhawe, Gosse, Pettorix.

I have said that the Abbess of Chatteris virtually ruled Foxton, Shepreth and Barrington. That is true, but the Law of the Land set stricts limits to her jurisdiction. With matters of crime, serious theft, murder, sudden death, etc., the Coroner or the Sheriff of the county naturally dealt at the Hundred Court or County Assize. When young Roger Lorimer, aged twelve, was found drowned in the mill-pond at Fowlmere, for instance, his mother who found the body was exonerated and a verdict of accidental death returned; but the vills of Stapleford, Trippelaw, Newton and Foxton ought to have sent men to the inquest as guarantors of their innocence, which they failed to do, and so each vill was fined 9s, the money going into the coffer of the King, not that of the Abbess. Another case which came before the county court instead of the manor court shows that the age-old feud between opposite sides of the river was still kept up:

1327. Thomas Stortford, parson of Barrington, complained that John Andrew, chaplain of Foxton, with others, assaulted him at Barrington and stole two horses. His brother William complained that the same persons assaulted him at Foxton.

Punishment involving prison or the gallows was beyond the jurisdiction of the Abbess, and such punishment, strange as it may seem, was comparatively rare in the lives of the common men. What did concern the Abbess, or her Steward acting on her behalf, to a very considerable extent was the everyday conduct of village affairs.

The Steward for more than twenty years was John of Cambridge. Twice a year at least, sometimes as often as five times a year, he would arrive at the 'hall' with his clerk and a bundle of parchment rolls, without which his task would have been impossible to perform. He seems always to have completed his business in one day, and to have dealt with Madingley and Over in the same day, though of course he may have spent the night in Cambridge, and the clerk may not have bothered to amend the date on the roll. In any case he must have had good horses, and the travelling conditions cannot have been nearly so bad as they were to become much later. If he was Steward of all the Chatteris manors, as seems most probable, he would often spend a week at a time on his travels. There would be many times when he was carrying as much as £30 with him to Chatteris, and it would be interesting to know what precautions, if any, he took for the safeguarding of such considerable sums. His task as administrator was simplified by the fact that all the demesnes were farmed out by this time; even the collection of 'common fines' (fees) was farmed out at Barrington in 1324; but his financial burden was thereby increased. There was still a Bailiff who was nominally responsible for the management of the demesne; he is not much in evidence, though he evidently acted as deputy for the Steward on occasion. The Bailiff was never likely to be popular; the nature of his office ensured that; but in 1324 the appointment of a friar as Bailiff seems to have provoked more resentment than usual:

It is found on the evidence of Brother Robert that Alice Barley would not allow the Lady's bailiff to take a lamb which she had seized from Hugo de Banns, so she is fined 3s 4d for contempt. And Robert Barley is fined 12d for contempt of the Lady and Brother Robert in obstructing him from doing his duty.

Foremost of the minor officials, and most important man in the village for the time being, was the Reeve. He was elected annually by the villagers from amongst their own number, free or bond. Originally he had always been one of the free men, and there had been a certain prestige and some perquisites attached to the office, but now there was little to be got out of the job but headaches and nobody really wanted it. Unfortunately, having been elected, there was no escaping from it except by paying a fine:

Thomas Leger pays the Lady 6s 8d for being quit for the present of the office of Reeve.

Richard Barley pays the Lady 3s 4d for relinquishing the office of Reeve.

It is easy to understand that reluctance to hold office. Vitally important as he was to the manorial system, the Reeve was forced to be a thorn in the flesh of his fellow villagers. To him fell the task of enforcing the rules for the organization of work, collecting fines, chivvying the work-shy, carrying out distraints, etc. He was the unpaid and overworked servant of manor and village alike, and could expect no thanks from either for his pains. On the contrary:

They present that Sir William de la Haye cut down a certain willowtree reserved for this manor, due to the negligence of the reeve; the value of the tree was 6d, which shall be paid by the reeve.

The reeve was ordered to distrain John Smith for customs and services now in arrears to the amount of 12d. The reeve so ordered says that he did make distraint of one young bullock, which he handed over to Brother Robert and the present reeve; they of their own volition gave it back to the owner, therefore he ought not to be charged with further responsibility, and seeks a verdict on this point. Verdict postponed until further inquiry, meanwhile let the money be paid.

That was the simplest way out for the Steward – let the money be paid. The rights and wrongs of the affair could wait for another day.

Then there were the constables, also elected by the whole village. These two men were responsible for the maintenance of law and order, for which in serious cases they were answerable to the Sheriff. Such cases, as already stated, were relatively few, and in the main the constables' task was not the onerous burden it might at first sight appear to have been. Not nearly so difficult as that of the modern policeman. For one thing, they knew everybody and everybody knew them. They knew where and when trouble was likely to occur and who was most likely to cause it. They obviously did not go around looking for trouble, and were sometimes caught unawares. When the 'hue and cry' was raised, as it was almost every time an argument reached the stage of blood-letting, or threatened to do so, then the constables had to do something. Just what they had to do is not clear, but, whatever it was, they had to do it quickly, otherwise they too were in trouble:

They (the jury) present that Robert Lef attacked William Brond with a weapon, whereupon William raised the hue and cry, and rightly so, therefore Robert is fined, but pardoned because he is a pauper. And they present that Richard Smith and Osbert Goodlok, constables, did not do their duty when the hue and cry was raised, so they are fined. (But one was pardoned because he was also reeve.)

There were many similar instances. It would serve no purpose to quote them all, except to point the fact that, if fraternity was the goal towards which man was progressing, he had got no nearer to it than he had to equality.

Finally, in the village hierarchy, there were the ale-tasters, likewise elected by the villagers. This office would appear to have been not at all unpopular, for it was frequently held by the same men for a number of years. I suspect – though I admit without any direct evidence – that there was some canvassing for the office, and perhaps even an element of bribery. The duty of these officers was, in theory, to ensure that the all-important beverage was sold at the right price in the statutory quantities of the correct quality; all of which criteria were fixed by the 'assize' of the assessors appointed for the county. In practice, so much ale was brewed, sold and consumed that standards could not possibly be maintained, and neither ale-sellers nor ale-tasters made any serious attempt to comply with the law. The infringements which are recorded number literally hundreds; those which went unrecorded must have numbered thousands. The assessors cannot possibly have visited any one village more than about twice a year; but since their visit was unannounced they never failed to catch out at least one of the ale-sellers, and usually caught the whole lot.

The fine was generally a penny or twopence, sometimes as much as six-pence. This latter sum might represent the profit on a single brew, or the sales of a single evening. The ale-tasters too were fined; but that, I am sure, was a matter easily adjusted at their next visit to the alehouse. Every set of court minutes contains this sort of thing:

Matilda Nutrex brewed and sold ale in her house and did not have a gallon measure; fined 6*d*.

John Aubrey and John Pake, ale-tasters, did not do their duty; fined 3*d*. Alice Dikeman brewed and sold contrary to assize; fined 6*d*.

Likewise Margery Lot, fined 3*d*; the wife of William Smith, pardoned; Tod Goddard, fined 3*d*.

And so it went on, all through that century and for centuries to come. The only real effect the regulations ever had was to provide a steady trickle of fines to put in the Abbess's money-box. One hopes that, now and then, those pennies helped to provide a little sustenance for the vagrant poor who knocked at the gate of the nunnery.

The court of the Abbess ought, strictly speaking, to have been two courts, a Court Baron and a Court Leet, the former to deal with transactions relating to land-transfers, inheritances, titles, etc., the latter to deal with minor infractions of the law. Indeed I think this was the case, but the distinction became rather blurred by overburdened clerks, especially when they recorded the proceedings directly on the parchment roll, as most of them managed to do. They used a system of standard abbreviations and set formulae, difficult to read at first but fairly easy after long practice. The biggest problem is the deciphering of their writing, a problem ren-dered more acute by the total erasure of some of the entries due to the chafing of sleeves and saddle-bags. Some of the entries, in particular those relating to disputed inheritance, run to a fantastic number of words and testify to the patience of Steward, clerk, jury and contestants alike. I think they must have derived pleasure from such cases, with the possible excep-tion of the clerk. He got rather bored at times, and betrayed the fact by doodling on the precious document.

In every case where there is any doubt, what finally settles the matter is what the jury unanimously declare on oath to be 'the custom of the manor'.

Furthermore the said homages of Barrington, Shepreth and Foxton say that such is the custom amongst them, namely that, if any heir who has claim to a holding by his neglect or inability leaves the land, then reappears after the holding has been granted in court to another person, and a fee paid, he can only recover one third part of the holding, and then only by special favour of the Lady of the manor. And because it is found that Thomas, by concession, paid the entry-fine, it is considered that John Dirgon shall gain nothing by his plea, and be fined for a false claim, and Thomas shall hold the land in villeinage according to the custom of the manor.

Re-marriage always provoked a dispute, as did the departure of a tenant overseas, whether on a crusade or in the service of the King. The case quoted above arose from the fact that Alan Eustace 'married a woman called Muriel, by whom he had a son called Robert who departed overseas and stayed there'. It was as important then as it is now that tenancy of land should be legally established, and there was no other legal basis than 'the custom of the manor'. This was one of the strongest rivets in the System. Security lay in keeping things as they always had been. This, it may be thought, operated entirely to the benefit of the lords, and was devised by them. But that is not true. When security of tenure was at stake, the tenants were as adamant as were the lords that things should stay as they were, as they 'always had been'. One real benefit which such a principle conferred on the peasants was that rents remained unchanged, in some cases for as long as five hundred years. Entry-fines – the sum paid on taking over a holding – did tend to increase over the centuries, but throughout the medieval period they remained remarkably stable.

Rents and fines, however, were not the only means of transferring money from the pockets of the peasants to the coffers of the lords. To pay rent for their holdings, or to provide services in lieu of rent, seemed reasonable enough; and the entry-fine could be excused on the grounds of legal expenses, perhaps. But the exaction of a 'heriot' – usually the tenant's best beast – on inheritance hit the peasants hard, and must have seemed the unfair extortion which it undoubtedly was; unfair because it no longer bore the slightest resemblance to its original form, which was the provision of arms and equipment by the lord. Equally unfair were the many other payments which plagued the peasant throughout his life and ensured that he should never rise above his station by becoming even moderately wealthy. He had to pay to get married; pay to be buried; pay to enter into an agreement with a neighbour; pay for not paying to enter into an agreement with a neighbour; pay to bring a case to court; pay for not bringing a case to court; pay for being at court; pay for not being at court. The only event in his life for which he did not pay was being born.

All those were individual payments. But the money-extraction process did not stop at that. There were numerous communal payments, exacted from a whole village or section of a village. Some were strictly legal; some were not; some clearly indicate that the burden of national taxation was being shifted by the lords from their own shoulders to those of their tenants; all were justified on the grounds of 'ancient custom'. Here is a selection of communal payments made to the Abbess of Chatteris between 1293 and 1324:

The homage of Shepreth pay a total of 12d by ancient custom for tithingpence.
The homage of Foxton pay a total of 13s 4d to the Lady for recognizance and aid.
The whole homage of Barrington owes 2s for the seal of the Abbess placed on their charter relating to the land which they have at farm.
The homage of Madingley pays a total of 14s 6d for tallage.
Fee for renewal of grants; vill of Foxton per capita 20s 7d.
All natives of Foxton for a fifteenth of their services and customs 13s.
Village of Foxton for common tallage 26s 11d.
Village of Foxton for common aid 13s 4d.
The homage of Foxton pay for common aid of their own free will 6s 8d.
From the village of Shepreth for burthsilver 12d.
From the village of Foxton for burthsilver 2s.
The village of Shepreth pays as usual 12d for Hevedbourhsilver.

Those last three items are payments for the upkeep of the manorial hall, and fully justified. As for the rest, I doubt whether the peasants understood them, or any longer tried to. They just paid. That they ever paid anything 'of their own free will' I find difficult to believe. That phrase must surely be a euphemistic formula, with more than a touch of cruel irony about it. One thing which still baffles me is how those peasants could possibly make those payments. Where did they get the money? Most of them were farming eighteen acres or less. On the produce of those few acres they had to exist, they and their families. There could not have been much surplus produce to convert into cash even in a good year, and none at all in a bad year. Perhaps many of the payments were not in fact made by the bulk of the peasantry, but by a handful of the better-off. Two things are certain: the bulk of the peasantry had no money at all to spend on themselves, and their standard of living was abominably low.

It seems then that equality and fraternity may be relegated to the status of pious hopes in the world of the medieval common man. What about liberty? Well, there are clear indications of liberty being wanted and sought for, by some, but not much sign of it being achieved. The distinction between free and bond was very real indeed. The word 'slave' was no longer used in England and had been softened to 'serf' in some countries; but a good two-thirds of the population of English villages were still virtually enslaved. Some of them may have been content with their lot, either from sheer apathy or because they really believed that bondage was the state of life to which it had pleased God to call them. Most of them, I am sure, smarted under the yoke, and would have cast it off if they could. Nor can the Abbess, I feel, have been altogether happy in the possession of these wretched people, body and soul. She may have stifled her conscience with the formula 'custom of the manor'. It was the System. It always had been the System. It always would be the System. She could not change it. Did she try? Other lords, laymen, had gone some way towards reducing the number of their bondmen by granting free status – for a consideration, of course. Perhaps they needed the money more than did the Abbess. In fairness to the Abbess as a person, let me say that her policy was not her own; she was obliged to fall into line with the general policy of the Church, and the Church did not favour freedom for the masses. Here is a statistical picture of the situation in two parishes in 1288; the figures are not, in all probability, complete; the missing numbers are certainly bondmen:

Manor	Shepreth		Foxton	
	Free.	Bond.	Free.	Bond.
Martin	16	8		
FitzFulk	11	2		
De la Haye	4	17	12	12
Chatteris	3	23	9	31
Mortimer			5	3

There were ways of escaping from bondage, apart from paying for freedom when given the chance. The most obvious, and most risky, was simply to run away, leaving everything. Not many did this, but here is one instance:

It is hereby ordered to seize and transport to the Lady's hall 4½ quarters of barley belonging to Robert Leger, and to arrest him bodily wherever he may be found.

Robert got away. He probably took refuge in Cambridge or some other town where, having remained undetected for a year and a day, his freedom was assured. But he could never again return to his native village.

Marriage, with or without permission, was only half an escape. It often meant accepting bondage of another manor, unless it was marriage to a man already free. No bond man or woman could marry without permission, which, of course, had to be bought.

Richard Brun pays the Lady for permission for his daughter to marry Warin West.

Christiana, daughter of Matilda Attgate, pays 2s for permission to marry a certain outsider.

Roger Legat pays 20s for permission to marry his daughter Amita out of the fee of the Lady (i.e. to another manor) namely to John Austin of Harston.

Robert Capon pays 2s to marry Agnes his sister out of the Lady's fee.

Matilda Tomme married John Caye, an outsider, without permission; and he has been employed on the land of William Tomme, a native of this manor; therefore it is ordered to seize all the animals of Matilda and all the land of William until they give satisfaction to the Lady.

Maddingley. It is ordered to seize into the Lady's hands a house and land which Matilda Kreyk held, because she has married a certain free man who is not bound to the land of the Lady.

Even when freedom was bought, there could be a hidden snag, as in this case of 1317:

Thomas Pate, younger brother of Henry, comes to court and says that the holding ought not to be granted to his older brother John, because at the court held at Foxton in 1302 John came and paid the Lady five shillings for permission to go wherever he pleased – The capital pledges of Foxton, Barrington and Shepreth say on oath that John is permanently excluded from any claim on the said holding and *on any other holding of the manor*, because he paid for permission to withdraw himself, and they say that this is the custom which has been in use since time out of memory.

There was the snag. Once you were legally out, you stayed out. That was no doubt why some preferred to stay in. The above example, which is by no means an isolated one, shows only too clearly that the peasants were slaves, not so much of a tyrannical Abbess as of a tyrannical system, and that the system itself was to some extent of their own devising. To be more exact, they may or may not have devised parts of the system, but they certainly acquiesced in them. And the reason for this acquiescence is, I regret to say, all too evident. In the case quoted above, the decision rested with the principal tenants in the three villages – as it nearly always did when the issue was of no financial consequence to the Lady of the manor. Those men could have struck one small blow in the cause of freedom. They could have bent the System ever so slightly and recommended that John Pate be reinstated in the holding he once had. They preferred to uphold the system and keep John out. Why? Because, the more they could keep out, the more land was available for those left in. We have met this attitude before in the common man, and we shall meet it again.

Freedom was sometimes sold with strings attached, so that the freed subject could not fly away completely, or very far:

Ben Tucker pays the Lady one capon for permission to dwell where he likes, for as long as he likes, and he shall come to the Lady's court at Foxton once a year.
Walter in the Heronry of Maddingley was given permission to live outside the manor for a fee of two capons, so that he need not do suit of court apart from one appearance after Easter at the great court.

One of the most popular methods of escape, less used here than in some places, was to enter the ranks of the Church:

– comes and pays the Lady 8s for permission to have his son John ordained to holy orders.
They say that Henry Swan had his son ordained to holy orders without permission, therefore he is fined 4d.
Alice Barley pays the Lady 5s for permission to have her son Peter ordained; granted by a letter from the Abbess.

This practice accounts for the prevalence of uneducated priests and chaplains at that time. Good men many of them no doubt were, but they remained peasants by nature, and it is clear that many of them had no real vocation. Some of the lads who took the 'first tonsure', whereby they became acolytes, probably intended to go no further along the road to priesthood. It was their only chance of getting a smattering of education. Two Foxton youths, William Tomme and Richard King, did go all the way; acolytes in 1337, they were ordained priests in 1345. The flood of ordinations towards the middle of the fourteenth century is best expressed in tabular form, the figures being taken from the Bishop's Register (Cambridge University Library). I do not suggest for one moment that these numbers are all of men escaping from bondage; they include many who felt a genuine call to religion, though I do not know how many; some of them in fact were monks. This list is for the whole diocese of Ely:

	1338	1340	1341	1343–4	1345	1348	1349	1350	1351
Acolytes	283	105	50	188	66	8	0	26	43
Sub-deacons	220	100	93	238	107	9	0	32	25
Deacons	217	77	75	202	100	12	0	18	35
Priests	159	108	63	202	108	7	0	12	55

There is a significance in those figures quite apart from their illustration of the escape from bondage; I shall refer to it later.

What brought most of the villagers to the manor court, apart from the summons of the constable that they should attend, was the necessity to register transactions relating to the sale, lease, sub-letting and inheritance of land and to pay the requisite fees. This had been going on for at least two centuries, perhaps much more, and was to go on for another five centuries without any marked change in form or procedure. It is not part of my brief to discuss the origins and nature of the various forms of contract in vogue, interesting though they undoubtedly are. There were hundreds of these transactions and no real purpose would be served by recounting them all. I will quote but one, chosen because it is typical of many yet unique in one small detail:

Emma, who was the wife of Theobald le Heye of Foxton, surrendered into the Lady's hands a cottage with one acre of land adjoining, situate between the house of Roger Lawe and the house of Thomas the Cowman, to the use of Roger Lawe and his wife Matilda. They pay 6s 8d entry-fine, and shall do the services and customs due. And Roger and Matilda, or whichever of them lives the longer, shall provide Emma with adequate lodging for as long as she lives, and two bushels of maslin each year as long as she lives, half at Michaelmas and the other half at Easter, *along with their good wishes each year*.

A bushel of mixed wheat and rye every six months would not keep old Emma alive for long, and a plank-bed in one corner of the single-roomed cottage was no doubt considered 'adequate' lodging for the poor old woman. Nevertheless, the court held on the Monday after the Feast of St Martin in the year 1300 must have been brightened up just a little by the humanity of that last phrase.

Everybody, at least once in a lifetime, must have been in court for some such reason. But there were many other reasons which brought the villagers there, some of them too often for their liking. One such was the ever-lasting matter of encroachment, overstepping the boundary marks or moving them. With literally hundreds of boundaries, between one strip and the next, between one shott and another, between arable and meadow, between field and road, between common and demesne; and with most boundaries consisting of a balk (narrow strip of turf), a stone, a stick, two bushes a quarter of a mile apart, or even an imaginary line, encroachment was as inevitable as the furrow was long. Some of it must have been accidental, due to failing eyesight, strong ale, working before daylight or after dusk, using a wobbly plough or driving an ox which could not walk straight. Much of it was undoubtedly deliberate, due to an irresistible urge to gain a few inches or feet of land at the expense of a neighbour or of the community. When John de la Haye or Constantine de Mortimer committed the same offence through the agency of their tenants or farmers – which they did with great regularity – the offence was noted and recorded, but no fine was ever imposed. The Abbess knew her limitations. Here are just a few of the many incidents recorded:

Henry Atthill ploughed a public way to the width of half a foot; fined 2d.
Alan Jeffery encroached on manor land, in length one furlong and in width three feet; fined 6d.
William Lawe shortened a balk at Goldrennishaveden by one foot; fined 6d.
William Cassandre removed a certain boundary-mark between him and Thomas Leger, which was placed by agreement of the court.
Peter Clark of Shepreth encroached on the furlong of Metlemadwe to a width of four feet, and has not made amends despite many previous orders.
Nicholas Werry fined 3d because he dug in the pasture of Schaldewellefeld damaging the roadway and causing a nuisance.
John de la Haye ploughed on the Lady's land at the Sheepfold, a furlong in length and two feet in width; fine 'nothing'.

There was no end to it; not, that is, until the Enclosure of five hundred years later.

Then there was the matter of 'morals', which needs to be dealt with rather cautiously, I think. Let me first present the evidence, or some of it:

They say that Matilda, daughter of William Cock, fornicated; fined 6d.
Matilda, daughter of Ate, fornicated with Richard Legat; fined 6d.
Beatrix, daughter of Matilda Attgate, fornicated with Peter Somersham; fined 3d.
Rosea, daughter of Matilda Lawe, fined 12d for lethewyte.
Richard Legat fornicated with Matilda Heyke, a kinswoman, whereby the manor land suffered serious harm; fined 40d.
Alice Gosse fornicated with William Overhawe; fined 6d.
Asselota, daughter of Alan Asselote, fornicated when at day-work of the reeve.
Matilda Thomas did likewise with Peter Woodward; fined.
Agnes Dirgon fornicated with a certain outsider employed by her father; fined 6d and Dirgon's holding is ordered to be seized.
Alice Fenner fornicated with John Taylor out of wedlock; let her be distrained until she shall pay the fine.

There are ever so many more, but that will do. I am not writing a modern novel. Had I been writing this book a hundred years earlier I would no doubt have omitted this paragraph altogether or dismissed its content with no more than a brief deprecatory reference to the 'immorality of the lower classes'. Such an attitude is no longer realistic or excusable. Yet I approach the subject with caution, not for any reason of prudishness, but because I feel that it may all too easily be misunderstood. There is more to it than just an attitude towards sex. To begin with, I do not suppose that there was any more carrying-on – or any less – in Foxton than anywhere else. Neither do I suppose that more than a small fraction of the carrying-on was detected and reported in the court. When everybody lives in a glass house, stone-throwing is not popular or profitable. I doubt whether the culprits who were detected, any more than those who were not, felt any real sense of guilt, any consciousness of having sinned, despite the teaching of the Church. I think that any loss of esteem which they incurred in the eyes of their fellow villagers would be attributable solely to their stupidity in having been found out. I am sure that, in dealing with this aspect of medieval life, we can dismiss the idea of any social stigma such as would have been incurred by similar offenders against the moral code of Victorian England.

Then why, in a rural setting where men and women lived in close daily contact with nature in the raw, was natural behaviour punished as though it were an offence? It could hardly be classed as an offence against God. Nor against society. Free men and women could carry on as much as they liked, and incur no fine. Lords and ladies had even more licence, though perhaps one ought to exclude the Abbess from this generalization. They incurred neither fine nor reproof. The unfortunate people fined by the court were all bondmen and bondwomen. *That* was their offence! The result of their tumbling in the hay might well be that one of them would be unfit for work for a time or that a little bastard of doubtful parentage would present a legal problem for future courts. Moreover, it undermined the Abbess's position as sole arbiter of the right to marry. That, I think, is the real explanation of this strange manorial custom. That, plus the obvious fact that it was yet another means of extracting a few hard-earned pennies from the helpless peasants. It had nothing to do with morality. Just simple economics and social expediency.

Many of the misdemeanours which landed the medieval peasants in the court of the manor were precisely those which land people in the magistrate's court today, and there is no real point in recounting and illustrating them all. There were brawls resulting in bloody noses; there was petty theft and housebreaking; there was debt and denial of debt; obstruction of roads and paths; cutting down trees; slander, trespassing, hooliganism. They committed all the minor offences you can think of, and some which you would not think of, such as dumping manure in the street or going on the road with a cart after sunset. There are however a few more items which I will mention and illustrate because they shed some light on a way of life and thought so different from that of today.

The first is pound-breaking:

Margery Attchurch and Alice Swan broke the manor pound and removed their geese; fined 4d (Barrington).
John Rose broke the manor pound and removed a cow impounded for trespass; fined 3d.

It was a surprisingly rare offence, surprising in view of the frequency with which it was to occur two centuries later. The pound was a fenced enclosure in the centre of the village, near the hall of the manor. In it the constables had to place all the animals found straying on the roads or in the corn or meadow (hence 'Little Boy Blue, come blow up your horn'), also animals seized for non-payment of debt, etc., and secured in such a way that they could not be removed by their owners except under supervision – or, unsupervised, by 'breaking' the pound. Originally this would have meant actually breaking the fence. The prohibition was not part of the manorial money-extraction campaign, but a measure of great antiquity devised by the community for the protection of the community. The manor had appropriated the jurisdiction and the fines, but the latter were negligible in relation to the damage which could be done by straying animals. It is of interest to note that the pound survived in many villages long after the manorial system had decayed.

Another item is poaching and here again is a surprise. One reads so much about the savagery of the forest laws and hears so many lurid tales about the brutality of much later methods of discouraging and punishing poachers – man-traps, spring-guns and the like – that one would expect it to be a prominent feature in medieval village life. Well, the fact is that, in three villages over a period of thirty-five years, only one case of poaching is recorded:

1320. Barrington, William, the servant of John Marchant, took fishtraps and set them in private waters at Archford dam; fine one penny.

As I shall not refer to this topic again, let me anticipate somewhat and quote the only other references which occur in later records. The first is in 1492:

John Hille of Newton, shepherd to John Thirlowe, at various times since the last court, was found fishing in private waters and banks called Barrington Re, in which he took fish where no one has the common right to do so; fined 4d, and ordered not to lay any more nets or traps for catching fish, on pain of a fine of 20s.

The next, and last, instance occurred in 1529:

A certain John Castell of Barrington came into this manor of Foxton and without right or official permission of the Lady fished in a certain pool next to Manhill and there took various fish, namely pike, roach and eels to the value of 12d and carried away those fish; so he is fined 12d.

This is of particular interest to me because I have in my possession a number of lumps of chalk, roughly fashioned, with grooves cut round the middle, which served to anchor the fish-traps at the right depth in the river. I also have the tool, unique as far as I know, which the bailiff used to locate and cut adrift the illicit traps, and the hook with which he retrieved the floating trap (made of osiers) and its contents. These objects were all found in the mud dredged from the river near 'Archford dam'. The number of such trap-sinkers and the smaller net-sinkers found in the same way all along the river suggests that fish-poaching was quite common, as one would expect it to be. Yet there is no evidence at all of the poaching of rabbits, hares, pheasants, ducks, heron and the other wild creatures which must have abounded in the large stretches of mere and waste which constituted half the area of the parish. De la Haye and Mortimer, like all the other lords, had 'right of free warren' on their manors, which meant that they could legally hunt everything furred or feathered except deer and boar. We can be quite sure that the peasants did not share this privilege. But those lords cannot possibly have maintained constant supervision over the whole of their territory. It may be that the Abbess, not being a hunter and secretly glad to have a subtle means of getting a little bit of revenge for the high-handed attitude of the knights, instructed her Steward to ignore the matter of poaching – except in her own private stretch of river, of course. It may be that Sir John caught the occasional careless peasant with a hare or rabbit in his wallet and promptly lopped off his ear or had him soundly whipped without reference to the court of the Abbess. But I do not really think so. I think that the men of Foxton, Barrington and Shepreth – and every other village in the land – were the ardent and skilful poachers that real countrymen always were, and that, safely relying on silence, stealth and darkness, they were never caught. Well, hardly ever.

Then there was the matter of 'foreigners'. Anyone who came from another village or another manor was a foreigner, or 'outsider', to lodge or employ whom was an offence:

John Dikeman lodged foreigners at harvest-time. Fourteen others committed the same offence; all distrained.

William Cock lodged foreigners at harvest-time to the detriment of the whole village; fined 6d.

Joan Parsons of Shepreth pays 2s fine for receiving men about whom there was suspicion.

There is more in this than the traditional parochialism which regards all outsiders as untrustworthy, a nuisance or having 'no right to be there', and which still lingers on in small measure, sometimes not wholly without justification. The attitude may have its roots deep in antiquity, may indeed be a survival of inter-tribal feuds, and is almost certainly a manifestation of the urge for self-protection on the part of the community. But here again the manorial system has seized upon an established thing and turned it to manorial profit, justified, no doubt, on the grounds of manorial security. A foreigner might well be a fugitive from another manor; if such suspects were lodged and given work in this manor, then the bondman of this manor might be tempted to take to the road.

One might well be led to ask, in view of all these prohibitions and impositions, whether there was anything at all which those peasants could do of their own free will without incurring the displeasure of the Church, the financial penalties of the manor, or both. I can only answer with surmises and deductions, lacking any direct evidence. They could, I suppose, get drunk. But getting drunk on ale in the fourteenth century would be rather like trying to get drunk on shandy today. The brew would have had to be exceptionally strong, and even then saturation point would be reached long before a state of jollification. They had lots of holidays – 'holy days' – when work was forbidden for all or part of the day. But the animals still had to be tended even on holy days, and it is by no means certain that the ban on work applied to working on their own holdings – although it did so apply two centuries later when the Church had assumed some of the former manorial authority. What did they do with those holidays? Did they sing and dance and play games?

The children and adolescents no doubt found ways of extracting amusement from simple things and pastimes, as children always have and, I hope, always will. Some of their pastimes were of such a nature – stoning a cockerel to death, torturing cats and dogs, tormenting lonely old women, and so on – that we can only be thankful for their falling out of fashion at last, though well within living memory. Others, such as hopscotch, cherry-stones, conkers, blind-man's-buff, etc., still survive here and there, mostly in junior-school playgrounds in rural areas. The parents of those children, I should think, were content to spend their brief leisure time in drinking, gossiping and making things. They still made with their own hands their furniture, clothes, shoes, table-ware (wooden), toys, ornaments, tools and implements, with some help from the smith and the carpenter in the case of the latter.

When the fair was started in 1310 and another one in 1325, it was easier for some of them to buy some of the things which they could not easily make, such as hones, knives, pots, trinkets, etc., and twice a year at least they were provided with an opportunity and excuse for a certain amount of merry-making. This was incidental to the main purpose of the fairs, the one instituted by Mortimer and the other by De la Haye, both by royal licence. The lords were motivated by no desire to provide entertainment for the masses, simply by the desire to increase their manorial revenue from the tolls paid by stall-holders. The Abbess does not appear to have applied for licence to hold yet a third fair. Perhaps she did not approve of such junketings, or, more probably, she was discouraged by the fate which befell the Mortimer fair in 1337, when Sir John de la Haye led a band of armed retainers who wrecked the show and prevented the tolls from being collected.

Despite the absence of much direct contemporary evidence, later retrospective evidence points clearly to the fact that the village church played a major role in village life, and we can be sure that the major saints' days and events of the Christian year were not called 'feasts' and 'festivals' for nothing. The Church from very early times had wisely recognized that ceremony and spectacle satisfied a basic need in the human mind and for that reason had grafted Christian ritual and story on to the old pagan stock of myth and custom, to produce a hybrid growth which still to some extent flourishes today. Plough Monday, Candlemas, Shrovetide, Palm Sunday, Maundy Thursday, Easter, Hokeday, May-day, Whitsun, Midsummer, Lammas, Michaelmas, Allhallows, Christmas, Childermas – to mention only the principal feasts – all had a significance for the villagers, not always entirely religious but mostly by this time inseparable from the religious aspect in their minds. The feasts provided something to look at, something to do, something to talk about, something to look forward to. They punctuated the working year, for farming practice followed the Church calendar. The cow did not calve on 25 August; she calved on 'the day after

St Bartholomew'. Rents were paid at 'Lady Day' and 'Michaelmas' – as indeed they still are in many cases.

The church, the building in and around which those festivities were largely held, had by this time been enriched by gifts and endowments until its nominal taxable value was just over £12 a year. In fact, with the growth of the village and consequent increase in the amount of tithes, it must have been worth at least twice that amount, perhaps three or four times as much. It had been enlarged in about 1240, when the former nave became the chancel and a new and larger nave was added. It was therefore a desirable financial asset to whoever 'owned' it, but it was not at all clear who did.

The situation was clarified in 1275 when the Prior and Convent of Ely appropriated the church. They had the official consent of Bishop, Archbishop and Pope, but carelessly forgot to ask the King, an oversight which cost them 500 marks. The Abbess had no say in the matter, beyond agreeing to share her pasture with the Rector. As for the Vicar and parishioners, I do not think that their opinion was sought. The continued growth of the village, coupled with the decay of the existing building, necessitated a fourth rebuilding of the church which took place between 1318 and 1338 and was mainly the work of Master Thomas de Foxton, who had his name inscribed on one of the beautiful stained-glass windows.

It was clearly intended that this new church should accommodate the whole population of the village, and I think we can safely assume that the whole population was frequently there. There was a moral compulsion to attend which few would have questioned or resisted. They might begrudge the Rector his tithes and mortuaries (payment at death, usually of the second-best beast); they might often wonder what the words of the service meant, for Latin did not come within their field of knowledge – it was often but dimly comprehended by the priest or chaplain, for that matter. But attendances at church did at least afford a respite from the everlasting round of toil. Furthermore, though this was perhaps even more dimly comprehended, it gave some sort of a meaning to life, an assurance that there was something at the end of it all, that there really was justice and goodness and mercy despite all appearances to the contrary. That vague something was represented and symbolized, not in the words of the service, but in the adornment of the church – windows, mural paintings, images – which at this time was more beautiful and colourful than it had ever been before or was to be again. Merely to be there, in the company of their own kind, was an experience which few would willingly have missed.

There were no doubt some who resented the interference of holy days with their programme of essential work, for the one fact clearly understood by all was that one had to work to live. I am sure that that was accepted as a natural law. What they did not accept as natural any longer was the fact that they should have to work for the benefit of somebody else. Simple people they may have been, uncouth, illiterate, narrow in outlook, slow to change, but they were not stupid. They could see that there was much that was wrong in the manorial system. Its injustices and impositions were too patent to be missed by even the simplest of them, and there must have been some who felt, though it was beyond their power to express, the worst wrong of all in the system, namely that it tried to keep a man in his place for ever, when his instinct was to move out of it, to move upwards. There did not seem to be much that they could do about it except, like recalcitrant animals, to kick, to jib, to refuse or deliberately bungle the task which was not to their liking or their own immediate advantage. There is ample evidence of this:

All the customary tenants of Foxton are fined 3s 4d for contempt in refusing to fetch the Lady's straw in the fields of Shepreth.

Henry Tucker refused to thresh the Lady's corn; fined 6d.

They say that Gerold Carpenter's wife did not tie her boon-work sheaves as she ought; pardoned.

All tenants holding half a virgate of land, except John Golde who was then reeve, are fined because they refused to do the carting when summoned.

All customary tenants fined because they refused to carry the Lady's hay out of the water on the day when they were mowing.

William Barley, Beatrix Gosse, Alan Asselote and Henry Werry each fined 3d because they did not come with their carts.

William Cock fined for contempt in saying that the tenants did not know that they were supposed to mow in a swamp.

Roger Capon fined because he refused to come to Barley when ordered.

Benedict Brewer fined for damage done at harvest-time.

Hugh Reeve, Sabina Alwyne, Robert Knyt fined 6d because they did not come to work when summoned by the reeve.

Nicholas Werry fined 6d because he reaped badly the Lady's corn.

Thomas Leger fined 12d because he reaped the Lady's corn when the weather was considered too cold. Likewise six others.

Agnes Dirgon gathered the corn badly; fined 3d. Likewise thirteen others.

Nine women and boys fined 2d and 3d for gleaning badly.

Ten of the tenants of full holdings (i.e. 18 acres) were each fined 2d because they made their sheaves much smaller with twisted bands when they ought to have made sheaves of the same size as they did when working for the Lady.

This last item, from the roll of 1326, is clear evidence of an attempt to cheat the Rector of some of his tithes, a practice which was perennial, and of which the Bishop indignantly complained in 1386. The Peasants' Revolt did not break out until 1381, when more articulate leaders had emerged and economic conditions were more favourable to the success of their efforts, but it is clear that revolt had been brewing for a long time before then in the villages of England.

I have by no means exhausted the store of interesting details contained in these documents; there is still much that I could say about the people, houses, crops, animals, field-names, etc., but I do not wish to tax too far the patience of my readers. Before the chapter ends, however, one topic so far omitted must have a place. It may have been noticed that I have not mentioned the Brook, and in consequence it may be thought that one of the threads of my theme has faded. I can assure you that it has not. The Brook has its lines in the script just as has every other feature of the village. In 1318 the following entries occur:

All the capital pledges of Foxton fined 2s for not putting right the brook which was stopped up by Thomas Roys.
John Kersey fined 12d for diverting the brook which flows through the middle of the manor, to a width of half a foot, and causing a nuisance.
Simon le Roo diverted the brook; fined 12d.
Roysia Kelle widened the stream by half a foot; fined 12d.
Ate Reeve did the same alongside his yard, widening the brook by letting the other bank fall in to a width of two feet; fined 3d.
Nicholas Werry allowed the brook to be unlawfully widened by neglect, to the extent of two feet; fined 6d.
John Goudlok allowed the brook in the public highway to run where it ought not to run, whereby the road was damaged to the public harm; pardoned, but ordered to put it right.
John, son of Richard Smith, encroached on the common brook; fined 6d.
Richard Pake fined 3d for encroaching on the road by digging at le Grenedich next to his croft, to the public annoyance.

What were they trying to do, with their half a foot here and two feet there? They were trying to gain a little personal advantage by making their own private ponds in the course of the Brook, to facilitate their own drinking and that of their livestock. If they had been allowed to get away with half a foot, they would no doubt have taken half a yard, two yards, three yards. Not only would half the high street have disappeared; those unfortunate people who lived in the east end of the village would have had no water, or only water in which the west-enders' cattle had already trampled. But they were not allowed to get away with it. Somebody – I wish I knew his name – spoke out and put a stop to it. The Brook was the Town Brook. It was for everybody, not just for those who lived in the west end. It was the life-line of the village.

5 Black Death

Most history books, except those dealing specifically with this topic, dismiss in a paragraph or two, several pages at the most, an event which affected the social and economic history of England and much of Europe to an extent which few other events ever did. The reasons for this are, I believe, lack of concrete evidence, difficulty in interpreting what evidence there is, and embarrassment at the implications inherent in some of the evidence. It is the first of those reasons which is responsible for the brevity of this chapter. Our last view of Foxton was that of a community thriving despite all the restrictions, with a population steadily increasing despite the seemingly adverse conditions, and more than one sign of the rebirth of a community spirit. Our next view of the same village will be that of the remnants of a community struggling, not very vigorously, to haul itself out of the slough of despair and despondency. Something, between those two phases, must have hit the village hard. Something did.

It came from the East, or so it is generally thought. We know it as bubonic plague, caused by a bacterium transmitted by fleas carried by rats. It apparently killed the rats but not the fleas, or not before they had tasted both rats and humans. It had a variant form known as pneumonic plague, contagious as between human and human. The speed with which it travelled and the distances which it covered suggest that rats and fleas may have been given an unfair share of the blame for it. Its effects and symptoms were – to put it mildly and briefly – nauseating and fatal. The people of Europe knew it as 'the pestilence'; the name Black Death was invented much later. In the course of a series of outbreaks lasting more than twenty years it killed rich and poor, young and old, good and bad with an impartiality and ferocity that struck terror and despair to the hearts of millions. It spread roughly north-westward across the continent, reached southern England in 1348, spread rapidly in the spring of 1349 to the rest of the country and raged pitilessly all that summer. Its course was as unpredictable as its cause was unknown. Some towns and villages escaped almost untouched; in others the population was almost wiped out. Some villages escaped the pestilence of 1349 only to fall victims to later outbreaks, especially that of 1361. It continued to break out sporadically over the next three hundred years.

Precise or even approximate casualty figures can never be known. Nobody had any specific reason for compiling statistics. Numerical statements made by later chroniclers are clearly exaggerations intended to impress rather than to inform. Ecclesiastical and manorial records are the only source of real information, and they are often incomplete or misleading; some even hint at a conspiracy of silence; many have been lost or destroyed; many were never made because those who should have made them were themselves victims of the plague. For all that, there are good grounds for believing that at least one third of the total population of England perished.

There is not one scrap of direct evidence that the plague hit Foxton in the fourteenth century, and the same could be said of hundreds of villages throughout the land. But there are facts both general and specific from which a conclusion may be drawn. I am well aware that, if one is determined to arrive at a particular conclusion, one will interpret facts in such a way as to lead towards it. The reader is free to interpret these facts in his own way. Here they are:

(i) In the year 1349 alone there were one hundred and eleven appointments of priests to vacant livings in the parishes of Cambridgeshire, which was something like ten times the normal rate. Several livings fell vacant three times within the year, and a good number twice. The vacancies occurred all over the county – but did not include Foxton; that is, no appointment was made at Foxton. How many of the vacancies were due to death by plague we do not know. The Bishop's Register does not once mention 'pestilence' – or, if it does, the word escaped my eyes. It does not even mention death in the vast majority of cases; it merely says that the living was 'vacant'. It is evident that there was a drastic thinning of the ranks of the clergy in this area. And yet, as the figures quoted earlier indicate, relatively few ordinations were made in the next two years. It is easy to see in this situation an indication that the plague was particularly virulent in the area; it is difficult not to see an indication that some of the priests deserted their post in the hour of crisis. If they did, it is not for me to justify or condemn; I merely adduce the fact as evidence of a plague-stricken area.

(ii) In the sixteenth century there are specific references to an unusual number – unusual for a village, that is – of people dying of 'the plague', and there were four houses in particular in which deaths occurred with such rapid frequency as to suggest that the plague was the cause. Foxton was evidently a village in which conditions conducive to the outbreak of plague existed, whatever those conditions were. And it is no use saying that the conditions were overcrowding, dirt, rats and fleas, because those features were common to every town and village in the land, and the plague often struck where there was no overcrowding and there was not – or should not have been – an excess of dirt, fleas or rats; in many monastic houses, for instance. It could be that the Town Brook in some way contributed to the spread or conservation of the disease. The plague virus could lie dormant for a long time, or it could be introduced afresh. If rats and fleas were needed, they would never be lacking.

(iii) The population of Foxton in 1327 was at least 320 – their names are known – and by 1349 it must have risen to well over 350. The next date at which an approximate count is possible is 1492, when the population was certainly not more than 150. Something drastic must have occurred to account for such a drop in the figures. One can confidently rule out flood, fire, war and enclosure for sheep-farming.

(iv) The Chatteris manor had 50 tenants in 1330; it had 18 tenants in 1492. The De la Haye manor had 24 tenants in 1330; the St George manor had 10 in 1492. Mortimer's manor had 6 tenants in 1330; none at all in 1492 apart from the farmer. The number of landless labourers may have increased in the meantime – I have no evidence that it did – but it could not have done so in a proportion to balance those figures. The size of the holdings had increased, obviously. Some men in 1492 held three houses and three '18 acre wares'. Two of the three demesnes were being farmed by men who were not resident in Foxton. They each had large flocks of sheep, but they had not 'enclosed' any of the Foxton land; they were using the 'commons' of Foxton, and incurring much wrath thereby. There are references to 'Waste' and 'more' in 1492 and subsequent years in such a context as to suggest that a lot of land had gone out of cultivation.

(v) There are well over seventy family names known in Foxton around the date 1330. Of these, only four are still to be found in the village in 1492. Families die out naturally and move elsewhere, or produce only daughters and so a change in name. In any period of 150 years it is likely that up to four-fifths of the names will change as was the case here in the period following 1492. There ought to have been at least three times as many family-names surviving from 1330 to 1492 as there were, perhaps six times as many, when one considers how much greater mobility there was in the period after 1492.

My conclusion is that two-thirds of the population of the village perished in the plagues of 1349 and subsequent years and that the effects of that disaster were felt for nearly two centuries afterwards. On the country as a whole the effects were not nearly so disastrous or so long lasting. Indeed it could be argued and demonstrated that the overall effect of the plagues was good rather than bad – depending on the ease with which one can discount the value of millions of human lives. The trend towards over-population was checked. There was more land available for the survivors. The shackles of the manorial system were loosened; the peasant found that his services could command a higher price. The hold of papal and ecclesiastical authority upon the consciences and purses of the whole population, but especially of the peasantry, was likewise loosened. All of which may or may not have been for the general good. As regards this one small village, there was nothing but bad in the outcome. There is but a single instance known of a village ceasing to exist as a direct result of the plagues; yet many must have suffered as Foxton did, and many must have faced the same long, slow, uphill climb to recovery.

Having already involved the Church in this chapter, it would perhaps be appropriate to continue the theme, for it fits in more neatly here than elsewhere.

The Church undoubtedly received a setback as a direct result of the plagues, quite apart from the thinning-out of the clergy and the loss of up to half the congregation. The faith of the survivors was badly shaken. Some blamed the Church for not having given timely warning of this divine punishment for their wickedness, if that is what it was. Some, and they included at least one bishop, said that many of the priests had failed in their duty and abandoned their flock. Some said that God had failed in his duty – he ought to have taken the wicked and spared the good. The overall effect seems to have been something of a paradox. On the one hand there was a bitter renunciation of belief and a denial of the authority of the Church. Nowhere, I think, is this more dramatically illustrated than by an incident which occurred at Foxton in 1377, when a murderer who had availed himself of the time-honoured privilege of sanctuary in the church was dragged bodily from his refuge and handed over to civil justice; one of only three such occurrences in the whole history of the diocese of Ely. On the other hand there was a determination to do even more than before to earn divine forgiveness or secure divine protection, a resurgence of faith and piety which resulted in a spate of church-building and embellishment; more chapels, more saints, more images. At Foxton the Guild of St Anne was formed. The cult of this saint – the mother of the Virgin Mary – seems to have been in abeyance for a long time; it now became prevalent here and in certain parts of France, where chapels were dedicated in honour of St Anne, particularly where the plagues had wrought most havoc. Pilgrimage once more became fashionable and belief in the healing powers of some saints stronger than ever.

By the middle of the fifteenth century this renewal of faith had gained the upper hand of despondency and disbelief. Hundreds of village churches testify to this fact in their outward appearance, which has remained substantially unchanged since then. Many of them were undoubtedly due for rebuilding in any case. Time, weather and neglect had played havoc with the lovely church which Master Thomas had built at Foxton, especially with its roof of thatch. And fashion was changing, as fashion always does. Plans were made for a better church – not bigger, as regards floor-space, for there was no need of more room, but higher – with a bell-tower, and a roof which would be sparrow-proof, weather-proof and a joy to behold from inside the church. Bishop Grey in 1456 launched the appeal for funds with an Indulgence promising forgiveness of sins, truly repented and confessed, to all who should contribute in any way to the 'maintenance of the lights or any of the ornaments of the said church, or to the fabric of the Chancel, or of the nave or of the bell-tower'. There was no rich benefactor to take the bulk of the financial burden; it rested on the whole village for a long time. Contributions were still coming in sixty years after the appeal was launched. When the work was finally completed in about 1540 – at least one major change of plan having been made in the meantime – the church looked very much as it looks now except for the glistening whiteness of tower and clerestory, and there were few people in the village who had not contributed to the cost in some way, as these extracts from some of their wills indicate:

1516 John Goodwyne:
    to the Rode loft on quarter barley,
    to the bells ii busshells barley,
    to the sepulcre ii busshells barley,
    to Saynt Annes gilde ii bushells barley.

1519 Anabull Fuller:
    to the bellys oon combe,

to the Roodelofte oon quarter mallt,
to the torches oon combe malte,
to the churche of Foxton xiiis iiii*d*.
to the Roodeloft in the churche of Foxton to the gilting of the same xixs vi*d*.

1519 Alice Pepercorne:
to the Rodlofte in the said church oon quarter barley,
to saincte Anne light ii bushelles barley,
to the belles ii bushelles barley,
to saincte Ann gilde oon table clothe flaxen,
to the churche of Foxton too half shetis for to make ii altare clothes.

1520 John Spencer:
to the bellys one combe barley.

1522 John King:
to the roode loft xxs.
to the Bells iiis iiii*d*.

1523 Lady Anne St George
to the Bells iiis iiii*d*,
to the Rode Lofte in the same Churche xx quarters malte,
to Seynt Annes gylde vi quarters Malte and one Cowe to lett to one poore bodie paying iis by yere and kepe same the stock and so the saide Cowe to be lett within the towne of Foxton.

1524 Robert Alanson:
to the Rood Loft vis viii*d*,
to the bells xii*d*,
to the torchys xii*d*.

1524 John King:
to the Roode in the saide cherche of Foxton vis viii*d* and xxs that I owe for the legace of my father to the saide Roode Loft,
iii shete to the Coverynge of the Rood Lofte and one shete to the newe Rood.

1526 William Fuller:
vi bushells barly to the sustentacion of iii tapers usually to be brint before the sacrament at the tyme of the consecration.

The Abbess, too, made her contribution, by increasing the fines for breaking the village bye-laws and donating one half of the fine to the church. The last contribution from a dying parishoner came in 1544:

William Styrmyn:
to the bells ther xii*d*,
to the Churchwarke of Foxton xii*d*.

There were no more, not because the 'churchwarke' was finished, but because the Reformation had begun. That put an end to many things, including St Anne's Guild, torches, tapers, quite a few of the saints' days in the calendar, and all this sort of thing:

to the iiii orders of Frieres in Cambridge to eche of them *xs* so eche of them singe one virgintall for my soule, my husbond's soule and all Christen soulles.

I bequeath ii mylche bullocks to kepe my obite yeerly.

I wille that xxx masses be saide for my soule and all christen soules after my decease at a conveniant tyme shortly after my death.

I will that one lientall of masses be celebrate for my soule.

I bequethe to the highte Aulter in the same Churche for my tithes negligently paide on cumbe barley.

I bequeth to the high Awter of my parishe cherche for my tithes and offerins negligently forgoten *xxd.*

6　The Middle Ages Linger On

Writers of history-books and compilers of examination syllabuses usually take the year 1485 as the dividing line between Medieval and Modern History. If one must draw a line somewhere, that is a convenient point at which to draw it. Of course there are, as everyone knows, no dividing lines in history; one era merges imperceptibly with the next, a fact which this chapter amply illustrates. The material on which it is based is a series of manor-court rolls of Foxton Bury which begins at 1492 and goes on almost continuously from there; and a continuous series of wills from 1516. It will be necessary for me to stray back into the preceding centuries to pick up the threads of my story, and I shall follow some of them through beyond the middle of the sixteenth century. Thus it will be apparent that the Middle Ages lingered on for a long time after 1485 in rural England, whatever momentous changes were taking place in the towns and in the world at large.

Even rural England was not without its momentous changes. In 1395, at the ancient manor-house which stood on the site still known as 'Hallyards' at Shepreth, there was a family gathering to celebrate some happy event or other, from which emerged a simple document of great symbolic significance. It read:

Let all know by these present that we, Baldwin St George, Knight, and Joan my wife, William Blyton and Mary my wife, have liberated from Bondage and set free William Cole of Shepreth and his wife with all offspring created and to be created by them for ever from all services and villeinage.

The significance of this is that lords of a manor have voluntarily and without condition abolished the slavery of one of their tenants, a procedure known as 'manumission'. It was not the end of all bondage but, in one manor at least, it was the beginning of the end. The same thing was happening on manors all over England; had in fact been happening for some time, but with increasing frequency after the plagues of the fourteenth century and the Peasants' Revolt of 1381. We need not here concern ourselves with all the reasons in detail. Suffice it to say that, fortunately, such things do happen, and that bondage died a natural death; and that by the year 1485 there were very few Englishmen who were not 'free'.

I need hardly state, I am sure, that this does not mean that henceforth all the land was free in the sense that it cost nothing, or that no more rents were paid. Lords of manors were not *that* magnanimous! They still had to live! What happened was this: tenants who, under the old system, had been bondsmen, now paid a fee or entry fine on taking up their holding, and paid an annual rent for it in cash, but owed no services beyond the obligation to attend the manor court and pay the statutory fee of a penny or twopence each time. All this was enrolled in the court minutes, and the tenant received a copy of the entry, hence he was called a copyholder and his land was a copyhold tenement. Those tenants who had previously been free continued to pay entry-fines and rents as before; their entry-fines were soon to be considerably increased, but their rents remained ridiculously low, sometimes as low as one peppercorn (meaning 'o'). They became 'freeholders' and their land was freehold. Thus it is evident that the old class-distinction was by no means abolished, either in fact or in name. Indeed it was not finally abolished until 1922. Moreover, though services and fealty and other traces of feudalism had ceased in fact, all copyhold deeds continued to embody the ancient formula:

– granted seisin thereof to him his heirs and assigns by the rod at the will of the lord according to the custom of the manor paying therefor so much in rent suit of court and all other services as of ancient custom due, and he did fealty and paid his fine and was admitted tenant thereof –

which continued to be written in Latin until 1733. The legal profession was most reluctant to allow the Middle Ages to come to an end.

Now let us fill in the manorial background, beginning with the De la Haye manor and briefly tracing its fragmentation; for, as the manorial system dissolved, so did many of the manors. The De la Haye line ended with a daughter, Margaret, who in about 1360 married Sir John Dengayne and took the Foxton-Shepreth manor with her as dowry. She died, leaving Sir John in possession. He married again, and had two daughters by his second wife. When Sir John died at Shepreth in 1392 his daughters inherited the manor in equal parts, and it was divided for the first time in two hundred years. Joan Dengayne married Baldwin St George of Hatley; Mary Dengayne married William Blyton. The Blytons had an only daughter, Margery, who in 1426 married John Wimbish, who thus acquired the half-manor which bears his name to this day. Two generations of male Wimbishes held it, then once more the male line failed, and it passed in equal portions to two sisters, becoming two quarter-manors. Both sisters married but neither had any children, so both quarter-manors came on to the market in about 1560–5, when John Swan of Newton bought one quarter, and the other was divided into two eighths, one of which was bought by Sir Ralph Warren, the other by Edward Ingrey. Meanwhile the St George family was thriving; they held the half-manor, along with their Hatley and Kingston estates, for four generations. Lady Anne St George actually lived in Foxton for a time after the death of her husband Sir Richard in 1511. The half-manor of Foxton-Shepreth became the dowry of her daughter Anne who married John Docwra in 1517; though she, or rather he, did not actually get it until old Lady Anne died in 1524. The name of Docwra has stuck to it ever since, despite all the vicissitudes and the fact that only one manor-court was held in that name. In about 1566 this half-manor likewise was up for sale. One half of it (i.e. one quarter of the original manor) was bought by Edward Ingrey; the other half was bought in roughly equal portions by Thomas Campion and Philip Welbore.

In view of all that, it now becomes clear, I think, why there are so many 'manor houses' dotted about the countryside. We began with one Lord of the Manor, and end up with five, owning respectively one quarter, one eighth, three eighths, one eighth and the final eighth of a manor. And all because the gentry produced daughters instead of sons, or needed ready money, or thought that, in buying a manor, they were acquiring a title and honours. What they were really doing was investing in land. But, assiduously encouraged by their lawyers, they kept up the illusion of 'honours' for a long time, and many of them purchased coats of arms to lend further substance to their notions of gentility. Many generations were to come and go before the title of 'Gent.' (it looked and sounded even better when latinized to *Generosus* or *Armiger*) was willingly abandoned.

Having gone thus far towards deflating the dignity of these new 'lords' whose lordship was founded upon hard cash, let me dispel one other illusion. It is all too easy to assume that one eighth of the original De la Haye manor meant a neat block of eighty acres of land in one corner of the parish, or a park surrounded by wall or fence, with a manor-house secluded in the middle of it. In the case of really large manorial estates that is precisely what did happen, but they are relatively few. What Warren, Campion and Welbore each bought was anything up to eighty strips of land scattered all over the two parishes, plus about twenty acres of pasture, meadow, woodland and waste similarly scattered. The process of consolidating holdings had begun, it is true, but it had a long way to go yet, and the face of the land in the early sixteenth century looked much as it had looked three centuries earlier. Some swampy ground had been drained; some woodland had been cleared; but the pattern was the same.

The Mortimers continued their loyal service to the Crown, as soldiers and as courtiers, which left them little time to devote to their Foxton lordship. Even when Sir John de la Haye wrecked the Mortimer fair in 1337 the Mortimers had made no reply, so far as we know. The male line of Mortimers came to an end in about 1375. The Foxton manor was inherited by one of three daughters, Cecily, who married Sir John Ratcliffe. He died in 1428, and Cecily married again, this time to Sir John Harling. Their son Robert married, in about 1458, Joan Gonville, and had one daughter, Anne. She must either have been a very attractive girl or endowed with much more than the Foxton manor of a mere two hundred acres, for she married three times, first Sir Robert Chamberlain, then Robert Wingfield, finally Lord Scrope of Bolton. So this, the smallest of the manors, was connected with one of the greatest families in the land. It remained in the Scrope family for more than two centuries. But the name of Mortimer never left it, and until quite recently there was a most impressive monument to Mortimer fame standing beside the moated homestead. This was the great barn which was originally built in the third quarter of the fourteenth century. A magnificent structure of massive oak beams with roof of thatch, it was clearly built to house the whole of the produce of the manor and the tithes of the Rector as well, and dwarfed for a time every other building in the village. Frequently re-roofed and patched up, it survived the storms of centuries and remained in constant use until a few years ago. A tractor accomplished in a few hours what it would have taken the elements another hundred years to do. When the last timbers were dragged away, a great gap was left, and the Middle Ages seemed that much further distant.

Throughout the period 1370–1538 the Abbess of Chatteris and her small group of nuns continued to support themselves, maintain their house, and provide candles for the high altar at Ely from the revenues of their Foxton and other manors. They cannot have indulged much in the luxurious living which was alleged against so many religious houses. The Foxton manor had been worth about £25 a year in the thirteenth century; it was worth little more, perhaps rather less, at the beginning of the

Mortimer's Barn

sixteenth. The total revenue of the convent was only £97 in 1538 when it was dissolved along with all the other houses. A reign which had lasted for 560 years came to an end and on 8 May 1540 the first court of the manor of Foxton Regis was held. We shall examine in greater detail presently the nature and events of the closing years of that long reign. Let us first continue the history of the manor to the point at which we left the others.

The title 'Foxton Regis' epitomizes the whole painful business of the Dissolution of the Monasteries. It really had very little to do with religion and even less with politics. It was the money which mattered. Foxton Regis did not remain the 'Foxton manor of the King' for long, even though, as a mark of royal clemency, the fee for suit of court was reduced from twopence to one penny. Very soon the manor, like hundreds of others, was put on the market. There was keen competition for these estates, for they were recognized as a good investment, and many a merchant and honest burgess saw in their acquisition an opportunity to rise in the social scale. Indeed, social advancement must have far outweighed financial gain in the promptings of many who purchased small estates such as this. Sir Edward Elrington bought the manor in 1544, held one court, then sold it in 1546 to Sir Rowland Hill, later Lord Mayor of London. He sold it in the same year to Sir Ralph Warren, Citizen and Alderman of London, who held it for the rest of his life, and enlarged it by the purchase of part of the Wimbish manor. (Hence the title 'Foxton Bury with Chatteris and Wimbish'.)

Now let us take a look at the village and the villagers during that half-century from 1490 to 1540 when the Abbess, safely ensconced, as she no doubt thought, in her distant refuge, seemed blissfully unaware of what was happening in the world outside, unaware that her way of life was tottering to its final collapse. Let us first, however, express a word of gratitude to her, to her Stewards and their clerks for so assiduously recording their transactions and preserving their records. Without those records, all would have been speculation and vague assumption. With those rolls of faded parchment before us, once we have learnt how to decipher the writing and mastered the system of abbreviations, it needs but little imagination to recapture the setting and bring back to life those villagers of centuries ago.

The court no longer meets with the former frequency and regularity; it might be twice a year, it is more often once a year, and sometimes two years elapse between meetings. But it still meets in the same old 'hall' standing on the same old spot, just opposite the church. Joanna Pokeryng's ale-house is not far away, and, if her supply of refreshment should be exhausted, there are three other ale-houses within easy reach. The location of the hall has its disadvantages, however, for just behind it stands Nicholas Thirlowe's dung-heap; the biggest dung-heap in the village, which Nicholas is in no hurry to move, for he never comes to the court and maintains a state of permanent hostility towards those who do come to it. The tenants are as impervious to the smell of Nicholas's dung-hill as they are to his hostility, but the Steward happens to be sitting near an open window, so Nicholas is threatened with a fine of twenty pence if the offending heap has not been removed before the next session.

There they sit – the Steward, his clerk, Robert Rayner, John Gerold, Tom Bryce, John Spencer, Will Symton, Will Herman, Robert Barret, Gilbert Amys, Tom Porter, John Lawe. A fair muster, but by no means complete. Several tenants who, holding land of the manor, live in neighbouring villages, have not bothered to make the journey; and their absence will cost them each three pence. The Master and Scholars of Michael-house, though holding fifty acres of freehold land in Foxton, never have attended the court, and never will, for which default they pay sixpence every time. Some half a dozen others, unable to attend, have taken the precaution of getting someone to answer for them and pay the statutory two pence; these are entered on the roll as 'essoined'. And so to business.

First come the transfers and inheritances of lands, messuages and cottages. There are far fewer tenants than there used to be, and so many instances of one tenant having acquired more than one holding, that these transactions are comparatively rare. Indeed it is all too evident that tenants have got into the habit of hanging on to what they hold, title or no title. Even when a tenant dies, it may be several years before his heirs or executors come to court to register the fact and pay the statutory fine and heriot. This state of affairs gets worse as time goes on, until it comes to the point where 'no one knows by what title he holds the land', 'no one knows who is his heir', 'no one knows what lands he held'. It is difficult to escape the impression that not only does no one know, but no one cares either. The old manorial discipline has gone. The Steward and Bailiff are slack in the execution of their duties; which is hardly surprising, perhaps, when the Steward's salary is only £2 a year 'to be paid out of the Foxton manor'. The Steward, of course, was steward of several other manors as well as this one; even so, he must have been prompted to seek ways and means of augmenting his meagre salary, some of them not strictly honest. However, that is not really our concern.

What does concern and interest us is the business of the court once the land transactions were dealt with. These men of Foxton, Shepreth and Barrington, gathered here in the hall at Foxton, guided rather than ruled by the Steward, they are Democracy in action. It is they who run the day-to-day affairs of their villages. In theory, that is. In practice it proves rather difficult, for a variety of reasons. To begin with, the jury of the court ('homage', as it is called) and the offenders against the bye-laws are all too often the same persons; passing judgement upon themselves. Then there is a weakness in the sanctions to be applied; penalties can be threatened – they are, with great frequency – but not easily exacted. There is no resident 'squire' to act as a natural leader, to inspire fear or respect. Lady St George is interested only in her own affairs, particularly the well-being and future safety of her own soul, and treats the court with disdain. The farmers of the Bury and Mortimer's, both living out of the village, do just as they please, ignore the court, and graze their flocks where they will:

John Hille, servant and shepherd of John Thirlowe, and Henry Sadeler, servant and shepherd of Richard Newman, with their flocks of sheep trespassed in the fields and stubbles and other growing pasture, contrary to the bye-laws; so they are fined 40d.

The fine was never paid; the offence was repeated again and again; the orders were repeated again and again; it made no difference. Not only the farmers:

John Everard, butcher, overloaded the commons and pastures of this village with his oxen and cattle, to the detriment of all tenants and residents; fined 10s.

Now that the Reeve was no longer a man of real authority, backed by the common will of the majority, the villagers had to be deterred by threats of penalties from doing what in the old days common-sense would have prevented them from attempting:

It is ordered that no one shall put on the pasture any animals except 'lez ploughbest' and milch cows and calves until All Saints Day in any year; on pain of 20s.
All tenants and residents of this village shall ring their pigs and piglets every year from Michaelmas to Christmas so that they do not grub up the soil or several pastures; on pain of 40d for every offence, 20d to the Lady of the Manor, 20d to the upkeep of the church.
Shepherds shall not keep sheep in the cow-pastures before St John Baptist's Day on pain of 6/8 fine, 40d to the Lady, 40d to the church.

But the indications are that they continued to put their animals where it suited them, and that they did not ring their pigs. To what extent the church benefited as a result of their transgressions I do not know; very little, I suspect.

It is not surprising to find that Barrington men are prominent amongst those who put animals in the wrong places. That bit of land which had been in dispute a thousand years before was still in dispute:

Thomas Norman, butcher, of Barrington, is ordered not to put any of his oxen or cattle in the commons or pastures of this village at any time of the year on pain of 10s.

Robert Wedde, miller, of Barrington, put his cattle nightly in Gosholme Medowe within the bounds of this manor where he has no right; so he is fined 6s 8d and ordered not to repeat the offence on pain of 6s 8d.

Thomas Bendish, Gent. of Barrington commoned with his cattle in a certain meadow called Gosholme where he has no common rights and never did have; so he is fined 3s 4d; pain of 40s.

The situation as regards pasturage for the animals, always a major problem, was not nearly so bad as it was to become in the course of the sixteenth century. It was bad enough, even though some land formerly arable had gone out of cultivation. Flocks of sheep were more common here than they used to be, yielding good profits at little cost in labour. Horses were gradually replacing oxen as draught animals, and they ate rather more. Animals were no longer killed off at the onset of winter simply because of the lack of feeding-stuff; they were fattened up and killed in the autumn in the normal way of husbandry, to provide a supply of salted beef, pork and mutton throughout the winter. The leaner animals were kept.

Purveyors of foodstuffs are now more numerous, and the weekly market brings bakers, butchers and fishmongers into the village from as far away as Cambridge. We never heard of meat being sold to the peasants of two hundred years before; now it is a common thing, and even butter is mentioned. The court minutes abound in prosecutions of ale-sellers, bakers and butchers for selling underweight, selling bad quality or overcharging, to the extent that one wonders whether people could really have been so consistently dishonest or whether it was due to sheer incompetence. Certainly the fines imposed, usually two, three or fourpence, do not seem to have made the slightest difference. The official ale-tasters too were fined for 'failing to do their duty', but they still continued to hold office, sometimes for ten years and more. The market, incidentally, seems to have come to an end in about 1540, as it did in many villages, from lack of business and inability to compete with the bigger markets which were now developing in certain villages better placed; these latter became the 'market towns' of the next three centuries; some still exist as such, though at the time with which we are dealing every village was called a 'town'.

Two of the entries relating to ale-houses are of particular interest:

1494. Ordered that no brewer or retailer of ale shall henceforth sell within or without the precincts of this manor *a gallon of good ale at more than one penny*;

on pain of outsiders forfeiting the ale to the Lady, and tenants or residents within the manor paying a fine of 6s 8d.

1529. Isabel Vyrley, Joan Wells and Joan Reyner are brewers of ale, and in various ways offended by selling ale contrary to the law of the land; each is fined one penny. And it is ordered that none of them henceforth shall sell, in or out of their houses, to subjects of the King, *a gallon of best ale at more than two pence*; on pain of a fine of 12d paid to the Lady for every infringement. And that each of them shall exercise and occupy the office of public sellers of bread, and continue to sell bread in accordance with the regulations, or pay a fine of 16d if they do not.

Here is perhaps a clue to the general contempt in which the authority of the court, and indeed the law of the land, was held. A penalty of twelve or sixteen pence was threatened if the offence were repeated, yet when the offence *was* repeated – in this case the very next year – the worthy ale-wives were each fined two pence. It must have been with a feeling of profound relief that the court made this declaration in 1528:

And as for any fine or penalty here imposed on bakers, brewers, fishmongers or any other food-sellers, or on the officials, none at present, so that the jury said as to those persons *all is well*.

Of course it may simply be that in that particular year the county Overseers of Assize failed to include Foxton in their round of routine visitations. It could also be that an outraged populace, exasperated at the vain official attempts to put an end to malpractices, decided to apply their own remedy, chased the offending trader all the way to Barrington and there threw him and his faulty balance into the river. This at least could be one explanation of the intriguing discovery of a fifteenth-century balance when the river was dredged in 1972. One last item on this topic: though inns and hostel-ries had been a common feature in towns and along main roads since very early times, here is an entry which suggests the evolution of the village ale-house into the village inn. The date is 1543:

It is ordered that all who sell ale, bread and other victuals shall put a *Sign in front of their door*. And further that they shall provide and prepare honest service and hospitality in accordance with the law.

This edict was simply giving legal force to what had been common practice for a long time; if it was complied with in remote villages it is more than likely that the 'sign' continued to be the traditional bush which good ale, like good wine, could well do without. Nearly two hundred years were to elapse before the village street was enlivened with a touch of exotic gaiety in the form of the 'Blackamoor's Head' swinging in the wind.

I will dismiss with no more than a passing mention a whole host of trivial and commonplace items which occupied the court's time and attention; such as distraint for debt, breaking of fences and hedges, encroachment on boundaries, failure to clean out land-drains, straying animals, pound-breaking, cutting down trees, obstructing paths, digging clunch from the road, and so on. These matters are not without interest; indeed many of them provided vital clues in the research on which the next chapter is based. They are common to all villages over a long period of time. But I want to concentrate on a few matters which, though equally common to all villages, help to throw a clearer light on what I believe to have been the general state of affairs in rural England at this period, or rather on the attitude of the common man towards that state of affairs. Manorial discipline had already gone or was rapidly going; the hold of the Church was weakening; baronial wars were a thing of the past; government was in the hands of a strong despotic monarch who, with his ministers, was too much involved in affairs of State to be concerned about the common man. The latter had more freedom and security than ever before in his history. What did he do with it? Just what one, being cynical, would expect. He did nothing, except look after his own interest. The community became a collection of individuals, each intent on feathering his own nest, not necessarily at the expense of his neighbour, but in almost total indifference as to the wishes and interests of his neighbours. We have already seen something of this attitude; I regret to say that there is more to come.

One redeeming feature of this gloomy picture however – and this in itself may be a sign of the times – is that there was nothing like the amount of lawlessness which might have been expected. There were, it is true, a few occasions when somebody assaulted his neighbour 'with a pike-fork, value 2d' or 'bloodily broke his head', but that sort of thing always has happened, and always will. There was the occasion when John Garolde 'took by night the sheaves of corn of his neighbours from the common fields at harvest time'. Now that, it may surprise you to learn, was not a common thing; it was very rare. The offending John left the village soon afterwards, encouraged no doubt by the open hostility of all the inhabitants, and never returned. There was no revolt of the kind we met so frequently two centuries before, because there was nothing to rebel against. Only one single instance is recorded of open defiance of authority, in 1515;

William Forester, tenant of this manor, *left the court and went to the alehouse*, with his name inscribed on the court-roll by the Steward for disobedience and grave contempt of court, despite being called to order. When he returned he was fined 12*d*.

I suspect that it was a combination of boredom and thirst which drove William to that extremity; though, of course, Thirlowe's dung-heap might have had something to do with it.

The outburst of John St George in 1521 would seem to have been due to different and more deep-seated causes. His family had for the past ten years been at constant variance with the manor court, and it looks as though John thought that the time had come to teach these upstart peasants a lesson:

John Seintgeorge and his servants under his orders broke the pound of the manor of Foxton *by armed force* and removed two geldings which had been impounded for straying in the corn-fields of Foxton, and broke the King's peace; he is therefore fined 3*s* 4*d* and ordered to be present to hear the decision of the Lady pronounced.

One can imagine him fuming as he listened to the tirade of his aged mother, Lady Anne, then hastily buckling on the sword which his great-great-grandfather had wielded at Agincourt. Summoning his faithful retainers from their task of mucking-out the pigs, he leapt astride the one remaining gelding and charged down the village street with the battle-cry of 'England and St George!' on his mind if not actually on his lips, whilst the village constable prudently retreated before this onslaught of knight-errantry. Such an action ought to have landed St George in the county court; but it didn't. And I doubt whether the fine was ever paid.

When we read that, in 1501, 'Edward Tanfield threw his kitchen-refuse in the highway, to the annoyance of his neighbours', and that he was threatened with a fine of 12*d* if he did it again, we might be led to suppose that the tidiness of the streets was as much a matter of concern then as it is now. Such a supposition would be a grave error. I do not know what it was that Lady Tanfield's son threw into the road, but it must have been something very nasty or very obstructive. Probably half the carcase of an ox, in an advanced state of decay, into which the constable blundered in the dark, or which caused a team of horses to stampede and overturn their load. For the road was the usual place in which to dump unwanted rubbish. As witness this:

All persons who from the scouring of the roads accumulate earth and manure in heaps called 'mire-heaps' and leave them in the streets shall cart them away before St John Baptist's Day on pain of a fine of 3s 4d, half to the Lady, half to the churchwardens.

If somebody delivered half a mire-heap on one of the unsuspecting church-wardens, he had only himself to blame! A few years later someone had a better idea, which promised to get the streets cleaned and mended at the same time:

No one shall carry away the common dung made in the street unless for every two cart-loads of dung he shall carry back one load of stones into the roads of Foxton.

Eventually, in 1578, the value of the manure was fully recognized, and the mending of the roads was relegated to the care of private charity:

No one shall cart away the manure called 'Compas' out of the street, on pain of a fine of 8s.

Which rather suggests that the precious commodity had by then become the perquisite of the churchwardens, to be carted away only under their supervision and upon receipt of due payment.

Every village had its stocks. This was – or these were – a simple device consisting of several stout pieces of wood, one of them fixed firmly in the ground, equipped with iron loops or pierced with holes in which the wrists of an offender could be securely held; sometimes the head and feet were secured also. There was quite a variety of design, but the object in every case was the same, to submit a person to the ridicule of all and sundry and facilitate a sound whipping by the constable if that punishment was ordered by due authority. It is impossible to say with what frequency this barbaric implement was used, but it is certain that it was kept in good working order until the end of the eighteenth century. Only one reference to it occurs in my records:

1542. They say that William Sturmyn junior set free a certain begging vagrant taken by the constable and lawfully placed and kept in the stocks. The said William of his own volition and without authority freed the said vagabond from the said stocks and allowed him to escape unlawfully. So William is fined 6s 8d which the Bailiff is ordered to collect and answer for.

This is typical of those cryptic entries in the records which tell us so much, but leave so much untold. Was young William's act symptomatic of youth's instinctive revolt against authority; was he being kind-hearted, malicious, or just mischievous? Six shillings and eightpence seems a severe fine to impose on a lad for doing an act of kindness; it would represent a month's wages if he was working, and a year's pocket-money if he was not.

Was the beggar cunningly persuasive, pitifully wretched, or noisily drunk? The reason for his being placed in the stocks is quite clear: he was a vagrant and he was begging. And he did not belong to the village of Foxton. That was his crime. Foxton had its own poor, and did not want poor people from some other place. If people were poor it was their own fault, the result of their own idleness. The way to cure them was to put them in the stocks, give them a good whipping, then send them away. That was the attitude of authority, backed by law. How far was it the attitude of the common man? It would seem that the common man largely acquiesced in that attitude, as he so often feels that he must. Hats off, then, to Master William Sturmyn, for daring to be different!

Likewise every village had its butts, or archery targets, the use and maintenance of which had been enforced by repeated statutes for several centuries. As was the case with many statutory measures, this was honoured in the breach more than in the observance. The men of Foxton were not very concerned about the need for preparedness to repel the French or the Scots or any other enemies equally remote. There was always the likelihood that they would have to repel the Barringtonians, especially round about fair-time, but they did not need bows and arrows for that; cudgels and pike-forks served perfectly well. So the archery-practice and the butts got rather neglected:

1523. The butts within the village of Foxton at present are inadequate, therefore *the whole village is fined* 2d. And it is ordered that the village shall sufficiently repair them before Trinity Sunday on pain of 6s 8d fine if they fail to do so.

I wonder who did pay that fine. Did the Bailiff, after vainly trying to divide 2d by 153, or whatever the number was, eventually take the two pence from his own pocket? Actually, I think it was a gesture of contempt on the part of the jurymen; their way of saying that they could not care less about the butts. A similar situation arose at Shepreth in 1529:

The targets called 'lez butts' are ruined and in decay. So the villagers are ordered to repair them adequately before the 20th of June next on pain of a fine of 6s 8d if they fail to do so.

No fine in that case, and the penalty of half a mark (6s 8d) looks like a bit of legal formalism. It seems clear to me that this was a case of ostensible compliance with a law which no one in fact had the slightest intention of obeying. One more gesture was made in 1540, doubtless prompted by the fact that the Lord of the Manor was now no less a person than King Henry VIII himself:

And they state that the targets called 'Le Butts' there are inadequate, so it is ordered that the villagers shall make them satisfactory and repair them before Pentecost next on pain of 3s 4d.

And that is the last we ever hear of the butts. Meanwhile there was another oddity directly connected with this matter, and illustrative of the wide gulf which still separated those in authority from the reality of life as it was lived by the common man. Authority wanted men to keep up their archery-practice; but men preferred other pastimes. So authority passed a law forbidding all other pastimes. Hence this:

1526. It is ordered by the whole homage that none of the inhabitants of this village shall henceforth play at 'lez bowles', on pain of each delinquent forfeiting 3s 4d to the Lady.

I do not think it will surprise anyone to learn that not a single instance is on record of that fine being paid or demanded. Neither is there any record of 'lez bowles' being played after that. But something tells me that the playing of bowls never ceased in the villages of England, and never will.

Now it is time to deal with an aspect of the village which tells perhaps more about the villagers than anything I have said so far in this chapter, and which, as it was gradually revealed to me by the slow and often difficult perusal of those faded rolls of parchment, caused me no little surprise and dismay. My account of it will probably have the same effect on the reader, particularly if he has in his mind a preconceived notion – as I believe most people have – of what a Tudor village looked like. We are all familiar with the image created and perpetuated on postcard and chocolate-box, in magazines, books and films – pretty black and white cottages with neat thatched roofs nestling among trees and flowers, inhabited by jolly folk glowing with good health and contentment. Modern villages, especially in eastern England, the west Midlands and West Country, only serve by their picturesque aspect to foster this illusion as regards their past. For, make no mistake about it, it is an illusion. The sad truth is that the houses in the real Tudor village were filthy, untidy, decayed, dilapidated and verminous; there were piles of muck and rotting straw where today the hollyhocks and roses bloom; and the people matched the houses, one can be sure.

The first hint of this state of affairs comes in 1496, with this entry relating to Shepreth:

John Awstyn, Will Lawrence, Will Newman, Robert Felde, Will Beton, Joan Hawsby and Alice Freeman have customary tenements in a state of decay, by virtue of defects in woodwork and carpentry, daubing and roofing. They are ordered to get these repairs done before Michaelmas on pain of a heavy fine.

Similar entries occur for Foxton and Barrington at the same date, and become more and more frequent, far too numerous to be quoted in detail. The repair work was not done, despite orders repeated over and over again. The fines and penalties were never paid. We need no reminder, of course, that all the houses, indeed all the buildings in the village – with the sole exception of the church – were built of wood; a timber frame of beams or 'studs', the spaces between the timbers filled with lath and plaster, and roofed with thatch. In some cases there were wooden ceilings at about head-level to make a sort of loft, but for the most part these houses consisted of one or two rooms only. Standing inside and looking upwards, one looked at the underside of the thatch, or through it! There were few chimneys, if any. The kitchen, if any, was outside. These houses were not so very different from those in which the villeins of two centuries before had lived. The floors of trodden clunch were the same floors on which those villeins had walked, and slept. The timber frame in some cases was that which had been erected two hundred years before, or contained members which had been taken down and re-erected half a dozen times. The provision of this timber in the first instance, and for subsequent repairs, was the responsibility of the Lady of the manor. But the maintenance of the fabric – that is, the renewal of the thatch and lath and plaster – was the responsibility of the tenants. It is quite clear that this responsibility was being neglected and ignored. A lot of people were living in houses which were literally falling about their ears. And all that the court could do was to record the fact.

William Rayner has a barn and other buildings in a very ruinous state.
John Spencer's messuage and croft are seized for failure to do repairs.
William Ketell has not yet repaired his houses.
William Rayner allowed his houses to fall down.

Official seizure of the property did not mean that it was repaired; on the contrary, it meant that it decayed all the more quickly.

John Thirlowe, farmer of the Bury, had recently built for himself a new 'hampstall' near the Bury, and the jurymen of the court decided in 1506 that he should have the responsibility of repairing 'all the dwelling-houses within the manor of Foxton before Michaelmas, on pain of a £10 fine'. They were wasting their time. For one thing, John Thirlowe was dead. His son Nicholas had no intention of spending money on houses for other people to live in. Two years later the threat was repeated on Nicholas; the fine was reduced to four marks (53s 4d); to no avail. Nicholas would not even repair the buildings of his own farm, and was certainly not going to repair the old hall of the manor, which was also falling down. By 1515 every single tenant of the manor had houses 'in decay as to timber, thatch, plaster and splentyng'. In 1513 Nicholas Thirlowe had died, and his successor John White had also died; the attempt to shift responsibility on to his executors provides us with a unique glimpse of the buildings in the centre of the village, and of their condition:

It is ordered that John King and Richard White, executors of the will of John White deceased shall adequately make good and repair all the walls round the farm called Foxton Bery, also that they shall roof *the great barn* and all other buildings there with straw and 'le thakke' before next Michaelmas, on pain of a fine of £4.

And that '*le GarnerHowse*', '*le Malte Howse*' and '*le Oldehalle*' of the said farm of Foxton Bery are also in decay, defective in woodwork and roofing. So it is ordered to John and Richard to repair those buildings before the said feast on pain of 40s.

Of course nothing was done, not even when the penalty was raised to 100s. Those silly men sat there and talked of fines and penalties, whilst the very building in which they sat was going to ruin. One would think that, having sat through one session with the rain dripping down their necks, they would have said amongst themselves: 'Right, since no one else will repair the hall, we will do it ourselves.' But no, they just went on talking, and hoped that it would not rain!

Newman, Rayner, Goodwyn, Wells, Symton, Ketyll, Flaxman, Bartilmew, Skynner, Ampes, Forster, Thompson – these are the names inscribed on the court roll as homage. These are the men who passed the resolutions about fines and penalties. And these are the men whose houses were falling down! In 1519:

Anne St George, widow, Richard Newman, John Skynner, Will Thompson, John Flaxman, Gilbert Ampes and Will Forster all forfeit the penalty of 3s 4d imposed at the last court because they have not carried out repairs. But the Lady, acting on advice, pardons them *because they did not have any straw* and for other urgent reasons, on condition that they do the repairs before the next court.

Because they did not have any straw? In a village surrounded by fields of wheat, barley and rye, they had no straw! It is just possible, of course, that a bad harvest followed by a severe winter had resulted in a scarcity of straw, and that what straw there was had been used up as winter feed for the animals. But this business had been going on for years, and went on for years to come. The Abbess cannot really have been so simple as to think that their excuse was genuine. I suspect that the inclusion of Lady Anne St George's name in the list of culprits has something to do with the Abbess's acceptance of such a lame excuse. Either that, or the Abbess just was not interested.

But how are we to explain this apathy? How can it be that two-thirds of the houses in the village are falling into ruins and nobody doing anything at all about it? The answer, I think, is this. Those men – Newman, Rayner, Goodwin and Co. – were looking after themselves. The houses in which they themselves lived were not falling down. It was the other houses which they 'owned', the copyhold cottages of their sub-tenants and labourers, which were neglected. Two hundred years, or even one hundred years before, the responsibility would have been clear and unquestioned. Now, it was not. The Abbess clearly thought that it was not her responsibility. Newman, Rayner and Co. thought that it was not theirs. The occupiers of the houses were certain that it was not theirs. So nobody did anything. One last half-hearted attempt was made by the court, in 1523:

Likewise *all other tenants* of this manor of Foxton have their houses and tenements in decay for want of repairs to woodwork, roof and plaster; all are ordered to carry out repairs before All Saints Day on pain of 3s 4d if they fail to do so.

That was the final despairing effort. We hear no more about it for thirty years or so. Either the occupants at last decided to do the job themselves – which, of course, they ought to have done in the first place – or the houses just fell down. And there is plenty of evidence in later years to show that the latter alternative was by no means uncommon. The time was ripe for a Building Revolution, and it was just round the corner. But before we deal with that, in the next chapter, let us take a look at some of the houses which were not falling down, and at the people who lived in them.

There is nothing morbid about the fascination which wills hold for me. I see them, not as symbols of death, but as the sole means of communication between people who were alive four hundred and fifty years ago and those of us today who want to know more about those people, to meet them, as it were, face to face. Confronted with one of these documents (in the University Archives, where there are hundreds of them in huge leather-bound volumes), one needs little effort of imagination to picture the scrivener at work on what was to him a routine job which he nevertheless performed with care, patience and a touch of artistry in the ornate flourishes of the capitals. Looking beyond his neat lines of 'secretarie' script as he faith-

fully copies the erratic spelling of the original, corrects the more out-
rageously difficult words in the interests of intelligibility but retains the
delightful blend of naïve simplicity and attempted solemnity of the
phrasing, with a little further effort of imagination one can see those old
people sitting on a stool or lying propped-up in bed; one can hear the quill
of the vicar, Mr Richard Birkenhead (who had great difficulty in spelling
his own name) scratching the parchment; one can feel the tension of the
tired mind striving to ensure that nothing and no one was forgotten.

But it would not do to print these wills in full, or even in part. The
magic would not survive the rendering into cold black print. Many a
reader would not survive the struggle with a labyrinth of words, and would
seek safety in flight. So I have extracted from them such details as I think
will throw most light on the houses, the custom of the time, and the people
both as individuals and as members of a community, and I present the
information in summarized form.

There are twenty of these wills covering the period 1516–45. They
provide a fair cross-section of about one half of the village society; that is
to say the testators range from the gentry, in the person of Lady Anne St
George, through the more prosperous yeomanry of the Fullers and
Wellses, down to the 'husbondman' with a house and from ten to twenty
acres of land. The list does not include any men classed as labourers,
though in fact some of the husbandmen probably were labourers some of
the time. It does not include any poor people; they did not make wills for
the rather obvious reason that they had nothing to leave to anybody;
nothing, that is, but a blanket or two, a couple of old pots and a bundle of
worn-out clothing, all of which would be put to immediate use by other
members of the family without benefit of testamentary justification. So we
only get a glimpse of one half of village society, for it seems fairly certain
that at least half, and perhaps as many as two-thirds of the people in the
village were poor even by the standards of the day.

The first feature of note in these wills is that, with one exception in
1542, all the testators are Catholics, as one would expect. The wording of
the preamble: 'first I bequethe my soulle to god almightie, to his mother
saynt Marye and unto all the holly company of hevyn' is not so much an
affirmation of faith as a standard formula dictated by ecclesiastical authority and custom. Immediately following the preamble come the bequests
to the church in respect of the altar, torches, bells, etc., which I quoted
earlier in dealing with the history of the church (at the end of chapter 5).
To what extent those bequests were dictated by ecclesiastical authority

and custom I cannot say. It would be unseemly, libellous even, to cast doubts upon the piety and sincerity of these good people, especially as some of them manifested that piety in other ways than by gifts to the church. It may nevertheless be permissible to suggest that in some instances piety was not wholly unmixed with other, more worldly, considerations. John Goodwyn in 1516, I think, managed to reconcile conflicting issues very neatly:

The Residewe of my goods – to Richard Goodwyn and John Teadisshe – myn Executors and administrators and thei to dispose yt to the Well of my Solle and all cristyn solls and to the profitte of my childerne.

The demands of the Church having been met, and the future security of their soul assured, these people next turned their attention to the bestowal of their property in this world. This for the most part consists of houses and land and the wills do not tell us much that the manor court rolls have not already told us, though they do often provide helpful confirmation. The property was handed on in accordance with custom already ancient and destined to remain unchanged for centuries to come; but one special feature catches the eye. William Pepercorne in 1520 declared:

I wille that Joan my wif shall have my Copyhold called Shephards in Foxton as long as she contineth single and unmarried. And if she marye, that then immediately I will that ye said copy be sold by my Execcutrice and the money thereof comyng I bequeth xxvis viiid to bye an abbe and a vestament wt the pertinences to my parishe Cherche of Foxton etc.

This attempt to place a ban on the re-marriage of a widow occurs with regular frequency during the next two centuries. I think it might be of religious origin, though I have been unable to trace that origin, and I find it difficult to explain, the more so in that, in this particular case, Pepercorne himself had married another man's widow with three children by her first husband. He increased the number of children to six, and it may be that his ban was motivated by the desire that there should be no more children to complicate the inheritance of the property. Be that as it may, the ban was satisfactorily circumvented and Joan did marry again – how otherwise could she have managed to run the farm, a widow with six children, five of them young girls? – and she did produce two more children by her third husband.

Still on the subject of wives and property, it seems to have been an understood thing that, whereas the houses and land that a woman owned before her marriage became the husband's property on marriage, she did not endow her spouse with *all* her worldly goods. At least, there was a good chance of her getting some of them back:

> I will that Alys my wyff have all soche goods cattell (chattels) and other stuff that she brought unto me.
> I will that my saide wif shall have all suche stuff of howseholde as she broughte unto me at the tyme of our mariage.

It was clearly limited to household 'stuff', which most husbands seem to have held in too much contempt to itemize and the return of which was not automatic but dependent upon the husband's magnanimity. Truly, it was a man's world! Most wives got their due, however, or what they had been brought up to consider as their due. Not so Philippa, wife of William Fuller who died in 1526; she seems to have been at the unlucky corner of one of those eternal triangles. Her husband left her, in addition to 'suche stuffe of household that now remaneth which she brought with her', three quarters of barley, one quarter of wheat and 'one grene Coverlet' – not even a bed on which to put it. Whereas a certain Alys Culpie got four quarters of barley, 'a Clooke, a fether bedd, a bolster & a matteres, one harness girdell, a towell playn stavid, a hutche, one panne of brasse, a basyn of pewter, a laten basyn, three Candelstickes of the best, a payre of pott hooks and hangles, a grydyron, a spitt, a payre of Cobyrons and a table both of the best', and much more besides. Mind you, all that was on condition that it did not 'fortune the saide Alis Culpie to departe out of this worlde or to be maried'. I have no idea who Alice Culpie was, but Mrs Fuller, I am sure, could have told us *what* she was.

The apparent modesty of the sums of money bestowed on the church, and the fact that the gifts were more often in kind than in cash, creates an impression which is amply confirmed by the rest of the wills, namely that there was not a great deal of money about. Some wills do not mention any money at all, and none of them mention much. The 'xx marks' (a mark was 13*s* 4*d*) of Lady Anne St George and the 'xx pownds of goode and lawfull money of England' of John Fuller are quite exceptional, and the latter right at the end of our period. The Fullers and St Georges were exceptional people, whose money does not impress me as perhaps it ought to; I find my heart warming more readily to David Alanson who left 'to eche of my godchildren one ew Lambe'. Even so it must be admitted that only in the Fuller and St George households, and in one other where there was money, do we get any suggestion of refinement or artistry, in the form of 'one half garnesse of pewter vesshel', 'my standinge coppe with the cover gylte', 'my harnest gyrdell with the barres' (this was a sort of belt of ornate silver links, the ends of which hung almost to the ground, all the rage at the end of the fifteenth century), 'my best Candelstickes', 'vi sylver spoones', etc. Gilbert Amys's 'holy watter Clock of laten' arouses both my curiosity and my cupidity, and Lady Anne's 'one girdill dansant sylver gylt with one flowre Columbyne at thende' conjures up visions of fair ladies tripping graceful measures in stately baronial halls – a long time ago, when Lady Anne was a girl. Alas for daughter Joes and daughter Kateryne, who received the other girdle, such things were soon to go out of fashion.

It looks very much as though those three houses – St George's, Fuller's and Amys's – were the only houses in the village in which fireplaces were to be found, complete with spits, andirons, pothangers and the rest of the ironmongery; the only ones in which there were beds, tables or chests ('bound with yrone' in the case of Lady Anne); the only ones in which there was any furniture at all apart from hutches, benches, boards and stools. As for cooking utensils, pots and pans of brass or pewter or iron abounded at Fuller's and Amys's (he even had a laver, proof that he at least sometimes washed), were somewhat scarce at Lady Anne's, and very scarce indeed at most of the other houses. If old Agnes Newman can be relied upon as running true to form in listing all her possessions, which elderly widows nearly always did – and I think she can, even though she was 'sycke in bodye and feebill in speeache' – then she only had two brass pots and 'one Skylett panne'. And she must not be thought of as poor; she had five sheep and two oxen, and was uncommonly generous towards those whom *she* considered poor.

Animals figure in the wills, of course, but it would be unwise to draw too many conclusions from the numbers mentioned because a lot could be included in 'the residue of all my goods'; indeed William Styrman goes on to say 'as all horses, oxen, bullocks, Croppe, Tylthe, Tymber', etc. Nevertheless a number of points do emerge with reasonable clarity. The first is that sheep were more numerous in 1520 than they were thirty years later; they seem to have been kept in fairly small flocks of about twenty, which would of course have to be merged into larger flocks for grazing purposes. The small farmer ('husbondman') usually kept two oxen, just as he had done throughout the Middle Ages. I was baffled for a long time by the term 'mylche bullock' – it seems so obviously contradictory – until I realized that the word 'bullock' was used instead of 'ox' up to about 1535, when there was a period during which both words were used before 'bullock' acquired the meaning which it still has. Throughout the period under review oxen were gradually being replaced by horses. Thomas Wells, who was farming about eighty acres, in 1537 lists five horses and no oxen. John Fuller in 1545 lists sixteen oxen, seven 'mylche bullocks' (which, in the context, must mean 'cows'), six horses and twelve sheep. As he was farming well over two hundred acres, besides land in other parishes, he probably had even more animals than are listed; some of his cattle were almost certainly being reared for beef; and, even so, he probably had as many draught animals as the rest of the village put together. In view of all this, I am prompted to wonder whether beef was not even more of a rarity in the Middle Ages than I had supposed, and whether the common man only became a beef-eater when the ox or 'bullock' ceased to be the prime drawer of cart and plough.

The price of animals is given quite clearly several times. A bullock was worth 20s, a horse £1 6s 8d. The only clue as to the price of corn comes from Nicholas Houson in 1534:

iii quarters barley to by one Cowe the whiche I will shalbe for xxd a yere for to kepe one yerely obit for me and my frynds.

From which we may deduce that the price of barley was about six shillings a quarter (i.e. about thirty shillings a ton), though the transaction sounds a bit like Irishman's logic to me. As for the crops, only wheat, rye and barley are mentioned – mostly barley, which was used almost entirely for brewing, and was in fact usually called 'maulte'.

The topic of clothes provides a double surprise, firstly in that it figures at all prominently, secondly in that it is the men who furnish most of the information. From the womenfolk (who, be it noted, are only four in number) we learn only of 'my best gowne', 'oon grene gowne' and 'oon Redd Cote'. Lady Anne mentions none; not, I am sure, because she had none, but because her four married daughters had ransacked her wardrobe before the final knell rang. The old lady was evidently anticipating trouble:

if one or all or any of my childern be abowtward to distrouble infringe to brek this my last will and testament that they he or she that so dothe or is abowtward to so do shall not enjoye nether take no profits.

The men on the other hand tell of doublets, jerkins, coats, cloaks, jackets and – believe it or not – 'my blue gowne' and 'my best gowne'. None, however, not even a Fuller, and certainly no ordinary yeoman farmer could rival the sartorial wealth and elegance of John Sharpe who died in 1536, leaving:

my best doublett, my blacke hose, one gyrkyn and one payre of shoys, my furrid doublett and one payre of white hose, my best Cote, my beste cappe, my best nyght cappe, one buck lether doublett, my best payre of shoes, on Cote.

I should think he was a retired tailor.

We have already had evidence of the shocking and dangerous state of the roads in the village. The local inhabitants had no doubt become accustomed to it, but in 1542 it seems to have reached a pitch of discomfort and danger which even they could no longer tolerate or ignore. Either that, or some official edict (Cromwell's Poor Law of 1536?) had decreed that some of the money which had previously flowed into the coffers of the Church should be diverted to public utilities. It did not work for long, and perhaps not very effectively, but at least a few people showed willing. Agnes Newman in 1542 left 3s 4d 'towards the reperacions of hye wayes therwithin the saide parisshe', and Thomas Flaxman left 'the valewe of five quarters bareley' to the same cause. Two years later William Styrmyn left twelve pence 'to the repayering and mendyng of hye wayes in the said Towne betwixt Nicholas Bawdrix gate and Poorys Waye' which, considering what William was worth, indicates either an extremely niggardly spirit or a reluctance to comply with an order.

Anyway, you might ask, how could a legacy of twelve pence, or even twelve pounds for that matter, make any difference to three-quarters of a mile of road? The answer, I think, is provided by the correctness of my guess that this is connected with the Poor Law, and a clause in Thomas Lavender's will in 1556: 'I will have carried forward the mending of the highe wayes x lodes of Stone.' Someone had hit on a bright idea for killing three birds with one stone by paying the poor to pick up the stones which littered the fields and cart them into the highway to fill up the ruts and holes. How many loads of stones did Styrmyn's twelve pence provide? How many poor people were relieved for how long by Lavender's ten loads of stones? How long did a few loads of stones affect the condition of the road? Sorry, I cannot answer any of these questions. I *can* tell you that the same technique was still being used two hundred and thirty years later, when the price paid for a load of stones was 1s 6d. My guess is that the poor wretches who were driven by hunger to accept the job in 1544 did it for a penny or two pence a load.

Was any help given to the poor by the rich, apart from this convict's pittance? I dare say it was; in fact it must have been, or the poor could not have survived. The Fullers, Amyses and Wellses, besides providing work and wages, must have provided food and clothing for many poor people.

And Lady Anne? Well, as we saw earlier, she provided one cow to be 'lett to one poore bodie paying ii*s.* by yere', but she seemed more concerned with the maintenance of St Anne's Guild than with the poor bodies, to whom she left not one penny in her will, whilst bequeathing £8 for masses to be sung for her soul ('and all Christen soules') and £5 to provide a memorial stone to her husband in 'Hungrie Hattley Cherche'.

The first person to remember the poor in his will was my old friend David (alias Robert) Alanson, who in 1524 left: 'to William Symton, John Gibson, William Baker, Joan Skynner, Elyn Godfrey, John Richardson and to Dionyse Curteyse my poore nighbours to eche of them iiii*d.*' To those same 'nighbours' he left his clothes – 'my blue gowne, my Russett Jackett, my tawny coote, my dublett and my Jerkyn', having made proper provision for his wife, his family, the church *and* his soul (to the extent of fifty masses at 4*d* each). He was a shepherd, living in a little one-roomed cottage with his wife, a son and two daughters. Close by was a three-acre close in which he kept his sheep and 'one Rede Cowe'. His total worldly wealth cannot have exceeded ten pounds. He need not have spent all that money on masses – *his* soul was safe enough.

Only three others during this period made bequests to the poor. Agnes Newman in 1542 left 6*s* 8*d*, Thomas Flaxman 12*d*, William Styrmyn, whose tightfistedness we have already had reason to notice, had no intention of encouraging idleness or extravagance in his poor neighbours, but at least he did remember them: 'to every poore howse in the est ende of the same Towne having no plowgh singlely ii*d*' and 'to Moother Gayler ii*d.*' Moreover, he had no intention of letting his sons get away with any attempt at thwarting his will after his death:

William Styrmyn my sonne to be my Executor and Nicholas Styrmyn with hym to helpe hym the best that he can to fulfyll it as they will gyve an answer before god at the dreadfull daye of doome.

With that awful warning ringing in our ears, and a fleeting surmise as to how Mother Gayler spent that twopence, we take our leave of them all.

Once again I have left the Brook until last. Once again we learn what the people were doing with their Brook by reading about what they were not doing, or were ordered not to do with it.

1492. John Everard, butcher, allowed his dunghill to drain into the common stream of this village, to the serious detriment of the tenants and residents; fined 4*d*; pain of 10*s*.

No tenant or resident within the precincts of this court shall allow his ducks or geese to frequent the common brook running in the middle of this village, but shall either sell them or keep them within their tenements or houses; pain of 3s 4d.

1495. John Fuller, John Roger, John Skep, Katherine Baret, John Lawe, John Spencer and Richard Pepercorne allowed their ducks to frequent and stay in the common brook running the length of the village, to the serious harm of the inhabitants and contrary to orders; fined 6d.

1507. Ordered that ducks, geese *and pigs* shall not frequent the common brook; and no one shall wash clothes there; pain of 3s 4d.

1521. Hereby ordered that Will Pepercorne, Will Forester, Will Rayner, Thomas Wells, John Raymond, John Skynner and Richard Newman shall adequately clean out the common water-course from Thomas Barrett's house as far as the manor of Mortymer's before St John Baptist's Day next; pain of 6s 8d each.

1541. Each tenant of this manor henceforth shall be ready and present at the cleaning and scouring of the watercourse called 'le Broke' whenever it shall be necessary, and they shall be warned to do so by the village officials or other inhabitants; pain of 12d.

No person shall wash linen called 'Clothes' in the common Broke; on pain of 20d for everyone caught in default.

1547. All tenants and inhabitants shall attend diligently on a certain day fixed among themselves to clean and scour the public 'rivulus' from the manor of Mortimers as far as the Conyngerth, each on the frontage of his own house and land, and from the Conyngerth as far as the village of Fulmer; pain of 12d.

1552. No one shall henceforth divert the course of the 'Riville' of this town; pain 3s 4d.

1562. All inhabitants are ordered that henceforth they shall not let out their *gutters and cess-pits* at any time before eight o'clock at night; on pain of 12d.

The Brook was still the sole source of water for every person – and every animal – in the village. One would have thought that it was an easy matter to come to a practical solution of the problem of its maintenance, but it quite obviously was not. Everybody wanted the water, but nobody wanted the work involved in ensuring that it flowed. Such an attitude, I regret to say, becomes more pronounced as the centuries progress. And there, with cess-pits, dung-heaps, sinks and gutters merrily draining into it from 8 p.m. to 4 a.m., we leave the Brook for the present. Do not ask me why the whole population was not killed off by cholera, typhus and the like. I do not know.

7 The Great Rebuilding

The transformation which was wrought upon all England during the reign of the first Queen Elizabeth is strikingly reflected and exemplified in the life and appearance of the village. That great national revival was the compounded result of expanding commerce, firm government, new ideas, a new outlook embracing wider horizons, renewed energy, pride in achievement, a spirit of sturdy independence and probably much more besides. The revival of the village could hardly embody all of those things, for it was still only a village when all is said and done, but energy, pride and independence are much in evidence in the latter half of the sixteenth century, and those are the very qualities which seem to have been most lacking in the people about whom I wrote in the last chapter.

Did those people, then, undergo a startling change in some strange way? Some of them, or the descendants of some of them, undoubtedly did. What the records tell about the Wellses, Fullers and at least one branch of the multitudinous Rayners clearly indicates that they were intent on climbing higher in the social scale. Though they did not achieve any great altitude, their efforts left their mark on the village. But what really brought the village back to life was an infusion of new blood. Of the old stock, the people who were here in 1500, at least a dozen families had gone, died out or moved elsewhere by 1523. A trickle of new names appears which, between 1548 and 1603, becomes a spate. Some forty new families came into the village during that period. They include the names of Campion, Beaumont, Brestbone, Mead, Singleton, Welbore, Hurrell – names which are prominent in village affairs for the next hundred and fifty years.

One might be tempted, as indeed I was until I carried my research a bit further, to suppose that this new blood came from far afield, from the towns, from London in particular. But that is not so. These new men came from neighbouring villages, at the most a distance of fifteen miles. Why did they come? Land was no cheaper here than elsewhere, so far as I can discover. Perhaps there were more sites 'ripe for development' here than elsewhere. But that would not adequately explain the situation, for what happened in Foxton happened in hundreds of villages all over England. Anyway, they came and, aided by the Wellses, Fullers and Rayners, they set the pace; the rest followed. There was still no one man to act as a natural leader, but it would appear that the communal spirit, or the combination of strong individual spirits, was such as to render a leader unnecessary.

What did those men do, then? Just this; between 1550 and 1620 they rebuilt the entire village. More than fifty houses were either erected on derelict sites or built to replace houses which were in a state of near collapse. Some were built in the old ramshackle way, or built entirely of old material re-used, and lasted no more than a hundred years or so. Most of them were built of new straight beams of oak, or of sound timbers salvaged from a previous house. They were built to last, and last they did, as witness the fact that in this one village alone twenty of them are standing at the present day. In this and neighbouring villages there are thousands of oak beams, mostly hidden by plaster on the outside, which were sawn from trees four hundred years ago, and amongst them are many which were sawn five or even six hundred years ago. They constitute a monument not so much to the material prosperity of an age as to the good sense and good taste of two or three generations of men, common men for the most part who believed in quality and durability. Did it ever occur to them, I wonder, that the beams which they were putting to such good use had come from trees which, in many cases, had sprung from acorns planted by man or by nature at about the time of the Norman Conquest? Did *they* plant any acorns? I do not think so, for if they had we would be reaping the harvest today, and the sad truth is that there is little harvest to reap. If there were any point in blaming these sturdy yeomen of England for their lack of foresight, we are surely not in a position to do it, for are we not also squandering our national heritage? They at least had the excuse that they were converting something of lasting beauty into something else of lasting beauty, possibly even more lasting and more beautiful.

To give a detailed description of the origin, structure and history of those fifty-one houses, with some account of the people who lived in them, fascinating though it is to me and to the present-day occupants of the houses, would take up too much space and might not be of general interest to those unfamiliar with the village. I propose therefore to present my picture in three parts: first a complete list of the houses; then an account of how the picture was achieved, for the benefit of any who may wish to try their hand at the same thing; then some account of specific features. Some of my dates are precise; where a date is approximate it is preceded by '*c.*' to indicate the fact, and I can guarantee its accuracy to within about five years; all dates, precise or otherwise, are supported by documentary or archaeological evidence, or both. The numbers in the first column refer to the plan on page 125. An asterisk after the number denotes that the original structure is still standing.

No. on Plan	Present designation	Date	Built by or for	Other details
1	West Hill Farm	c. 1595	Henry Fuller	rebuilt c. 1884
2*	No. 1 High St.	c. 1550	John Fuller	enlarged and rebuilt c. 1720
3*	No. 5 High St.	1586	Richard Dunnidge	
4*	Cottage on the Green	1583	Thomas Campion	much of 1501 house survives
5*	No. 2 The Green	1555	John Fuller	enlarged c. 1660
6*	No. 1 The Green	1570	William Yewell	enlarged 1678
7	'Maltings', High St.	1585	Anthony King	demolished 1956
8	No. 15 High St.	c. 1600	Thomas Sympton	burnt down c. 1790
9	No. 17 High St.	c. 1578	Thomas Campion	collapsed c. 1795
10	'Old Black Boy'	c. 1550	Simon Campion	rebuilt c. 1730
11	next above	1561	Walter Pate	demolished c. 1880
12	No. 19 High St.	c. 1578	John Rayner	in ruins 1932
13	'The Forge'	1587	George Poynet	rebuilt 1754, demolished 1964
14*	'Michaelhouse'	1575	Trinity College	
15*	No. 18 High St.	c. 1550	John Fuller	rebuilt c. 1662
16	No. 33 High St.	1583	John Aunger	demolished c. 1695
17	Dovehouse Close	c. 1560	Richard Fuller	demolished c. 1810
18	No. 37 High St.	c. 1552	William Jacklyn	rebuilt 1792
19	next above	c. 1620	John Welbore	demolished 1967
20	War Memorial	c. 1620	Thomas Marris	demolished 1907
21	Univ. Tutorial Press	1578	Philip Welbore	demolished 1879
22*	No. 22 Station Rd.	1570	John Rayner	
23*	No. 18 Station Rd.	c. 1582	Thomas Wells	
24	No. 10 Station Rd.	1586	John Aunger	rebuilt 1871
25	School	1578	Robert Ayre	School built 1883
26	No. 43 High St.	1572	John Willcock	demolished 1936
27*	Nos 32 and 34 High St.	c. 1560	Robert Alleyn	
28	Post Office	c. 1575	Nicholas Mathewson	demolished 1845
29	'White Horse'	c. 1553	Henry Sturmyn	burnt down 1880
30	next above	c. 1560	Richard Curvey	demolished c. 1835
31	opposite above	1553	John Rayner	demolished 1840
32	No. 42 High St.	c. 1614	Edward Rayner	demolished c. 1850
33*	Nos 44 and 46 High St.	c. 1590	Edward Rayner	enlarged 1637

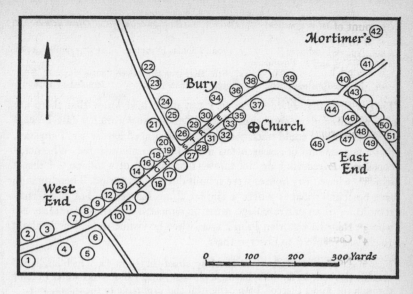

Map showing the location of houses built or rebuilt from 1550 to 1620. Blank circles indicate sites of houses whose history cannot be traced.

No. on Plan	Present designation	Date	Built by or for	Other details
34*	The Bury	1593	Sir Richard Warren	much altered and enlarged
35	Village Hall	c. 1570	Thomas Sympton	demolished c. 1850
36*	'Pound Cottage'	c. 1580	William Brestbone	
37*	No. 50 High St.	1560	John Everard	
38	No. 65 High St.	c. 1600	Thomas Wells	rebuilt c. 1745
39*	Nos 73 and 75 High St.	c. 1620	Richard Allen	
40*	Nos 1 and 3 Mortimers Lane	c. 1575	William Gybson	
41*	No. 5 Mortimers Lane	c. 1600	Thomas Hurrell	much altered
42	Mortimer's	c. 1548	William Sturmyn	rebuilt c. 1836
43	No. 2 Mortimers Lane	c. 1585	John Fuller	burnt down 1788
44	No. 2 Fowlmere Rd.	c. 1553	Thomas Lavender	burnt 1788, rebuilt, demolished 1968
45	Way's End	c. 1580	—— Rayner	demolished 1956
46*	Barron's Farm	c. 1565	George Wells	altered and enlarged 1890
47	No. 2 Barrons Lane	1620	Edmund Ostler	demolished c. 1770
48*	Nos 8 and 10 Fowlmere Rd.	c. 1574	Matthew Goodwin	

No. on Plan	Present designation	Date	Built by or for	Other details
49*	No. 20 Fowlmere Rd.	c. 1600	Thomas Sympton	partly rebuilt c. 1780
50	Nos 25 and 27 Fowlmere Rd.	c. 1618	Barnabas Brightwell	burnt down 1788
51	No. 31 Fowlmere Rd.	c. 1560	William Cock	demolished 1708

That is the tally, as complete as I can make it. I know that there are several omissions, several sites which do not come within my date-bracket or about which I could trace nothing definite. I need hardly say, I am sure, that a fair amount of research was needed to compile that list. Whether it constitutes a record I do not know. I have read of a village – I forget which – where forty houses were rebuilt during this period. There must in fact be many villages where a similar thing happened, but the virtual rebuilding of an entire village must be almost if not wholly unique. No wonder that the historian John Layer, when he visited the village in about 1622, was inspired to observe that:

Foxton is a pretty village, dry and healthy, situate in the midst of its bounds, and containeth about 60 families, having a pleasant small rill of sweet water running through the midst thereof, both delightful and profitable to the inhabitants.

I have reason to be pleased with John Layer for many things, not least for that charming reference to our Brook. But what a blessing it is that he did not see it – or taste it – between 8 p.m. and 4 a.m.

I can well imagine some of my readers asking at this point: how is it done? Is it all written down somewhere? Is it mostly guesswork? Well, in some instances, all too rare, the manor court rolls do actually give a precise statement and date. In the case of No. 6, the roll of 1571 says: 'William Yewle recently and unlawfully erected and built part of a house upon the highway, 30 feet in length and 6 feet in width.' In the case of No. 25, Robert Ayre and his wife in 1578 were granted 'a piece of pasture of the manor land, 40 feet long and 20 feet wide, that they might build a cottage there'. (The rent for that piece of land, incidentally, was 3d, i.e. per year.) Dates on buildings still surviving are rare, and none at all survive from the period under review, but later dates provide useful clues. There is the date 1678 and initials J.R.M. on No. 6, indicating its enlargement by John and Mary Rayner. The dovehouse bears the date 1706 and initials J.R.S. for James and Susan Rayner. No. 33 has 1637 and R.B. in plaster on a chimney-breast, indicating its enlargement by Richard Beaumont. No. 48 has 1652 carved on a beam, the date when the parlour ceiling was inserted. And that is all. But the rest is not just guesswork, I assure you.

Starting with the Enclosure Award and Map (1830 in the case of Foxton; much earlier in the case of some villages, and much later in others; such documents are, or ought to be, in the County Record Offices) one learns exactly who owned what at that date, and where it was located. Then, given time, patience and an almost continuous series of manorial records, one can work backwards from there and trace every change of ownership and many changes of occupation. With a bit of luck – an awful

Richard Dunnidge's house (No. 3) as it appeared a few years ago

lot of luck actually – this process may take one right back to the fifteenth century, as it did in the case of No. 3. More often it leaves one in mid-air somewhere around the middle of the seventeenth century, where there are some large gaps in the series of records. Then one starts at the beginning of the series and works forward, again ending in mid-air. The problem then is to link up the forward-moving trails with the backward-moving ones, and this is where the process gets really interesting, for it becomes a search for clues, a sort of detection game and jig-saw puzzle combined. One turns to other sources of information – wills, inventories, terriers, parish registers (which may turn up in the most unexpected places, though actually I got most of my information from the University Library, University Archives and County Record Office) – collecting in the process thousands of scraps of knowledge, most of which appear quite irrelevant to one's immediate purpose, but any one of which may prove to be a vital piece of the puzzle.

The most difficult part is the location of the houses. Rare indeed is an exact location given in the records. I found only one: No. 37 was 'lying opposite the churchyard' (*jacens ex opposito cimiterium*) and even that was not all plain sailing, for in fact the house is *alongside* the churchyard now, the bounds having been altered since 1492. Sometimes a location is given which, though complete enough for the man who lived there at the time, is tantalizingly incomplete for someone who does not know where that man's neighbours lived. No. 16, for instance was:

a messuage with croft adjoining, between the land of Trinity College on the west and a tenement of John Starke on the east, and the messuage abuts on the highway to the south.

There are far more vague locations than that, however. Often the house was 'situated in the West End' or 'in the East End by Mortimer's Lane'; all too often it was simply 'in Foxton'.

As the search continued, I began to notice details the significance of which had previously escaped me. The rents, for instance, remained unchanged for centuries. A house and eighteen-acre ware paying an annual rent of fourteen shillings in 1500 was still paying the same rent in 1770, and if it had in the meantime acquired more land in two different lots the rent would be stated as three separate items. A freehold property was easier to trace than a 'copy', for there were fewer freeholds. One had no difficulty in tracing No. 44, with its annual rent of 2*d*, or No. 30 'freehold, paying a rent of one penny', and the three freeholds 'for one peppercorn' were eventually sorted out. (A peppercorn rent meant that the tenant paid nothing. In the later jargon it became 'one peppercorn on demand', but I do not suppose that anyone ever demanded one peppercorn, or was expected to; I think it originated as an expression of weak jocular slang, the peppercorn referring to the 'o' in the accounts, just as we refer to an unlucky batsman's score as a 'duck' or a 'blob'.)

Another feature which proved of great help was the practice of naming a house after its first owner and retaining that name over a long period. No. 5, for instance, was 'John Fuller's' for a hundred and fifty years. Simon Fuller's name clung to No. 15 for a similar length of time. 'The house where John Starke lived' was in use a hundred and sixty years after John Starke had died. The same practice applied to land, and No. 46

furnishes the outstanding example of it; very early it became a substantial holding made up of three eighteen-acre wares, one of which belonged to a Coxall in 1485, another to Richard Perry in 1490 and the third to Will Sympton in 1507; in 1824 the names of Coxall, Perry and Sympton were still used to designate the land.

Names could also prove a pitfall. 'Everard' looked exactly like 'Ward' in its abbreviated form, and eventually became 'Everett'; 'Newman' became 'Newling'; 'Bartholomew' changed to 'Matthewson' and became 'Materson'; 'Ampes' became 'Amys', and so on. There were sixteen different ways of spelling 'Dunnidge'. One soon got accustomed to this sort of thing, but 'Edward Rayner' presented a problem which I cannot honestly claim to have solved. At one time there were five Edward Rayners all holding land, and three of them were 'son of Edward Rayner'. Several instances occur of two brothers having identical names, usually John. And then, of course, there was the obvious difficulty of offspring consisting entirely of daughters, usually three for some odd reason, all of whom changed their surname on marriage. No. 18 provided the most intriguing instance of this. In 1669 Philip Brightwell left the property to his wife Katherine and after her to his daughters Susan and Mary. Katherine outlived the daughters and left it to her son John. But Susan and Mary had married and produced between them three daughters, called Katherine, Susan and Mary, who claimed the inheritance. John died, leaving the property to his own three daughters, called Katherine, Susan and Mary. That baffled me somewhat; the manor court never did sort out the tangle – but time did.

Perhaps the most helpful clue of all was the fact that, when a man built his house, he was almost sure to find himself in trouble with the manor court for obstructing paths, moving or overstepping boundaries and the like. When for instance in 1501 'Richard Peppercorn obstructed the paths leading from le Merketstede' it is clear that he almost certainly did so with the materials needed to build a house and so I was able to date my own house, No. 4, the oldest of the village. When Walter Pate in 1561 was fined for 'digging clunch in the highway' he must have been engaged in making the floors and walls of a house. Clunch was the standard flooring until the mid-eighteenth century, and even when bricks were introduced they were laid on the original floor of clunch. That Walter Pate chose to get his clunch from the public highway in front of his door is another illustration of the general attitude towards roads.

A terrier, i.e. a detailed description of an estate, made when the property changed hands, is a veritable treasure and relatively rare. Sometimes it describes the land in great detail, merely referring to the house as a 'messuage', 'tenement' or 'homestall'. But the Michaelhouse (No. 14) terrier of 1579 included this:

There is conteined in the same Homestalle a howse wth a chimneye, in the Northe ende there is a chamber wth a soller, and in the Sowthe ende a chamber wth a soller.

In 1594 the description has shrunk to 'twoe Cross Chambers, one at ether ende', and although in 1631 Edward Myles made a 'perfect terror of the Michael House Farm' he barely mentioned the house.

A study of the fabric of those houses still surviving, wholly or partially from the period of the Great Rebuilding reveals several features of interest, though few surprises. A wealthy man like one of the Fullers used nothing but new straight thick beams of oak. The less wealthy invariably incorporated in their construction as much material as they could salvage from the old home; those are the beams which cause the most trouble

Michaelhouse (No. 14) today

today, being reduced almost to powder by age, damp, woodworm or dry rot. Oak was by no means exclusively used; indeed there are clear indications that it was already becoming scarce towards the end of the period. Quite a lot of elm is to be found, especially in the rafters; often whole branches, far from straight, and with the bark still on them. Iron nails at this time were rarely used; nearly all the joints are mortice and tenon, secured by the insertion of a dowel peg about an inch thick.

It is impossible to determine how much of the actual construction was done by the owner and how much by the village carpenter or by an outside craftsman. I would venture to suggest that there were not enough carpenters in England to have done all the work, and that, apart from the sawing and joining, which needed special facilities and tools, the houses were largely erected by the men who lived in them. The chimneys must have been built by the local bricklayer – except that in No. 38, which was built of blocks of chalk – but the brick foundations were, to judge by the look of them, often the work of amateurs with more zeal than skill. Damp-proof courses were unknown and, I imagine, unthought of. The previous generation of houses – several generations of houses – had had, as their sole foundation, horizontal beams resting on the earth ('sleeper beams'). Incredible though it may seem, some of these lasted for more than four hundred years; I have removed several – mostly in the form of a fine brown powder, admittedly, but still recognizable as oak beams. The only house with really durable foundations is No. 34, the Bury, where two large cellars with walls four feet thick were made; on these the present house stands.

Windows were for the most part still unglazed. The usual practice was to contrive within the framework an opening about two feet square, often much less, with two or three vertical wooden bars. A fine example of this type of window survives in No. 46; it was certainly not glazed. The only mention of glass occurs in connection with No. 21, the Welbore mansion, which was also wainscotted. Decoration and ornament does not appear to have been a feature of these houses, though there are two references to 'painted cloths', which must have covered the interior walls. The kitchen of the yeoman's house prior to about 1500 was nearly always a separate building set apart from the dwelling; the kitchen of the new houses was usually the space at the back of the chimney-base, though the actual cooking was done at the one and only fireplace in the 'hall', as the living-room was called. A summary of wills, given later in this chapter, shows what was in the kitchen and around the fireplace.

I have not been able to find out what it cost to build a house of this period, but there are a few vague hints here and there which lead me to believe that the figure would be in the region of £100 for a house with chimney, two rooms and one loft or chamber. I do have one precise record of the cost of a building site. When Richard Dunnidge bought a 'kitchen and a parcel of land adjacent, in length 6 perches and 6 feet approx., in width 3 perches and one foot' (No. 3) it cost him £11 12s 4d. That works out at just over one halfpenny (one quarter of a new penny) per square foot. The yard and outbuildings were thrown in free for good measure. Finally, since we are on the subject of finance, a few observations not specifically related to houses, but rather to the land, which continued to be the primary concern of the manor. The rents, as already stated, remained unchanged for centuries despite the change in monetary values of everything else. The entry-fine steadily increased from about eight shillings for a house and nine acres of land in the mid-sixteenth century to about £8 a century later. In addition to this fee, a heriot continued to be paid. It had for centuries been 'the best beast'; then it was frequently commuted to cash, usually twenty pence. Then in the early seventeenth century heriots begin to reflect something of social status, and we find payments of 'one feather bed', 'one gown of woollen cloth, value 10s', 'one silver cupp value 40s', though we still find 'heriot one cow value 10s', 'one grey horse value 30s'. One must treat these valuations with a certain caution, however; a horse valued at £4 by the Steward had been valued at 24s a few weeks earlier by the men who made the inventory of the owner; it depended whether the valuer was a prospective vendor or a prospective purchaser.

Fascinating though it was, this research into the construction of the houses would have been somewhat of an academic exercise had it not brought occasional glimpses of human comedy and drama, and here and there some insight into the character of those common men, those yeomen of England. This was the age of the sturdy, thrusting individualist, of whom no better example could be found anywhere, I think, than that provided by John Rayner. Born in about 1518, he inherited a house and eighteen acres of land from his father in 1538. He also inherited, or developed, a total lack of respect for manor courts and disregard for the interests of his neighbours, an attitude which he resolutely maintained over a period of fifty years. Here is a list of his transgressions as recorded in the minutes of the manor court:

1541. He refused to appear with others to enquire into the unlawful lengthening of a hedge; fined 12*d*.

1543. He encroached with his plough on various balks in various places; fined 4*d*.

1550. He was ordered to mend the fence between him and Bartholomew Mathewson.

He encroached with his plough at Whytmoreshot; fined 4*d*.

1551. He assaulted Richard Day and drew blood; fined . . .

1553. He enclosed part of the public way with a wall; fined 12*d*.

1554. He was ordered to remove the hedge between him and Mathewson.

1558. He failed to widen a drain as ordered; fined 4*d*.

He failed to repair a hedge next to John Kyng; fined 3*s* 4*d*.

He kept a dog which was in the habit of worrying sheep; fined 3*d*.

1559. He trespassed on the land of Will Fuller and did damage to the extent of 6*s* 8*d*.

He trespassed and did damage on the land of John Kyng to the extent of 10*s*.

1561. He occupied ½ acre of enclosed pasture without title.

He was ordered to mend the fences between him and John Calcott.

He was ordered to mend the fences between him and Elena King.

1562. He ploughed up the common balks; fined 12*d*.

He was ordered to mend the fences next to John Smith.

1566. He removed the common boundary-marks in the fields; fined 12*d*.

He cut branches from two willow trees of Agnes Crosse; fined 3*s* 4*d*.

He was ordered to replace boundary-marks in Hayditch Shott.

1568. He was ordered to repair the fence at Andrews; fined 12*d*.

He failed to clean out the ditch there; fined 12*d*.

He made a ditch somewhere else; fined 6*d*.

He encroached on 5 roods of Trinity land in Chawdwell Felde; fined 12*d*.

He set a bad example by taking the oath negligently in court; fined 12*d*.

1571. He encroached on manor land at Andrews and stole a tree; fined 20*d*.

1576. He encroached on the road-way in Woodway Shott; fined 12*d*.

He ploughed over a boundary in Woodway Shott to the extent of one furrow; fined 12*d*.

He encroached with his plough at the Shot, using his fork, at Flag Pyghtell; fined 3*s* 4*d*.

He ploughed and encroached on a balk-end; fined 12*d*.

He failed to amend the encroachment at Andrews; fined 10*s*.

He trespassed when mowing upon the manor land of Richard Fuller to the extent of a swathe and a half; fined 2*s*.

He ploughed 5 roods in Downfield contrary to orders; fined 2*s*.

1578. He was ordered to mend the fences between him and Thomas Wells.

1581. He let loose his beasts at Apletons; fined 12*d*.

He lopped two willows of John Fuller; fined 4*d*.

1586. He was ordered to mend the fence between him and Perrys.

How many transgressions he committed and got away with we can only guess. Living next door to him must have been a bit of a nightmare. I am pretty sure that he complained bitterly about the 'interfering busybodies' who were 'always meddling in his affairs', and the events of 1576 do rather suggest a concerted effort to put a stop to his activities. In vain, for he carried on almost to his dying day. Yet, for all that, it cannot be said that he was a bad man. He never, so far as I know, broke the law of the land. He served as churchwarden on two occasions, and never fell foul of the Archdeacon. He did duty as ale-taster for several years but, understandably, never served as constable.

John Rayner witnessed only one will; never wrote his name – he could not write his name (there were only three men in the village who could). He owned three houses at one time, one of which (No. 22) still stands today. He did his duty by his own family; when he died, aged eighty-one years, he left to his wife: '£4 a yeare soe long as shee lyveth, a bedd with all that belongeth to yt, with a chamber to lye in soe long as shee lyveth yf she will.'

Thomas Campion was John Rayner's closest rival in the defiance of authority, incurring much heavier though less frequent fines. When he died he not only left his wife nothing but completely ignored her existence. He was one of the party caught playing illicit 'games', i.e. gambling for drinks, in Margaret Sympton's ale-house in 1576, a party which, incidentally, included the vicar, George Awder. A little higher up the social ladder than these thrusting outspoken yeomen was Fuller Mead, Gent. Not that he was any less thrusting, but instead of thrusting against authority he chose to thrust with it. His father had married money – the Fullers' money – and he was determined to ensure that, though his contemporaries might ignore the fact, posterity should know that he was a man of no mean merit. Here is what he had engraved in letters of brass on a marble slab in the church in about 1620:

Here lyeth the body of John Fuller who departed in April 1588, who married Dorothy, Daughter of Thomas Chichely of Wimpole, Esq. by Maryan his second wife, the daughter of Hussey of Lincolnshire; the which Thomas Chichely was the Sonne of William Chichely and of Alice his wife, the daughter of Bruges, grandfather to the first Lord Chandos, the which William was Sonne of Henry, the sonne of John, the sonne of William who was Brother to Henry, Archbishop of Canterbury, and Robert Chichely twice Mayor of London, the sonnes of Thomas Chichely of Higham Ferrers.

This stone was laid here at the charge of Fuller Mead the sonne of Robert Mead borne at Much Easton in Essex who married the Daughter and Heire of John Fuller by Dorothie his wife; wch Fuller Mead married Rose the daughter of Francis Brakin of Cambridge, Esq. who had issue by her Edmund Mead and Fuller Mead.

What Fuller Mead did *not* mention on his marble slab was that his great-great-grandfather John Fuller was fined 3*d* for stealing a horse, which John Fuller was brother to William Fuller who assaulted Will Rayner 'with a pyke-fork, value 2*d*', was fined 4*d* for allowing his pigs to stray unringed, and broke the manor pound to remove his horses impounded for straying in the corn. Perhaps there was not sufficient room on the slab. It was Robert Mead, incidentally, who planted a vineyard at Mortimer's in 1598, but it only seems to have thrived for about twelve years. His son's marble slab likewise had a short life – the anti-popery iconoclasts smashed it and stole all the brass.

In these matter-of-fact records, comedy is rare. Tragedy, when it occurs, does so in such a way as to make one realize that it was never far away, and that these sturdy bustling yeomen, for all their seeming self-confidence, lived under the constant menace of something which they did not understand and were powerless to prevent. The 'pestilence' was still liable to break out again at any time, and many other ills, equally mysterious, could put a sudden end to a man's social ambitions or nullify a lifetime of hard work. That is why, along with whatever religious faith a man might hold, and whatever religious practice royal edict might prescribe, there still persisted practices inspired by superstitious dread of the unknown. Even the most cynical of those yeomen, when building his house, would take care to incorporate in its structure a talisman to ensure that it and its occupants would enjoy some measure of protection from bad fortune, evil spirits, witchcraft and the like. This talisman usually took the form of animal bones, or a shoe, or a piece of iron, embedded in the chimney-stack, under the threshold, at the base of a wall, wherever the evil spirits were most likely to sneak in when the occupants were asleep or off guard. In the case of my own house the protective talismans were half a sheep's jawbone, complete with teeth, and a little old shoe.

When John Aunger built house No. 24 in 1586 he may well have omitted the necessary talisman. It is evident that he was a speculator; he bought three building sites in the course of a few years and erected houses on them to sell. The practice, something of a novelty at that time, was frowned upon but tolerated by the manor court until Aunger's son took over his late father's property and refused to pay rent or fees on the grounds that he was not a tenant of the manor, thereby forfeiting the said lands. As for No. 24, Aunger sold it to Will Feere as soon as it was built.

Feere moved in with his three children, Edward, John and Katherine, his wife having recently died. On 20 February 1588 Will Feere made his will, leaving the new house to his son John 'at the age of 21 years, and if the saide John do departe this worlde then I will that Edward Feere my sonn shall enjoye it'. A week later Will Feere was dead. Son John did not 'enjoye' the house for long; as soon as he reached the age of 21 he sold it to Will Ayler in 1602. Will Ayler lived there for a few months, then he died. He had made his will, leaving the house to his son John for life, and after him to Will Cock. John Ayler and his wife Elizabeth moved in; a few months later they both died. So Will Cock moved in; before the end of that year 1603 he was dead. Talisman or no, there was certainly something about that house which made it a target for ill fortune.

It is fairly certain that Will Feere, Will Ayler, John Ayler and his wife and Will Cock died of the plague, which was never far away. It was just round the corner, at house No. 28, in 1581. Margaret Mathewson's husband had just died of the plague. Let Margaret's will tell its own story:

In the Name of God, Amen, the 28th day of September in the Yere of our Lord god 1581, Margaret Matheson of Foxton – wyddowe, beinge in perfect mynde & memorie but sicke of bodye, did make and declare hir will and Testament Nuncupative in manner and forme followinge. First she gave her soule to allmightie god and hir bodye to the earthe. Item, she havinge twoe of her children ded of the plague & lyeinge unburyed, and haveinge two other children verye sicke & she her selfe beinge sicke of the same decease, did give all her goodes that she had what soever unto Ralph Wade and Margary his wife, sister of the sayd Margaret Matheson, to burye her and her said children.
These Wittnesses, Walter Pate & Thomas Campion.

If by chance you read that quickly, may I ask you, please, to read it again, slowly, and ponder awhile upon its content. You have rarely read, I imagine, a matter-of-fact statement of such poignancy.

The plague was likewise next door, at house No. 25, the one which Robert Ayre built in 1578. The vicar, Nicholas Staniland, had to live there because his vicarage had been burnt down. He had a wife and four little girls in 1625. Three years later he, his wife and four little girls were all dead. Of course the only real link between those tragedies and the practice of incorporating protective talismans in the houses is that the former go a long way towards explaining belief in the latter.

The John Rayner mentioned earlier was clearly no ordinary man, though one of the common men whose lives are my theme. The explanation, if one were needed, may be that he belonged to no ordinary family. In the general run of things it seems that the male line in most families dies out after five or six generations. It also seems that one or two families in every hundred defy all the laws of genetics, if there are any such laws, and do the most remarkable things. The Cock family, for instance; they were here in Foxton in the thirteenth century and did not disappear until the early nineteenth. The Rayners had a slightly longer innings and made a much higher score. There were Rayners at one time or another living in more than half the houses on my list. The same could be said of many isolated families in many villages, I am sure, especially villages in isolated regions like the Fens, but few families can have lasted so long or been so prolific as the Rayners of Foxton. I know of 60 Rayners born between 1450 and 1660; 78 were baptized between 1690 and 1810; 74 were buried in Foxton between 1680 and 1810. And that is by no means a complete count, for some were never baptized, some left the village and some died in infancy. In fact many died in infancy. Infant mortality must always have been high; it is not until the early seventeenth century that we get a clear idea of its incidence. I will quote just one example to illustrate both Rayner productivity and infant mortality; it is by no means a special or isolated case. Philip Rayner married Elizabeth Bevin in 1611. These were their offspring:

1612	Mary	1619	Frances, died 1619
1613	William	1620	Edward, died 1620
1614	Stephen, died 1617	1621	Thomasine, died 1627
1616	Bridget, died 1617	1624	Thomas
1617	Elizabeth, died 1617	1624	Edward

The mother, not surprisingly, died in 1629.

In dealing with the vast amount of information supplied by the documents at my disposal, I have done my utmost to omit from these pages everything not strictly relevant to my theme. I may have omitted much which would have interested some of my readers. I hope I have not included too much which does not interest them. In either case, please accept my apologies. I propose to deal with just two more topics, one relating to crops, the other to houses.

It will be noticed that in subsequent pages there is frequent reference to saffron, a commodity which perhaps many people today have never even heard of – with the special exception, of course, of those living in north Essex.

It was extensively cultivated in south Cambridgeshire in the sixteenth and seventeenth centuries, usually by people holding a small amount of land; it was not then the 'poor man's crop' which it tended to become later. It was suitable for growing in gardens and closes, but seems to have been mainly grown in the open fields in plots ranging in size from half a rood (one eighth of an acre) to two acres. The corms of the crocus were left in the same ground for three years, a crop being harvested each year over a period of about two months, then lifted and moved to fresh ground. 'Harvesting' consisted in picking off the yellow stigmas of the flowers in full bloom, a finicky job which women and girls could do best. These stigmas were dried in a special kiln, pressed into a solid 'cake' and sold for use as colouring and flavouring in cakes and biscuits, also as a dye for woollen cloth. An acre of corms in one year would yield perhaps 25 lb of stigmas, which when dried would weigh about 6 lb, worth about £6 in cash. It was therefore a very profitable crop, provided that plenty of unpaid labour was available; unpaid labour was one of the basic features of farming then and for another two centuries. One apparent disadvantage of saffron-growing is that it would interfere with the normal rotation of cropping and fallowing in the open fields. This could be overcome by fencing in the saffron-ground with wattle hurdles – the plants would welcome a bit of shelter in any case – and so arranging things that several saffron grounds were adjacent. By this time (sixteenth century) the rigidity of the ancient field-system had been considerably relaxed and modified. A holding still consisted of a large number of small strips, varying in size from half an acre to two acres, dispersed in the fields, but there are indications that the holder could now grow what he wished to grow, so long as the triennial fallowing was not interfered with. The saffron-ground, certainly, was outside the normal scheme of things and was treated as a possession distinct from his normal holding of land.

Finally a word about house-plans. Most of the houses on my list consisted of two rooms when built, the hall and the parlour. Two and a half rooms, to be precise, for there was nearly always a small area at the back of the chimney which was used either as the kitchen or as the buttery; the latter was where the brewing was done. Some of the houses would have a ceiling of beams and planks over the parlour, thus creating a chamber, or 'soller', or loft. This was not intended originally for sleeping in; it was rather for the storage of seed-corn, wool, cheese, bacon, saffron and suchlike things too precious to be entrusted to the barn, where they might be a prey to rats, damp and thieves. In the first half of the seventeenth century it became fashionable, indeed necessary, in view of the increasing amount of furniture and improved standard of living (not to mention large families), to insert another ceiling over the hall, or over both hall and parlour. This meant that stairs had to be fitted in to give access to the upper floor, and a window (rarely more than one) made in the roof to give light. It also meant that head-room was severely restricted on both ground floor and first floor, for in the majority of cases the original timber frame did not allow for two storeys. Whenever you walk into an old thatched cottage and crack your head on a solid oak beam across the middle of the room, you can be sure that you are in a genuine Tudor house and that your head has encountered a seventeenth-century insertion. If you do not bang your head, either the floor has been lowered, or the house has been rebuilt, or you are not as tall as I am.

As for the daily life of the people who lived, loved and died in those houses, by far the most eloquent testimony is provided by their wills. Once more I will restrict myself to a summary only of those relating to the period 1550–1630. To quote them all, even omitting the lengthy preamble, would be to tax the patience of the reader, for they number well over fifty, and the details which have so much significance for us today were of little interest to those who listened with bated breath to the first reading of the will four hundred years ago, just as the items which interested them most are those which interest us least today. It would seem that all but the poorest people at this period made a will, usually a very short time before they died 'beinge sicke in bodie but in perfect good memory of minde'. Some of them indeed – and this is particularly true of elderly widows – were of such perfect good memory of mind that they were able to recall and list every single item in the house and yard, and account for every rood of land which they possessed.

The foremost preoccupation of all of them, rich or poor, was the equitable disposal of their houses and land: 'all that my messuage or tenement wherein I nowe dwell, called Matheyson's, together with all the arrable lande, meadowe-grounde & pasture thereunto belonginge', etc. The eldest son always inherited the bulk or the best of the property, due provision having been made for the widow 'soe longe as shee lyveth', and her portion was often dependent 'upon this condition that she kepe herself wyddowe'. Provision was frequently made, on a modest scale, for 'servantes', which could mean both domestic servants and farm-workers. Responsibility for aged parents was generally admitted and translated into practical terms: 'my wyfe shall pay unto my Mother yearlie duringe her lyfe tyme thirtie shillinges fower pence a yeare'. No grandchild was ever omitted from the list of legatees, a fact which helps enormously in revealing the size and composition of families when Parish Registers are faulty or missing, and provision was made even for children still on the way: 'to the childe that my wife is with, if it be a sonne 43s 4d, if it be a daughter three quarters Barleie and a cowe the price 18s.' Boys, of course, were always treated more generously than girls, not only as regards the size of their share but also the age at which they could inherit, which could be at 14, 16, 18, 20 or 21 years whereas a girl usually had to wait until 'the daye of her marryage' or 21 years, whichever came soonest. On the other hand it is pleasing to note that in numerous instances the daughter who had stayed at home to look after an ageing parent, having postponed or abstained from marriage, was given first choice of the household goods – 'she havinge her choyse of them' – and thereby enabled the more easily to marry late in the day. It was never too late to marry, and a woman with a little bit of property would not remain for long without a suitor, whatever other attractions she might lack.

Money, inevitably, figures largely in the bequests, and the sums specified range in size from £300 in the case of a very wealthy man like Philip Welbore, through '£40 in moneye', '£30 of good and currant money' of the average yeoman, down to '12d lawfully demanded', the latter being a deliberate slight on a headstrong son or daughter who had most probably married contrary to the father's wishes. A similar bequest to a godchild, of quite frequent occurrence, is an indication that the role of godparent was taken more seriously then than it is nowadays. There were, however, some men for whom money, as such, was clearly a commodity of secondary importance. Old Simon Campion, for instance, who died in 1563, made twenty bequests of barley totalling more than eighty quarters (160 sacks) and specified less than ten shillings in cash.

Scarcely a single will fails to mention animals and crops. Indeed it would be almost possible to calculate the animal population of the village and make a survey of the crops from the many references to cows, bullocks, horses, sheep, pigs, barley, wheat, rye, oats, beans, peas – not forgetting saffron. Moreover, and this is of particular interest, we get the occasional indication of the value of these things in terms of cash:

two horses the pryce £3 13s 4d.
two bullocks one black pied and one browne heifer, or foure pounds in monie.
two horses the pryce of £6 bothe.

a cowe the price 18s.
one gode carte the price 40s.

With the exception of carts, 'shod' or unshod, and 'plough geere' (collars and traces), farm implements get no mention at all, which may come as a surprise until one realizes that most of the tools and implements used in sixteenth-century farming were made largely of wood, were made by the user with a bit of technical assistance from the village carpenter or blacksmith, were highly expendable and certainly not to be reckoned as hereditable possessions. Old Thomas Sturman, for instance, in 1607 saw fit to specify 'my shedd as it standeth in the yard, two stockes of bees and the hedge owerthwarte the yarde', but he made no mention of any implements.

The matter wherein these wills are most revealing, like the examples mentioned earlier and the inventories which come later, is the actual content of the houses, and here we can trace a steady improvement in the scale of furnishing and equipment which can only denote a rising standard of living, with more comfort, more privacy and more refinement. It is clear that no household – none at least of those whose owners made a will – was without a bed of some sort, and that bed takes pride of place amongst the owner's possessions. We are frequently told in detail what was on the bed – its 'furniture', as they put it – and sometimes exactly where it stood:

a bed with allthings perteyninge therto, as mattris, fetherbed, shete, Bollster, pillowe, a Blanket and a coverlet with a Bedsted standinge in the parler by the strete.

Notice that it was downstairs. Only towards the end of the period do we find beds upstairs 'in the chamber'. Feather beds and 'flock' beds are about equally prevalent, with occasionally the super-comfort of 'a coverlett of downecke', which must have been a sort of quilt stuffed with the finest feathers of goose (the very thing which in recent years has been extolled as an 'innovation' from Sweden). Sheets, pillowcases, tablecloths, towels, napkins were of flax (linen) or the somewhat coarser tow (hemp); blankets of course were of wool; all of these items were obviously meant to last for a long time and a sheet would have to be very threadbare indeed before it was given away or torn up for other use.

Next in importance and prestige-value came the table. Boards laid on trestles were still much in use and continued so for a long time yet, but tables, usually 'round' or 'square', often 'littell', became common around 1570, and by the end of the century 'joyned' tables were all the rage. 'Joined' furniture – beds, stools, forms, chairs as well as tables – represented a major advance in home furnishing, and a landmark in the social and financial status of the owner, also a landmark in local craftsmanship. It would however, I think, be a mistake to visualize in these yeomen's houses any of those magnificent Elizabethan or Jacobean tables which now command such fabulous prices in the antique shops. Most of the 'joyned' tables which filled their owner's hearts with pride in 1600 were, I am pretty sure, made in the village, and all of them were firewood by 1750. The only other items of furniture, as we understand the term, were chests, 'hutches' (for clothes, not rabbits), cupboards, coffers and presses, all of which were virtually the same thing, that is boxes with lids, either vertical or horizontal, nearly always with locks. This was the only means of storing things, especially clothes, in safety. Not infrequently the chests were also used as beds, as they invariably were in the Middle Ages. Few of these likewise have survived the ravages of time and woodworm, though plenty of imitations abound. Two instances occur of an item which must have been a prized antique in those days; John Fuller in 1558 refers to 'all the paynted clothes', and Margerie Rogers in 1604 to 'all the painted shetes which be aboute'. These could well have been handed down from medieval times, and were probably of religious inspiration although fulfilling the mundane office of keeping out draughts. They would be priceless possessions today had they survived, which of course they could not possibly do.

Then there were the kitchen utensils, the pots and pans of brass, pewter or 'latten' (an alloy of copper and zinc). In some cases they seem to have been limited to a 'brasse potte and a little kettle', leaving it open to suggestion that food was still being eaten from wooden platters and ale being drunk from wooden goblets. In most cases however it is clear that the house was well stocked with pots large and small, kettles, cauldrons, frying-pans, posnets, skillets, platters, mortars, dishes, even a few 'great chardgers'; frequently all lumped together as 'all my brasse and all my pewter'. Margaret Sympson, widow, in 1580 itemizes such a wealth and diversity of equipment, including 'a quart pott of pewter' and 'twoe brueinge tubbes', that one is left in no uncertainty as to her occupation as an innkeeper. Every substantial yeoman's house was equipped with the necessary tubs and vats for brewing ale (frequently of lead, and kept always in 'the buttery') and it is clear that most of those yeomen could easily have dispensed with the services of Dame Margaret, though it is equally clear from other sources that few of them did.

Cups do not figure in the lists, except for the occasional silver cup evidently treasured as an heirloom, but there are two references to a 'sawcer'. It cannot possibly have been what we understand by a saucer, and must, I think, have been a small dish for sauce or gravy. Spoons, when mentioned at all, are nearly always of silver, and they also seem to have the quality of heirlooms. The common workaday spoons were of wood, and were as low down the social scale as is the 'wooden spoon' today. Knives are never mentioned, presumably because they were such a commonplace that nobody would ever think of mentioning them specifically. Forks are never mentioned for a totally different reason – they were not used. Table-forks had not been invented, but fingers had. That explains the number of 'napkins' to be found in the more refined households. In the not-so-refined households, where napkins were lacking, tongues were not. Candlesticks seem to have become common in the 1570s, yet there is no mention, as one would expect, of candle-snuffers or of moulds for making the candles, which must have been a home occupation.

That bread-making in the home was as much a commonplace as the home brewing of ale – particularly after the disappearance of the weekly market in about 1540 – is testified by the numerous mentions of a 'kneadinge kymnell' (a trough for kneading the dough), and the inglenook fireplace so appealing to popular imagination today is brought vividly to the mind's eye by the many references to 'andyrons', 'a payre of cobirons', 'the best spytt', 'the pott hangers' and so on. I can find no reference to ovens – they became a common built-in feature of the fireplace about a hundred years later – unless the solitary mention of 'a fyre' is in fact referring to an oven; and I wonder just how the bread was baked. I can only suppose that it was done on a 'girdle' or 'griddle' plate (though that is not mentioned either), an iron disc about two feet in diameter, placed on top of the fire to make smallish flat loaves.

And what about the fuel for that fire? Most of my readers, I imagine, will say without hesitation that wood was always used. So would I had I not come across a reference in one of these wills, dated 1566, to 'colefayer day nexte comminge'. This I find really intriguing. There can be no question about the 'cole', but was it 'coal-fire' or was it 'coal-fair'? Was there a certain day in the year on which coal-fires could be started without incurring a charge of extravagance, cold-footedness or breach of ancient custom? Or did the supply of coal come once a year, on the occasion of one of the annual fairs? In any case, how and whence did it come? My guess is that it came by sea from Tyneside to Lynn, and thence by river all the way to Cambridge. An expensive business even in those days, and the price of the coal must have put it beyond the reach of all but the more prosperous of the yeomen. The others would certainly use wood – there is more than one mention of 'the ould wood in the yarde' – and the poorer people would eke out the ever-diminishing supply of wood with dried cow-dung, as they had done for a thousand years, and as they were still doing two hundred years later.

I was surprised to find only one 'spinninge wheele', belonging to Agnes Starke, widow, and only one 'warming panne', that of old Richard Beaumont in 1615. Both articles feature so prominently in the picture one imagines of a Tudor house. Perhaps they really were as rare as they would appear to have been. I was further prompted to wonder just how much do-it-yourself activity went on in these houses by at least three references to 'the woollen cloth at the weavers'. It would seem that there was little spinning done, and even less weaving. It can however, I think, be safely assumed that, though the cloth was made elsewhere, the clothes worn in the village were made in the village. The wills have plenty to tell us about those clothes. The womenfolk were proud to hand on to their daughters 'a russett petticoate', 'my blacke frocke and my redd petticoate', 'all my woollen apparrell', 'one double kercher', 'my best gowne, my best hatt, a wascote and one neckercher', 'my working day gowne', 'my two gownes', and so on. Hardly enough material from which to design a fashion-plate, but let us remember that the setting was hardly one for the suitable display of fashions. Let it be noted, too, that clothes-consciousness was by no means confined to the gentler sex, nor to the more affluent of the not-so-gentle sex. William North, a labourer, who died in 1620, left to his younger son: 'my best suit of apparrell, that is to say my best blacke fustian dublett, my beste russet cloake, two hose of the same peere, one payer of high shoes'.

Though he only had three shillings to distribute amongst his children, his 'second suit of apparrell' was deemed fit to be handed on, and his elder son was the recipient of 'one black staffe'. That gives scope for speculation as to what might have been the occupation of William before he descended to the status of labourer. Thomas Flacke, a shoemaker who died in 1626, was so well endowed with worldly goods that it comes as no surprise to find him leaving to his son 'three paire of breeches, two dubletts, two hatts and two jerkins'. His will, incidentally, contains two other small items which are of interest though nothing to do with clothes. The four pounds which his son Thomas is to receive must be paid 'at or in the churchyarde of Foxton'. This stipulation occurs again and again; as often as not it is 'in the churche-porch'. It is an interesting reminder that, whatever changes in dogma and ritual might have taken place in the meantime, the church had retained its role as a guarantor of good faith and honest dealing; a man might cheat in the ale-house or the market-place, but he would not dare to cheat in the shadow of the church. Let us hope that their simple trust was not misplaced. The other item is that the will was witnessed by 'Matthew Dunnidge and *me* Matthew East'. I knew that Matthew East lived in the village, and that he was a professional 'scrivener'; I suspected that he must be the man who was writing these wills. It was particularly gratifying to have the fact confirmed by his own hand.

Back to clothes. There was no finery about the clothes, and few adornments. Such items of jewellery as these people had they obviously regarded as commodities to be treated in the same way as their clothes; that is to say, used for as long as they lived then handed on to be used by someone else until there was no more use left in them. Nothing was ever thrown away if it could still be used, but it would seem that decency forbade a man to dispose of his late wife's clothes until he himself was dead. Stephen Wells in 1566 left to his sister Elizabeth 'the gowne which was my wyffes with the sylver pynnes and silver howkes' and 'an owlde kyrtell of worsted which was my wyffes'. There are numerous such instances, and one, much later, which seems to point to the fact that a man's second wife ought not to be permitted to wear the clothes which had belonged to his first wife. Margaret Sympson, the possessor of perhaps the last 'harnesse girdle' to be seen in Foxton, put equity before aesthetic considerations when it came to the disposal of her other precious heirloom:

I will that Marye shall have my payer of beades and the best pece of sylver that hangeth one them, and Elizabeth the next peace of sylver, and Joan to have the third peace of sylver thereone.

John Fuller, who died when the Spanish Armada was on its way to England, left 'to my Mother two Aungells to make her a Ringe' (an 'aungell' or angel being a gold coin worth about eight shillings at that time), a reminder that gold, whether used as money or as ornament, was still gold. His wife Dorothy had evidently long held that view, for the sole items in her will, made in the same year 1588, were:

to Mr Chichley of Wimpole one Ringe of goulde,
to Mistress Sterne of Melborne berye one ring of gould,
to Mistress Wood of Fulbourne a Ring of gould,
to Mistress Rutlysse of Gamlinghaye one ringe of goulde.

Whether the rings were tokens of friendship, rewards for past favours, or given in expectation of favours to come, we cannot know. Of all the families in Foxton at that date, only the Fullers were in a position to make such gestures. Incidentally, I wonder whether the general practice of giving a gold wedding-ring dates from this time?

John Fordham, another shoemaker, who made his will in 1583 'though sycke in body yet, praysed be the lyveinge god, of good and perfecte remembrance', obligingly demonstrated both his good memory and his honesty by appending the following:

Debts oweing to me John Fordham.
Johnson the miller of Barrington owethe me for a paire of heighe shoes iis.
Thomas Sturman of Foxton the carpenter for mendinge a paire of shooes iiiid.
Mr Fuller for a paire of shoes for one of his men & for mending a paire xixd.
Richard Calcotte for soleinge of shoes xid.
Thomas Whitby for mendinge a paire of shooes iiiid.
Debts which I John Fordham doe owe.
to Josephe Parker for killinge my bullocks and shepe xs.
to my father in lawe xls.

He thereby provided us with an insight into the cost of living, an indication of the way in which Mr Fuller, mentioned above, treated his men, and proof that at least one village craftsman was also a part-time farmer. In fact there is ample evidence to show that shoemakers, blacksmiths, carpenters, innkeepers, bricklayers, etc., were all of them part-time farmers. Or were they part-time shoemakers, etc.?

I have said nothing so far in this chapter about food, apart from bread, nor would one expect to gather much information about this vital topic from documents dictated by people who had little further use for it. Even if the testator had specified what sort of a meal was to be provided for the assemblage at his funeral, which none ever did – though one old lady did specify in a spirit of defiant pride 'to be disposyd for me at my buryall xxs and better' – it would obviously bear no relation to the norm of daily living. The only items of food actually mentioned are 'a flyche of bacon' and 'two flitches of bacon', which, when one thinks about it, were the only items sufficiently durable to be mentioned, with the possible addition of cheeses.

It can be assumed, from the various articles, animals and crops listed, that some of the people sometimes consumed beef, pork, mutton, ham, bacon, eggs, chickens, cheese, beans, peas, lentils, bread, butter, honey, milk and ale. It can be assumed from general inference that they also ate fruit and vegetables. What proportion of those commodities produced in the village was sent for sale in neighbouring markets there is no means of knowing; nor can one know who ate how much of what, and how often.

Consideration of one item alone, roast beef – the most expensive item then, as it is now – will show to what extent the whole business is a matter of speculation. It is clear that beef was roasted and eaten; the mention of spits and 'drypeinge pans' is, I think, adequate confirmation. But a closer study reveals that all the five spits mentioned were in the possession of elderly widows. Does that mean that they alone possessed spits and that other people brought their joints to be roasted by those old ladies, just as throughout the Middle Ages all the bread in the village had been baked by two or three 'public bakers of human bread', and just as, within living memory, people in towns used to take their Sunday joints to be roasted by the local baker? And, if so, were the old ladies paid partly in kind with 'a cut off the joint'? Or, as seems more probable, does it mean that only elderly widows saw fit to list their possessions in such detail as to include those items which all the menfolk dismissed in the one phrase 'the rest of my implements of householde'? We know that Simon Campion owned three bullocks when he died. We do not and cannot know for sure that he ever intended to eat any or all of them if he had lived. And yet my own firm belief is that Simon and his son Thomas and his grandson Nicholas and his great-grandson Samuel, all enjoyed a regular joint of beef roasted within a few feet of where I am sitting now. It is no mere surmise, but a fair certainty, that many of the people living at the other end of the village tasted roast beef, if at all, only a few times between the day they were born and the day when they were 'buryied in the churcheyarde of Foxton'.

Equally a matter of speculation is the degree to which extended the comfort and refinement of which I spoke earlier. That it included facilities for personal washing is attested by the existence of basins and towels, and there were obviously means of washing the increasing amount of 'linnen' other than in the Brook, which, though expressly forbidden, was probably still the only facility available to some people. When, however, we look for evidence that any of these people ever had a bath, we find little, and none that is very convincing. It could be, of course, that some of the many 'tubbes' referred to in the wills were bath-tubs, though for the most part they are mentioned in a context which makes it clear that they were used primarily for brewing ale. It may be that they were used both for bathing and for brewing – not simultaneously, of course. It must, I think, remain a matter of speculation.

There is a risk that the evidence for the improved standard of living provided by these wills might obscure another fact, namely that the increased prosperity was enjoyed only by some of the people, not by all. It is true that a number of 'labourers' left wills during this period and that they were, generally speaking, as well-off as some of the small farmers of the earlier period. But it is also true, as it was earlier, that there were a lot of people who did not make wills because they had nothing to leave. We know neither their number nor, except in a few cases, their names. We know of their existence, mainly through the various statutory enactments necessitated by the menace which they constituted to society. This 'menace' may have been exaggerated by comfortable burgesses fearful for the safety of their property and purses – 'the beggars are coming to the town – oh!' But they undoubtedly did have cause for alarm. Many of the desperately poor were driven to take to the roads, to beg, to steal, to form up in gangs, in company with habitual criminals and cut-throats. Such poor wretches soon became criminals in their own right. Officialdom did at least recognize that the root cause of vagrancy, violence and lawlessness was poverty, though it accepted no responsibility for it, and tried to cure it by putting the responsibility on the parish or village. The harshest measures, some of them brutally inhuman, were directed towards keeping a poor person in the parish to which he 'belonged'. It was, in a sense, a reversion to the conditions of the Middle Ages, when 'outsiders' were shunned, punished and evicted. The wills tell us nothing of that aspect, but they do tell us something indirectly about the way in which the village people dealt with the poor in their midst, the poor who did belong to them.

It is clear that, from about 1550 onwards, there was some sort of organized system for the relief of the poor, for which the churchwardens were responsible, but it was on a semi-voluntary basis until the Poor Rate was levied in 1601. Of the twenty-eight people who made wills between 1550 and 1601, only eight made any bequest to the poor. The bequests continued at the same rate after 1601, then in 1630 they ceased altogether apart from three rare instances, presumably because the collection of the Poor Rate was more efficiently organized after that date. We must not however assume that the bequests made by people in their wills was the only assistance given to the poor. For what it is worth, here is the complete statement of such bequests:

1556 Thomas Lavender:
  'to everie poore housholder in this parisshe iiii*d*. a peece – to old Humfreys a shurt, to old White a shurt, to old Casbold my Freese coate and to old Aymes a payer of hussen.'
1560 John Rayment: 20*s*.
1566 Stephen Wells: 'every poore housholder one pecke of maulte'.
1576 Marg. Chapman: 5*s* 8*d*.
1580 Marg. Sympson:
  'my aker of rye when it is brought home shalbe threshed oute and the corne after it is dighte shalbe distributed amongst the poore people of Foxton everye one of them to have a pecke oute of yt so far as it will goe.'
1583 Agnes Starke: 'poore persons boxe 5*s*.'
1588 John Fuller: 40*s*.
1589 John Rayner: 'poore mens box 10*s*.'
1603 William Campion: 12*d*.
1606 Thomas Simpson: 2*s*.
1615 Philip Welbore: £4.
1617 Philip Gardiner: 5*s*.
1620 William Fuller: 20*s*.
1626 Thomas Flacke: 5*s*.
1630 Thomas Wells: 20*s*.
1630 Elizabeth Wells: 20*s*.

It may be of interest to note that twenty shillings at that date would provide sustenance – of a kind – for one family for a whole year.

One does not look for humour in people's wills, but I trust that I shall not be charged with impropriety if I end this survey with a quiet chuckle at the expense of dear old Margaret Sympson who, amongst so many other things, left:

my roode & a halfe of barlye & my roode of pease to be equallye devyded betwixt Nicholas Brasyer's children which he had by my daughter at the sight of my Executor.

8 Noysome Synkes and Puggell Water

The Brook, which is after all one of the main characters in my story, got little mention in the last chapter and will be similarly neglected in the next. I propose therefore to give it a short chapter to itself, consisting entirely of quotations from the village bye-laws relating to it. Comment or explanation on my part would, I feel, be superfluous, once I have said that the bye-laws from 1594 on were written in English, which provides much more interesting reading than my translations from the Latin.

1587. It is ordered that all the inhabitants of Foxton shall 'caste the brooke' so far as it fronts their lands or tenements before the feast of Pentecost next on pain of 12d for every default.

And that henceforth no one shall wash anything in the said brook on pain of forfeiting 12d to the Lord for every offence.

1590. Whoever has not appeared within one hour after the ringing of the bell to clean out the common brook shall forfeit 4d to the Lord.

And whoever shall not clean out the brook fronting his land within the time appointed by the Heyward shall forfeit 12d.

No one shall wash any cloth in the brook before 8 of the clock at night on pain of forfeiting 12d for every offence.

1594. No man shall lett out there sesterns or other noysome synkes untill eight of the clock at night uppon payne for every one doinge the contrary to forfeite unto the Lord for every tyme xiid.

No man shall keep any geese or ducks in the Comon Broke in pain to forfeit unto the Lorde for every of them iiiid.

1598. [Latin] It was ordered as previously that all inhabitants of the town of Foxton should scour the 'comon broke' from the land of Henry Fuller as far as the 'Vyneyard bridge' before the eighth of October next on pain of five shillings.

None shall harm the Brooke with any Sesterne Pond or Sinke water, nor lett out the same before eight of the clocke at night, on pain to forfeit 12d.

1600. That noe man shall annoye the Brooke with anye Cesterne, Pond, washynge or sinke, nor to lett out the same before eight of the clocke at night uppon payne to forfaict for every such offence xiid.

1611. No one before eight o'clock on any day shall wash, shall drain, shall lett out or shall cast any pond or sinke or shall wash any bucket of clouthes whereby dirty water or anything unhealthy shall run into the brook, on pain of 3s 4d. [That one was half in English, half in Latin.]

1612. Ordered that every one shall clean out and scour the brook alongside his land from a certain place called 'Henry Fullers' to the Vineyard Bridge before the feast of St John Baptist, on pain of forfeiting 3s 4d to the Lord.

1643. No person shall through out his puggell water into the stream at any time of the day before sunset, on pain of iiiid.

No person shall allow the water in his cestern to run into the stream at any time before sunset, on pain of xiid.

1665. None shall suffer or permitt any Sinks to come into the runninge brooke or common rivulett which runnes through this towne upon payne of forfeitinge for every offence 12d, one halfe to the Lord of the Mannor and the other halfe to the Informer.

Every inhabitant of this Towne shall cleanse and scoure the comon brooke or rivulett which runnes through this Towne soe far as it runnes against their grounds att such tyme and tymes as the Churchwardens of this Towne shall limitt and appoynt under penalty of forfeitinge for every offence 3s 4d, one halfe to the Lord, one halfe to the Informer.

Noe person or persons whatsoever shall lett out or suffer to runn out any of their Sinks or puddles out of their yards into the Common runninge brooke or rivulett in this Towne att any time from fower a clocke in the morning untill eight of the clocke att night under payne to forfeit 12d etc.

1698. Item that any person who shall suffer any ducks to come into the Common Brooke shall fforfeit for every such offence 6d to the Lord of the Manner.

Item that every inhabitant that shall not cleanse the Brooke or rivulet which runns through the towne of ffoxton soo far as is abutting upon their grounds att such time or times as shall bee appointed by the Church-wardens of the said towne shall fforfeit for every such offence 3s 4d to the Lord of the Manner.

Item that any parson that shall lett out or suffer to runn any of their sinkes or puddles out of their yards into the Common Running Brooke of the town of ffoxton shall forfeit for every such offence (if it bee att any time from ffoure of the clock in the morning until eight of the clock at night) 6d to the Lord of the Manner.

9 Many Yeomen but no Squire

I must ask forbearance of the readers who like their history in strict chronological order, for, though this chapter deals mainly with the middle and later half of the seventeenth century, I shall in fact wander back to the days of King James I and forward beyond the reign of Queen Anne when it suits my purpose. In the weaving of my tapestry there are threads, left hanging some distance back, which have to be picked up, and others which have to be continued for some distance forward lest they be forgotten. My purpose, let me remind you, is to portray a truly rural community far removed, both physically and metaphorically, from kings and queens. It would be gratifying to an ardent royalist such as myself to think that, when King James lodged at Royston and hunted in the neighbourhood, or when King Charles passed by Thriplow Heath on his way to or from Newmarket, the populace of the neighbouring villages flocked to line the roads, pay their loyal respects, wave their caps and be cured of the King's Evil by a touch of the royal hand. A charming thought, but remote from the truth, of that I am quite sure. Very little evidence has survived as to the political sympathies of the local populace. Officially they were not credited with opinions or the ability to form any; they did and thought as their betters told them to. Such evidence as does exist suggests that the bulk of them were anti-Establishment. If they were pro-anything they were pro-themselves.

When the Civil War broke out, the local villagers had little choice as to which side they were on. Their betters, particularly one Oliver Cromwell who had family ties with this and many other villages in East Anglia, decided for them, and there was no strong Royalist interest to raise any doubts in their minds as to the ultimate triumph of the Parliamentary cause. We can be sure that Foxton provided its quota of recruits to Cromwell's army – the sudden disappearance of certain men from the records just after 1641 can be explained in no other way. Foxton itself, though fortunately well clear of the main areas of military activity, came perilously near to involvement in August 1645, when the war had already been lost at Naseby. King Charles with a force of cavalry attempted to force his way into East Anglia, hoping to enlist support from the isolated nobility and gentry there. After the relief of Newark, Huntingdon was taken and Cambridge attacked, but the defences of Cambridge held firm. Parties of Royalist cavalry attempted to force their way across the Rhee at various points, in particular Harston, Barrington and Malton. At every possible crossing-point they were opposed by Parliamentary artillery and repulsed, with considerable losses at Harston. For several weeks Cromwell's gunners were billeted in Foxton, in the house at the eastern extremity of the village. For one glorious half-hour – or it might have been only five minutes – Foxton was in the front line. One ten-pounder and one six-pounder cannon – maybe more – were positioned at the last corner on the Barrington road, covering both the bridge and the ford. As soon as the leading Cavalier appeared at the ford – which, like the bridge, had obviously been barricaded – the gunners opened fire. And that, as far as I can tell, was that. There might be more cannon-balls somewhere in the vicinity of the ford, but I have only found two, one ten-pounder and one six-pounder, in the mud dredged from the river. I cannot help thinking that any Foxton men who were watching the engagement – and I am confident that there were some – got a secret satisfaction from the fact that the cannon were pointing towards Barrington.

If this and other villages in the neighbourhood had little sympathy for the Crown, they had even less for the Church. For this the Church itself was largely to blame. I do not mean the parson; he, poor fellow, was doing his best to attune himself to the mood of his parishioners, and to survive in a ruinous vicarage on a stipend of £4 13s 4d a year, to which handsome figure it had been 'augmented' in the mid sixteenth century. No, the trouble was with the Archdeacon, backed by the Bishop, vigorously striving to maintain ecclesiastical control over matters which, in many cases, ought really to have been left to the individual consciences and common-sense of the parishioners. The result was a constant niggling, backbiting, prying into private affairs, which did not raise moral standards one little bit, rather the reverse. The churchwardens joined in the witch-hunt, if only to save their face and divert official stricture from themselves. Then, as the churchwardens had their hands pretty full with looking after the more mundane affairs of the village, two 'inquisitors' were appointed, whose specific duty was to spy out and report the moral and religious shortcomings of their neighbours.

Here is a series of extracts from the records of Archdeacon's Visitations and Consistory Court proceedings (Ely Diocesan Records, University Library, Cambridge), which shows the situation developing over a period of some fifty years:

William Yule has not received communion for a year and more.

Elizabeth Awsten of Foxton is vehemently reported to be with childe.

Dorothy Wilson was delivered of a child unlawfully begotten by Richard Carlton of Kings Colledge, as she sayeth.

Mr Meade was presented for not receavinge the Communion at Easter.

Thomas Sturman was reported by his wife that he and Mary Rayner did live together incontinently.

Mr Brampton (vicar) was presented 'for not catachizinge our Servants nor our Children, neether have wee anie minister Resident in our Parishe'.

Edward Lithell of Melbourn was presented 'for being at Foxton ffayre on the Sabath daye'.

Thomas Campion was presented for begetting his wife with Child before they were married.

'Neyther the vicar nor his curate doe use the Clokes appoynted for them.'

Andrew Osborn was presented 'for that he had carnal copulacion with his wife before the daye of their mariage'.

We payne oure Minister as he him selfe saithe is not licenced by his Orders to preache and yet he preachethe.

Will Breastbone presented for absenting himselfe often tymes from the Churche.

Nicholas Campion presented for cartinge uppon Hallowmas daye.

Thomas Adleson presented for suffering of play in his house ye 29 December being Sunday.

Wee present Elizabeth – singleton of this parish for committing fornication with one John Tomlin as is supposed and as the common fame goeth.

Mistress Meade was presented for goinge out of the church two Sundays together & being called back by the minister shaked her hands at him & spake some contemptuous speech against him & so went away.

It was almost inevitable that sooner or later Valentine Phipps should find himself involved in an unholy rumpus. It came in 1638 when, under the influence of drink, he addressed one of the churchwardens, George Wells, as 'a base rogue, a base rascall and a whoaremasterly Rogue'. That is what Wells said he said; I doubt whether the whole of Phipps's speech was reported. Phipps was charged with absenting himself from church on thirteen consecutive Sundays and holy days, and that he was seen 'ridinge upon horseback on the Sunday towards St Ives market to buy Cattell'. When told that he would be reported to the Archdeacon, he answered that it was his trade and added 'I care not a turde for Dr Eden and his Court.' No right-minded person would condone the behaviour of a drunkard who 'did fall off the bed, most beastly spew, defile and bewray himself'. But it soon became evident that many people in the village shared Phipps's views on ecclesiastical authority.

Bishop Matthew Wren, newly appointed to the see of Ely, made a visitation of the whole diocese in 1638. His spiritual messengers, as they were called, found fault everywhere, just as they had done in the diocese of Norwich a few years previously. At Foxton the reading-desk faced the wrong way, the fence round the churchyard was broken, there was no terrier, and the vicar was ordered to repair his vicarage before Pentecost (it had been burnt down and rendered uninhabitable thirty years before). Not only that, the churchwardens had to fill in a written questionnaire of 146 questions relating to the way in which the services were conducted, the attendance of people at church, their moral conduct, public and private. In some villages the churchwardens obviously welcomed the opportunity to expatiate on the subject of their neighbours' transgressions. Not so George Wells and Samuel Campion. The fact that only one of them could write, and that with difficulty, may have influenced their decision, but they wisely refrained from answering most of the questions and declined to attend the Consistory Court held at Great St Mary's, Cambridge, thereby earning for themselves severe admonition and suspension from office. Such was the widespread animosity aroused by Bishop Wren that he was attacked in a public petition bearing two thousand signatures – that must have been pretty well all the laymen in the county who could write their name. The Bishop was removed from office and imprisoned, though it should be stated that the imprisonment was of his own choosing.

The pendulum of reform having started to swing, it was allowed to swing too far, as is so often the case, and became a sledgehammer. In 1643 Parliament passed an ordinance designed to strip the churches of everything which might conceivably be taken as representing a continuance of the Catholic faith and form of worship. It was well known that previous edicts, such as that which had demanded the dismantling of rood-screens, for instance, had not been strictly observed. There were to be no half-measures about this latest order. There were few Catholics in the area; none at all in Foxton – the last one had died over sixty years before – but there was plenty of material in the church which reminded people of the distant past. When the agents of William Dowsing, parliamentary Commissioner for the Eastern Counties, came to Foxton in March 1644, they 'Brake 60 popish Superstitious Pictures & gave order to brake down and take down 2 crosses & Mr John Welbore pson to levell the chancell'. John

Welbore was not the parson; he was not even the Rector; he was the farmer of the Rectory – not that it mattered. They smashed the beautiful stained-glass windows, hacked down the rood-screen, scraped the pictures from the walls, removed candlesticks and muniments, broke the statues in fragments, flung out the altar – they reduced the interior of the church to an indescribable shambles.

And what, one wonders, did the villagers do or say about it? The records are silent. Perhaps the villagers were silent too. In some villages, not many, there are indications that the iconoclastic activities were curbed by the hasty application of a coat of whitewash to the walls and the removal of some of the ornaments before the arrival of the vandals. There are two clues pointing to the fact that this official vandalism did not meet with wholehearted approval in Foxton. The crosses on the outside of the church and many of the carved angels and bosses in the roof escaped damage. So, either the 'workmen' were too lazy to get a ladder to do their job properly, or – and I hope that this was the case – the villagers refused point-blank to lend them a ladder and hid any ladders which might have been borrowed. Furthermore, Mr John Welbore did not level the chancel; nor did any one else; the recent discovery of over a hundred medieval tiles in their original position in the extreme N.E. and S.E. corners is clear evidence of this.

The effect of this measure of 'reform' was soon apparent. Popery was not abolished; where it had previously existed it was strengthened – the Scropes, owners of Mortimer's manor, for instance, were ardent Catholics and remained so; likewise the Huddlestons of Sawston, and many other notable families of the area. Those who had most to lose were the most tenacious in their faith. The vast bulk of the villagers had nothing to lose and nothing to gain by their religious beliefs, if any. And there can be little doubt that this general apathy was greatly enhanced by the action of Parliament, which virtually abolished religious observance for the space of nearly half a century. The vicar, Mr Vaughan, was able to build for himself a new vicarage, thanks to his marriage to a wealthy young widow (later in this chapter you can see just what was in that vicarage and how much space there was for a family of seven children), and he did continue to hold services in the church, though there must have been many a winter Sunday when the icy blast blowing through the broken windows was too much even for the vicar. People did continue to be married and buried at church, and they did bring their children to be baptized. The Parish Registers tell us that much. But they do not tell us how many attended the Sunday services.

When bishops returned to favour, the aged Matthew Wren amongst them, in 1660, an attempt was made to restore the old order. The visitations were now, however, concerned more with the churches than with the congregations. The non-conformers were recorded and admonished for the sake of form, but no one pretended any longer that people could be made to worship if they chose not to. In 1666 the following observations were made on the church of Foxton:

– chancell out of repaire – church to be new whyted & plaistered – chancell to be mended in the wall forward – dore to be amended & a lock to be made – fyrewodd laying in the church to be removed – the water of the font runnes into the churche – Chest to be repaired & 3 locks made to it – etc.

Twelve years later, not only had these faults not been remedied, many more were noted:

– Church to be plaistered and whited, made cleane and kept soe – pavement and ye seats to bee mended – ye font to bee made cleane – Dirt, Duste, Tiles and straws to bee removed – windows to bee glazed and ye Pullpit to be new painted – Side Isle which is Nasty to be made cleane – a partition to bee made in ye Northeast parte of ye Church to separate the Lumber from ye Church – to sett up ye Chancell dore – etc.

Which lends substance to the stories often recounted of cows and pigs being kept in the churches 'at one time'. And still nothing was done for many years. There were few people left who cared. The vicars, more often than not, were university dons serving several parishes and resident in none. The Rector, Mr Hatton of Longstanton, was too far away to worry unduly about a ruined chancel or a rickety door in a parish which would not pay its tithes. The congregation was not there. In 1685 the 'freethinkers' numbered thirty-nine, who were holding meetings in Nathaniel Singleton's great barn at Mortimer's, which was no doubt a good deal more comfortable than the church. The number of churchgoers is not recorded. Nor is the number of those who had lost all interest in religion, though a few entirely new doctrines make their appearance – at least one old lady was a 'Muggletonian'.

The manor court of Foxton Bury struggled gamely on as the administrative body in the village, but its powers and authority were diminishing year by year. In 1611 a homage of fifteen men was present, all Foxton men; eleven men, four not of Foxton, sent their excuses; thirty-seven tenants who ought to have been there did not bother to attend or make an excuse, and fifteen of them lived in Foxton. A similar situation existed in 1649. In 1665 the attendance was about the same, but no one seemed to bother any longer about the defaulters. The rental of 1669 lists forty-one copyholders paying a total of £22 5s 0d in rents and fifteen freeholders paying £2 16s 9d. What was happening in Mortimer's manor no one knew – indeed no one had known for the last hundred years – and no one cared, so long as the rents were paid. In 1692 we find:

A return made by the Constables of the names of the inhappitents that is warned to apere at the Court Lete and Barron houlden at the Berry.

It lists thirty names, including the constables. Some years earlier, in 1683, Edmund Ostler, as constable, had been fined £10 for failing to present a list of residents and not appearing at court. I am pretty sure that Edmund Ostler – whom you will meet again at the end of this chapter – never paid that fine. The Steward, I am equally sure, never seriously intended that he should pay the fine, but was trying desperately to assert his own authority, knowing full well that he no longer had any authority – except to collect rents.

The court nevertheless continued to 'legislate' – we have already seen their edicts relating to the Brook – on matters becoming more and more restricted in scope:

1665. Noe person or persons whatsoever shall putt or keepe his or their sheepe in the heard pasture of this towne from Mayday to Midsomer under payne of forfeitinge 3s 4d for every offense every time, one halfe to the Lord of this Mannor and the other halfe to the Informer.

Noe person or persons shall keepe or lead any Cowes or bullocks upon the small balkes lyinge betwixt the grayne in the feilds of Foxton at any time from Mayday untill harvest bee home –

1689. We order noe Horses nor Horse shall be kept uppon the small Balkes while Harvest is don.

Nor no gedines or Infitters Horses [I had better translate that; it is 'geldings or infected horses'] shall be kept or put one the common.

No Hoggs shall be put in to the fields without being sufficiently ringed.

No Ducks shall be suffered to be kept in the Comon brook, no they shall not com in to the cow pastor nor in maddows after the time they usealley use to be laid.

[I feel sorry for those poor ducks. Where *could* they go?]

1698. Any parson that shall lead or suffer to bee lede any Cow or horse in or upon any small Bawkes shall fforfeit for every such default 3s 4d to the Lord of the Manner.

These weighty injunctions are repeated once more, in 1712, and then – finis. The curtain falls on the Court Leet after a run of 500 years.

The Court Baron continues its existence for a long time yet, though it is no longer anything other than a legal device for collecting rents and registering transfer of property, as which, of course, it fulfils a useful and necessary function. The lawyers – and most Stewards were by this time lawyers – kept up the traditional show of formality to the bitter end, adding to their dignity – and adding even more to their fees – by indulging in verbosity to an extent which knew no bounds. As the next century progressed and the cost of legal documents rose steadily, the lawyers developed the art of using 2000 words to say what could quite easily have been said in twenty. I do not wholly condemn this practice, for, though it adds enormously to the difficulty of finding information which is lurking in a forest of words, it also means that much information is there which with greater economy of words might have been lost for ever. Tenants developed the art of leaving things to the lawyers and keeping away from the court for as long as they could, and only attended when their material or monetary interest was threatened. The days were not far distant when the Steward would find himself holding a court at the Bury with only four people present, including himself and his clerk. As for the management of village affairs, that was taken over by the Vestry. In theory this was all the ratepayers of the parish meeting once a year to elect its officials and supervise their conduct of affairs – a truly democratic institution. In practice it was something rather different, as we shall see in the next chapter. The last ale-taster in Foxton was appointed in 1609; the last 'heywood and pinner' in 1714.

This would seem to be an appropriate point at which to pick up the threads of manorial history and carry them through to the end of the line. We have seen how manorial discipline, then manorial authority, gradually crumbled away. We are at the stage in our story when, in many villages up and down the land, by one of those curious paradoxes in which history abounds, the lord of the manor enjoyed something like a reversion to feudal status. Justice of the Peace, monarch of all he surveyed, petty tyrant or benevolent despot according to his temperament, hard drinking, hard riding, in the saddle six days a week, half the time in pursuit of the fox, in his own special pew on Sundays, half the time asleep. The Squire. How much of the picture is founded on fact, and how much is the result of the novelists' skill in creating, exploiting and perpetuating a picturesque character, it is hard to say. He will not figure in these pages, for the simple reason that, in my documentary territory, he did not exist. All the men who might have filled the role, as will be readily seen when I round off the manorial history, were townsmen, lawyers, speculators, farmers; few of them ever set foot in their manorial domaine, let alone ride over it.

Sir Richard Warren probably only once saw his coat of arms, moulded in plaster on the chimney-breast of his new manor-house of Foxton Bury, before he died. He left the manor to his sister Joan, already married to Sir Henry Cromwell of Hinchinbrooke. Their son Oliver Cromwell (not *the* Oliver Cromwell but his great-uncle) inherited it in 1597. Sir Oliver Williams, alias Cromwell, when his first wife died, married the widow of the famous Sir Horatio Palavicine of Babraham. Henry Palavicine married Catherine Williams, his stepsister; Toby Palavicine married Jane Williams, *his* stepsister; Baptina Palavicine married Henry Cromwell alias Williams, her stepbrother. The net result of this multiple family link-up, as far as we are concerned, was that Toby Palavicine inherited the Foxton manor in 1615, along with a goodly share of a fortune which was, or had been, reckoned as somewhere in the region of a hundred thousand pounds. But even that, apparently, was insufficient for the needs and tastes of Sir Toby. Within fifteen years it had all gone. So had his mansion of Babraham Hall; so had the Foxton manor; so had Sir Toby. The story of how that vast fortune was amassed has already been told; some day I might tell the story of how it was spent – a very different story. The manor was bought by Edward Boston, passed to Richard Taylor, then in 1682 to Christopher Hatton of Longstanton. The Hattons held it until 1767, when it was bought by William Mitchell who in 1772 sold it to Thomas Parker. The latter sold it in 1787 to Richard Bendysh of Barrington for £7400 and it remained in Bendysh hands until 1928.

The Docwra manor in Foxton (actually a quarter-manor, as you may remember) eventually came into Welbore hands, where it remained until shortly before the death of John Welbore in 1725. Now there was a man who could have been 'Squire', and ought to have been, but fate decided otherwise. Rescued from financial ruin at the age of fourteen, he had a successful career in Law, and became a very wealthy man. It seems probable that his whole life was influenced by the tragic circumstances of his childhood (another story to be told some day). He never married, spent most of his time in London except for business visits to Foxton and died alone in his lovely Foxton house. His estates passed partly to the Hattons, partly to Samuel Herring of London, then to John Seddon, who did live in Foxton for a time, then to Thomas Parker, and so to Richard Bendysh in 1787.

The Manor House of Foxton Bury – 'The Bury' today

Mortimer's manor remained in the Scrope family until 1699, when Simon Scrope of Danby sold it to Thomas Bendysh, and it stayed with the Bendysh family. From 1787, then, the Bendyshes were Lords of the Manors of Foxton Bury with Wimbish and Chatteris, Docwra's and Mortimer's. With a title like that, how could a Bendysh *not* have been Squire? The opportunity was there. The resources were there. The man was missing. The Bendyshes were not even at Barrington Hall much of the time, but in London or in Bath for 'the Season'. I feel somewhat cheated at not being able to draw a portrait of the Squire, and disappointed that nearly a thousand years of manorial history should have to peter out in such an inglorious way. But then, my theme *is* the common man, so let us return to our common men – our yeomen.

Yes, yeomen. Whatever the title may have meant originally, it now meant 'farmer', one who cultivated his own land, as distinct from 'labourer', who mainly cultivated someone else's land and was paid for doing so. Farming was still the be-all and end-all of village life, and village life was still the life of the vast majority of English people. It is true that in the village there were butchers and bakers, blacksmiths, carpenters, bricklayers and shoemakers. But those men lived by serving and supplying the farmers; not only that, most of the small tradesmen and craftsmen were also farmers, even if they only had three or four acres. To what extent had the farming pattern changed in the past hundred years or so? Very little indeed. There was, as I have already said, a relaxation in the rigidity of control, and a man could grow pretty well what he chose to grow, within limits. He could not grow clover, turnips, kale, lucerne, sugar-beet, maize, potatoes – because he did not know of such crops. And if he had known he could still not have grown them because the age-old three-fold rotation system was still in operation: winter-sown crop one year, spring-sown crop the next, fallow the third. This still applied even where there were four fields, or only two, for the divisions between fields was quite arbitrary. Much of the waste and woodland had disappeared. Most of the marshy patches were brought under cultivation, thanks to extensive draining and ditching. By the end of the seventeenth century only the names remained to serve as a reminder that what was now good arable land had once been swamp and mere, and those who mowed hay in Oslock soon forgot that it had been a 'muddy lake', whilst those who ploughed in Flag Pightle no longer thought of digging turves of peat there.

Two men in particular, Campion and Welbore, were able to some extent to opt out of the system. They bought a fair slice of Docwra land which had been made into a 'sheepwalk' in the fourteenth century, and so were able to indulge in the revived fashion of sheep-farming.

1649. The Jury present that 600 sheep can and should be kept on the common fields of Foxton, whereof 300 belong to the Lords of the said Manor, 100 belong to Mortimer's, and 200 belong to the Connigree lands of John Welbore and Samuel Campion, which 600 sheep, by the ancient custom of Foxton, ought to be kept in two flocks and two folds, i.e. one for this manor and the other for the Connigree Lands and Mortimer's Manor.

This revival of sheep-farming was short-lived in this part of the country, even more short-lived than the previous revival of the late fifteenth and early sixteenth centuries, when a lot of enclosure had been made in some areas. The days when England's wealth and political bargaining power largely depended on wool were gone for ever. Indeed the wool trade was in such straits in the sixteen-eighties that statutes were passed compelling burial 'in woollen' in order to boost the trade.

By 1689 it was all arable farming once more in Foxton and neighbouring villages: hundreds and hundreds of narrow strips all over the parish, separated by narrow 'balks' about a foot wide which were left to produce a crop of grass and weeds. Once again I am baffled by a problem. How did a man find his own strips of land amongst all the others? The only way to designate a particular strip in a title-deed or terrier was to say in which field it lay, in which shott, and who owned the strips to the north, south, east and west of it. Fine, the owner knew all that, but one half-acre of plough or stubble looks remarkably like any other half-acre of plough or stubble. They may all have been labelled in the document, or on the map if one existed (and if one did exist it has never been found). But I am pretty sure that they were not labelled on the ground. When a labourer set off to plough half an acre in the middle of Chardwell Field on a misty morning in December, how *could* he know that he was ploughing the correct half-acre? He *did* know, we can be sure of that, but how? It would be all right if there were a dozen men setting out at the same time to plough the adjacent strips, and of course this must have been a frequent occurrence. Twenty plough-teams constantly rubbing shoulders, so to speak, on their furlong shuttle would be a common sight, and the frosty air would resound with ribald remarks, perhaps even a more or less tuneful song, interspersed with 'Come hither!', 'Whoa back!' and 'Gee up, then!' But there would be times also when a man was on his own, having left the yard

163

with such instructions as: 'Go down Woodway till you get over the brow of the hill, turn left along the second wide balk, down that for four furlong, turn right on to a headland, past another wide balk on your left, then it's the fifth land on your right facing Newton, and don't come back till you've finished it.' Neither farmers nor labourers could read or write, and such instructions, or whatever instructions were given, would have to be transmitted verbally and retained mentally. Even if the farmer said something as simple as, 'Go and plough the one acre in Deadman's', it still meant that the labourer had to carry in his head a mental picture of the whole complex pattern of strips. Which prompts the reflection, and not for the first time, that farm-labourers cannot have been anything like as stupid as they have often been portrayed, especially by townsmen.

I did think of drawing a map of one of those fields to show you what it looked like, but I had to abandon the idea in sheer frustration. Even if I had complete terriers of all the holdings at a given date I could not do it, for it is impossible to determine the boundaries of the various shotts. Although I know, for instance, that Down Field consisted of Brook Shott, Further Downhill Shott, Homeward Downhill Shott, Littlefield Shott, Woodway Shott, West Hill Shott, Townside Shott, Clunch Pit Hill Shott, Golden Haven Shott, Baldwins Shott and Burrow Shott, and although I know roughly where they were situated, I have no idea of their shape and orientation. I could quote for you in full a terrier of several farms, but if I did, I rather think that you would abandon me in sheer frustration. So I will simply summarize one for you, and leave the rest to your imagination. This is a farm of forty-six acres (nominally two 'eighteen-acre wares'; the difference of ten acres is due to the amount of reclamation which had been done) owned by Stephen Wells in 1673 and farmed by John Rayner (*one* of the John Rayners).

In Hoffer Field he had 20 strips of from $\frac{1}{4}$ acre to $1\frac{1}{4}$ acre.
In Hill Field   „   19   „ $\frac{1}{4}$ „ $1\frac{1}{2}$ „ .
In Ham Field   „   2   „   of 1 „ and $\frac{1}{2}$ „ .
In Newton Field   „   1   „   of 1 rood.
In Chadwell Field   „   15   „   from $\frac{1}{2}$ acre to 2 „ .
And 7 'doles' of meadow in Oslock and Ham, from $1\frac{1}{2}$ poles to 9 poles.
That is 64 strips in all.

And if it was difficult to locate a strip of plough, what must it have been like to find a strip of meadow?

I spoke earlier about the fascination of wills and the way in which they serve to throw light on the life and times of those who made them. By the mid seventeenth century the manner of will-making began to change. People no longer made comprehensive lists of all their belongings, and as the fashion changes do does the fascination fade. There is an increasing tendency on the part of testators to concern themselves solely with money and property, and dismiss all those items about which we are most anxious to learn as 'the rest of my goods and chattels'. There are a few survivals of the old style, in particular the will of Mistress Anne Vaughan (dated 1666, though she died in 1658); she lists no less than eighty-six separate items of furniture and household stuff, including 'one striped carpet', 'my wicker chayre' and, to son Roger, 'the bookes if he will accept them'. More about that later. Several others, mostly widows, make specific reference to beds and bedding, brass kettles, tables, chests, etc., but not one of them after 1666 makes the sort of list which was a regular feature a century before. However, a new feature crops up by way of compensation, as we shall see presently.

Not that these later wills are wholly devoid of interest. Far from it. Provided one has the patience to plod through the welter of wordy jargon one can be sure of a reward in the form of an unexpected glimpse of character, an indication of a family quarrel, or a reference to a once familiar custom long since fallen into disuse. In addition to the satisfaction which this affords to one's natural curiosity, there is the further satisfaction at the confirmation of the Yorkshire adage: 'There's nowt so queer as folk.' Why, for instance, did John Welbore in 1661 leave to Mrs Elizabeth Oxford 'dwelling in the house she dwells in for six years from the Feast of St Thomas next if she live so long, she paying *one penny* and keeping the house in repair'? Was it pure benevolence which prompted him to leave 'to Wendy Oxford and Philip Oxford £3 6s 8d a piece towards their being put out as Apprentice'? It could well have been; he was a very generous-natured old man. Incidentally, in case you think, as I did, that Wendy Oxford is a delightful name for a girl, and in case you are as surprised as I was at the apparent putting-out of a girl as an apprentice, let me tell you that Wendy Oxford was a boy. Wendy was the surname of an eminent family living in Haslingfield. The use of surnames as Christian names occurs with increasing frequency during this period.

As further evidence of John Welbore's generosity we find him leaving 'to Charles Baron my ancient servant £5' and 'to Anna Beatham my ancient Cooksmaid 40s'. He himself was seventy-three years old; how old, then, must Charles and Anna have been? I think he was using the word 'ancient' in the archaic sense of 'former', for neither of the servants died in the parish, having no doubt been compelled to return to their native parishes by the Poor Law exigencies. That same will of John Welbore hints at trouble with his son Philip, and Philip's own will of only fourteen years later (1675) amply confirms the hint. The family fortunes so assiduously built up by his grandfather and father have been largely squandered and converted into debts, some clearly the result of gambling. How much this was due to Philip's own temperament, how much to the shattering blow of losing his wife and two young children within five years of his first marriage, and how much to his disastrous second marriage, cannot be said with certainty. Philip was relieved of further trouble by death at the early age of thirty-seven. His eldest son John – the one who ought to have become Squire – must have lived through enough anguish and turmoil between the age of three and eleven years to mark him for life. Which it did.

Bransome Rayner (another surname Christian name, and another short life of hopes unfulfilled) was comfortably off, with two houses, but at the age of thirty-two he had not yet plucked up courage to get married. He at least made his intentions clear by leaving 'to Ellina Bowles my loving sweetheart £5 within one year of my death'. But poor Ellina, cheated of a husband, was cheated of her legacy as well. Brothers John and James quarrelled over their inheritance for seven years after Bransome's death, and when a will was eventually produced before the manor court in support of James's claim it differed on five major points from that originally proved and made no mention of Ellina Bowles. Another man whose good intentions were thwarted by Fate – with a little human assistance – was old John Cock who died in 1712. He left 'to my well-beloved kinsman John Dunnidge £10', 'to my well-beloved sister Elizabeth James £20', and 'all the rest to my well-beloved nephew Samuel Cock'. All he possessed in the world was a bed with mattress and bolster stuffed with straw, two old hutches, two kettles, four sheets, three shirts, two drinking-pots, a Bible, his clothes – the whole lot worth just over two pounds – and £2 in cash. The £30 which he bequeathed to his well-beloved kin had all been 'borrowed' by his less well-beloved kin.

Old Ellena Collins had a hard time of it in the six months by which she outlived her husband, with her substance dwindling week by week in the mere struggle to keep alive, but at least she knew what she had, and where it was. To son Henry she left 'a chest standing above next the stares one the left hand as yoe goe into the chamber', and 'to my daughter Elling all the bed and bedding that lyeth upon the bedstead in the loft over the parlour'. She believed that children too should have their place – 'my brother Edward Chapman and my brother John Starke to have the ordering and command of my two childring for their good until they come to age to shift for themselves'. Thomas Eversden, who died in 1694, was equally clear about the proper place for his wife, to whom he left

the £5 which is in the hands of William Symonds the younger of Thriplow – halfe the fowles in the yard and one quarter of the hogg now a fatting when he is killed – two bushells of wheat, two bushells of barley, two bushells of rye, one busshel of pares & one busshel of apples.

And that was all, except for 'the trunk marked with S.B.', which was her own anyway, and the gift of which looks very much like a firm hint that she should pack it and go. I believe she did, for there is no further trace of her. It is to be noted that Thomas's first wife had died nineteen years previously, having borne him eight children, two of whom died in infancy, and that he had remarried rather late in life. I have said elsewhere that it was never too late for a woman to marry. True, but the woman who married a man who had been married already for twenty years or so was often putting herself into a difficult situation. She might get reasonable treatment from her husband – especially if she had some possessions of her own – but she rarely hit it off with his children. The legendary jest about unpopular stepmothers is based on cruel fact.

We tend to think that the problem of parental control – or lack of it – over children is peculiar to our own times. It must be one of the oldest problems in the world. I could quote scores of instances of filial defiance merely from the narrow circle of experience with which I am dealing. I will quote but two. Edward Chapman (mentioned above) in 1709 took the normal step of cutting off his son George with the traditional shilling for marrying against his wishes, then added insult to injury by referring to George's wife as 'my daughter Phumphred' (her maiden name). Edward Rayner in 1721 got in first with a firm preventive measure:

my mind and will is that my aforesaid son William Rayner shall not receive any thing of the abovementioned one hundred pounds if it shall happen at any time hereafter that he shall take to wife one Susannah Good living a servant with me at this present time.

That put an effective stop to Master William's carrying-on with servant-girls. Well, to be more exact, it stopped him from marrying Susannah. He married Elizabeth Gilman six years later.

James Rayner, who died in 1726, had seven daughters, all of whom got fair treatment, and one of them the kind of protection which Rayners understood best:

to my daughter Judith, wife of William Stallibrass, 40s per annum for her sole use and exclusive always from her husband so that he shall have no control thereof.

Finally, as regards the wills, another John Rayner in 1738, being 'something indisposed in body', left

to Catherine my well-beloved wife the use of all the household goods and furniture she brought with her during her life if she so long continue my widow, she subscribing to an Inventory thereof to be taken immediately after my decease.

I do not know what the Women's Liberation Movement would make of that, but I think it must be the best example of arrogance, impertinence and hypocrisy that I have ever seen in writing. To give a woman permission to use what is her own; to make that permission subject to her remaining a widow; to insist that a list of her belongings be made at her own expense; to leave her *absolutely nothing else* (though he possessed property worth more than £400) – and then to refer to her as his 'well-beloved wife'! Perhaps we may withdraw the charge of hypocrisy on the grounds that the term 'well-beloved' was at this date a mere formality, a manner of speaking (like the 'darling' of today). But the arrogance and impertinence charges must stand, even if such conduct was in keeping with the custom of the times. I need hardly say that Catherine was not his first wife. He had married, in 1720, Elizabeth Rayner, one of the seven daughters mentioned above – the only instance known to me of a Rayner marrying a Rayner. They had six children, the last of whom died at birth, followed by her mother three weeks later in 1729. John Rayner, like his first wife and her parents and two of her sisters, was buried in the nave of the church beneath a stone slab from which, it may give you some satisfaction to know, all trace of inscription has been obliterated by the passage of feet and time.

And that brings me to the new feature which compensates for the lack of information in the wills. John Rayner did not hatch the idea of the Inventory in his own small mind. It was a very old idea which was given legal force by a statute of Henry VIII, whereby the probate of wills in ecclesiastical courts was authorized subject to the presentation of an inventory of the deceased's belongings made by two disinterested persons, reputable neighbours. The reason for it is not quite clear; partly a measure to prevent tax-evasion, I think; partly a means of ensuring that too much was not given to the Church. It does not appear to have worked well for the first hundred years or so. If it had been fully complied with there would be as many probate inventories as there are wills, which is not the case. Many of them have no doubt been destroyed or lost. There is, however, a good crop of survivals from the latter part of the seventeenth and early part of the eighteenth century; by no means complete, but adequate. I have copies of twenty-six of these documents relating to Foxton for the period 1658–1725. They are well worth studying, but, for various reasons which I trust are obvious, not the sort of thing to print in full. Anyone who wishes to see the originals, and many others, may do so at the Cambridge University Archives.

The reason why so few inventories exist from before 1660 is probably that, in this and many other villages, it was impossible to find two reputable neighbours who could write – or even one. These lists, written on tattered sheets of rather flimsy paper, all bear at least one signature; as often as not the other signature is 'So-and-so his marke'. The first thing that strikes one on seeing an inventory is the appalling writing. In order to decipher it you have to unravel the spelling at the same time. A lifetime of schoolmastering ought to have made me recoil in horror before this mutilation of our mother tongue, but to tell the truth I rather enjoy it. Not because it is something to laugh at – though one cannot help but chuckle at some of the efforts of these worthy yeomen grappling with intractable words much as they would grapple with intractable animals – but because these men obviously spelled as they spoke, and one is thereby enabled to recapture something of the actual speech of the times. Not with any great degree of certainty, mind you. For instance, if they could spell 'inventory' with this variety: invenfetory, invtory, inventorey, invetory, invatory, invetry, invetorey, invenentory, invitory – how did they pronounce it?

No sooner was the deceased decently buried 'in woollen' – actually there are two instances where the deceased had obviously not yet been buried but still lay on his bed – than the two 'appraisers' entered the house and went from room to room noting the contents of each one, then into the yard, barn and outhouses, writing down all that they found and making an estimate of its value in cash. *Their* estimate of its value. It is terribly important to bear that in mind. You think you are going to learn a great deal about the dead people, about their houses and furniture and farms; and so you do. But you learn almost as much, in a sense even more, about the appraisers themselves. Especially when you study a batch of consecutive inventories in detail. The prime object of the exercise was to provide a financial assessment, to find out how much a person was 'worth'. This was achieved, relatively. We learn that Nathaniel Singleton, with £823, was five times as rich as the average yeoman in the village, worth about £150, and that the below-average yeoman with £40 was ten times as rich as the worn-out labourer with £4. We learn that there were two or three wealthy people in the village, half a dozen comfortably well off, perhaps forty or fifty who could just manage on what they had; we must assume that the rest were paupers or near-paupers. But really there is no such thing as 'average' when considering people. Generalizations are misleading, meaningless and futile when studying documents such as these. What would have been a confusing picture in any case is rendered doubly so by the hopelessly haphazard valuations of these appraisers. Just when you think that you have got the measure of their fairly consistent undervaluations, you come across an overvaluation which shocks by its grossness. Let me give you a few examples.

Mistress Anne Vaughan had 'one bond good Bible' in the house (it was not her property; it belonged to the church, but that is beside the point); it was valued at £45. Fifty years later old John Cock's Bible was valued by two different men at two shillings and sixpence. Mrs Vaughan had 'In Pewter 3 great Platters, 3 lettell Platters, 4 smale dishs of Pewter, one ould quarte, 17 Pewter spoones, 3 okemy spoones' – valued at £1 the lot. (I shall come back to her later.) Nathaniel Singleton had

one Feather Bede, Boulster, 3 Pillowes, 2 Blanketts, a Coverlead, Curtaines and Vallence and Beddsteed, One chest with 6 paire of Flexen sheets and other Linnen with a silver Cupp and Gold Ring in it, foure leather stooles, One chaire, One cushion, One Carpett, One Joyne stoole, with other things.

That was in his best bedroom. We can be sure that it was his best furniture, and that it was good stuff in good condition. And the value of the whole lot – £12 10s! I know that there is a risk of being misled by the inflated values to which we are perforce accustomed today. To go round the shops and buy similar articles today would involve an outlay of perhaps £300. To possess those actual articles and be in a position to sell them in the right market would ensure a return of perhaps £3000 (perhaps a great deal more). What their true worth was in 1675 we cannot know for certain, but it was a good deal more than £12 10s. Why did these appraisers make such absurd undervaluations? Was it the instinctive reaction of the peasant to what he thought was an attempt to exact money from him? Or did they really have no idea what things were worth? Their valuation of corn and land is consistent and seems accurate. So, in the main, does their valuation of animals, though one sometimes has a suspicion that the figure which they quote depends on whether they are hoping to buy the animal or sell it. They could count the money in a man's purse, but when it came to adding up their own list of figures the result was often wrong, and sometimes the addition was not even attempted. All in all, then, we need not place too much faith in these documents as evidence of economic history.

No matter; they still tell us a lot about people and things. One of the most interesting features is that, for the first time, we get a clear picture of all the rooms which made up the house. The interest is heightened for me by the fact that, in about a dozen instances, those rooms listed three hundred years ago can still be clearly identified in houses in the village today. Generally speaking, the normal house contained five rooms:

(i) The hall or main living-room, which one entered on opening the front or back door, and which contained the fireplace.

(ii) The parlour, downstairs next to the hall, which was still often used as a bedroom, especially for a sick person.

(iii) A chamber or 'loft' over the hall, reached usually by stairs, but still often by a ladder; used as a bedroom, but also as a storeroom.

(iv) Another chamber over the parlour, also used as bedroom or store-room – in one case it is an apple-room, and in several a cheese-room – often described as 'little' because the stairs had reduced its size by perhaps three or four square yards.

(v) The buttery or kitchen, which was the space downstairs at the end of the house, behind the chimney-stack, accessible from the hall on one or both sides of the fireplace.

Needless to say, there are wide variations from that pattern. Singleton, living at The Bury, had Parlour Chamber, Middle Chamber, Cheese Roome, Parlour, Hall, Little Buttery, Little Parlour, Maides Chamber, Kitchen, Dairy and Drinkehouse. His hall – the only one in the village justifiably so called, for it was in fact the 'Hall' of the manor, where the manor court had sat, and still sat – contained only 'a Cuppboard, 2 Tables, a Forme with other things'. Eloquent testimony, that, to the decline of the manor court. Time was when ten forms would have been needed to seat the assembled company. In marked contrast to that, Henry Chapman was existing in one room containing only 'one Jene (joined) bedsted with all the beding there unto belonging and a ould huch'. Anabel Hurrell likewise lived in one room (which could have been one room of a house consisting of several more) containing 'one beadstead, one feather bead, one feather bouster 2 pillows one blanket one coverlead a pair of sheats and a pillow beare, a pair of curtains and a box'. In case you should form a picture of utter destitution from that, I must add that the old lady had £80 in cash which, presumably, she was hoping to take with her. Philip Browne only had 'pearler', 'hoall' and 'chiteng' (that, I think, takes first prize for spelling oddity, closely followed by 'citkion') indicating that his house had not yet had ceilings inserted.

Roger Nelson, in addition to the usual accommodation (which, incidentally, was later converted into *three* dwellings) had 'the shop'. If I tell you that it contained 'one paire of Bellowes, one Anvill, one Trof with other Impliments' (valued at £4), I need not add that he was the blacksmith. Oddly enough, the word 'house' only occurs once, in a context which seems to indicate that it is a variant of 'hall', though as it contained only 'One long Table, two shelves and four pewter Dishes', and as the house, that of an elderly widow, contained also 'one Copper and two Tubbs, one Barrell, one Kneading Trough', it may well have been one of the last of the ale-houses, now fallen on lean times. Mary Baker (1690) had almost certainly been an alewife, even though she was no longer in business; her house was of ample size and well stocked with furniture and equipment, including 'thre barrels, five tubbs, foure Flaggons, one maltquarne' – all of which was valued at less than £10.

Having given you a further reminder of the economic unreliability of the valuations, I want to say a word now about another aspect of them. It may have occurred to you already that the assessment of a person's belongings must have been influenced by the attitude of the appraiser towards the person whose belongings he was assessing. We get a graphic example of this in the case of Mrs Anne Vaughan (pronounced 'Vane') the widow of the vicar. Her will gives the impression of a genteel lady comfortably well-off, benevolently bestowing as widely and fairly as possible her prized possessions – about £45 in cash and a houseful of furniture and equipment. Her inventory reveals that the house consisted of 'hall', 'chamber' and 'buttery', i.e. one room downstairs, one room above that, and a space at the back of the fireplace. In this little house she had borne and reared seven children, two of whom died in infancy. Her will listed 86 separate items. Her inventory lists 107 items. The value of those 107 items (excluding the Bible) was assessed by Roger Nelson and Thomas Eversden at £14 1s 10d.

Just another case of undervaluation? Oh no, there is more to it than that. For one thing, this is the only inventory on which every single item in the house is listed; there is no 'with other things' or 'other lumber in that

John Fuller's house (No. 15) as rebuilt in 1660

room'. Then as you go through the list you notice the recurrence of phrases like 'one oulde cubbard', 'one oulde livery cubbarde brockken', 'one ould lettell wickker chayre', 'one ould fryen pane'. It stands to reason that, when a person dies, many of his possessions are old; it does not need to be said. Now, in Roger Nelson's list (he was the one who could write) of

Mrs Vaughan's things the word 'oulde' occurs seventeen times, and the word 'little' (or Nelson's rendering of it) ten times. Am I being too sensitive in seeing these words as deliberate insults, too imaginative in reading into their use a scornful contempt on the part of Roger Nelson? I don't think so. When I tell you that Nelson was one of the leading Freethinkers in the village, I think you will agree with me that he was taking a rather mean knock at the Anglican Church. His colleague Eversden was a churchwarden, but could not read or write, so Nelson had it all his own way. Which of the two, I wonder, valued the Bible at £45? One final query; what do you make of 'okemy spoons'? I thought that it was an attempt to spell 'mahogany', but I am told that mahogany had not been introduced into this country at that date (1658). It is in fact 'occamy', i.e. imitation silver. One final observation before leaving Mrs Vaughan for good – I wish I had the 'one Righting deske with certaine bookes in it' which Nelson valued at 2s 6d. I would give quite a few half-crowns for it!

As regards furniture and utensils, there is not a lot to add to what I have already said on the evidence of the wills. The bed was still the most important possession inside the house. Fashion had endowed it with curtains on rails to give the more refined people complete privacy, and a 'vallence' round the edge of the bed to hide its legs and whatever was underneath the bed. There must have been a utensil there – a stroll down the garden or round the back of the house on a cold winter's night was out of the question – and it must have been made of pewter. And yet I have never seen it mentioned in either wills or inventories; perhaps it was already an 'unmentionable' – or one of the 'other things in that roome'. The well-to-do slept on feather beds, the less well-to-do on 'flock' (a mixture of wool and shredded cloth) and the poor on straw mattresses. Beneath feathers, flock and straw alike there were plain hard boards – 'a borded bedstead' – the luxury of metal springs was many generations away yet. The very poor slept on straw on the floor, as they always had done. Bolsters and pillows are much in evidence, and 'coverlets' in general use. 'Trundle bed' occurs frequently; this was a small bed with wheels on the feet so that it could be moved around. When one works out the ratio between the number of people known to have lived in a house at any one time and the number of beds which they appear to have possessed, it is obvious that sleeping three, four or five to a bed must have been a common practice. The old joke about 'when father turns we all turn' isn't really a joke at all; it's just fact.

Tables, of course, were mostly 'joined'. Chairs were quite common; so were stools, but forms were still much in use; Singleton's 'leather Chaires' and 'Great Chaire' were exceptional. Chests and hutches are as frequently met with as they were a century before, though cupboards are on the increase – not yet built-in, but movable. The first 'dresser' appears in 1728, i.e. the first mention of it. Kitchen utensils are what they were a hundred years before. Cooking was still done on or before the open fire, with the use of 'hobirons', 'cobirons', 'spitts', etc. The first 'Iorn grate' is mentioned in 1725, in conjunction with '2 cobirons, a fire shovel and tongs and one spit'. Baking went on in practically every home; 'kneading trof', 'kneading kimnell', 'flower Trof' occur everywhere. Ovens do not yet get a mention, but there must have been one or two installed by 1730. Warming-pans – usually called 'bed-pan' – are more common than they were, but still rare enough to suggest that they were a luxury without which the countryman could well manage. Spinning-wheels only occur three times; Mary Oliver had 'one wooling whell' and 'twoe linen whelles'. There is something odd about this. It may be simply that this was not an area where cottage industries were carried on. It may be that the spinning-wheel was, and always had been, a symbol of impoverishment. (When I say 'always' I mean during the previous two or three centuries. In Saxon times, and in Norman times, the spindle-whorl and distaff were symbols of gentility and femininity.)

I have mentioned the decline of the ale-house. There was a time when every village, even the smallest, had three or four ale-sellers. The time was coming when every village would have at least one pub, sometimes three or four. In between there seems to have been a period when in some villages, of which Foxton is one, there were neither ale-sellers nor pubs – roughly between 1660 and 1730 as far as I can judge. (I have failed to pinpoint the beginning of 'The Blackamoor's Head'; the first actual mention of it is in 1775; but it must have existed well before that; the house looks as though it were built about 1730.) Has this strange gap anything to do with Puritanism and Nonconformity? Does it mean that one bit of rural England abandoned for a time its traditional beverage, lost its appetite for beer? Not in the least. Several prominent citizens had part of their premises designated as 'drinkhouse', notably Nathaniel Singleton, whose Drinkehouse contained 'One Pipe, 5 Hoggsheads, 2 full of Beare, a Mashing Tubb, yielding Fatt (vat) with other small Tubbs, a Querne and Coales and other Lumber.' And Singleton was the most rabid Dissenter of them all. They all had their tubs and barrels and coppers and vats and skimmers. Including the vicar. This was the heyday of 'home-brewed ale" when home-brewed *was* home-brewed.

What about farming? Well, we know already most of what the inventories have to tell us, but at least they provide confirmation. The crops are

Reconstruction of the Malthouse, from details revealed during restoration. The boy on the cart is young Stephen Rayner, carving his initials and the date 1743

wheat, oats, barley, rye, lentils, peas, hay and saffron – what they were a century before. The animals are as before, except that there is now no mention whatever of oxen. As regards horses, there is something of a mystery. Over a period of sixty years, only twenty-five horses are mentioned, owned by only eight men, of whom one man owns ten horses. It would be easy to explain this by assuming that lots of inventories are missing, as some are known to be. But that still leaves the problem as to why nine men who *ought* to have had horses – they had carts, ploughs, harrows, etc. – did not in fact have any. Were horses in short supply? The implements are not all that plentiful either. Was the standard of farming much lower even than we had supposed? We know that sowing, weeding mowing, reaping, threshing and winnowing were all still done by hand, just as they had been throughout the Middle Ages. It looks as though English farming of the seventeenth and eighteenth centuries was not far removed from the medieval pattern. Even Nathaniel Singleton's farming differed more in scale than in manner. He was farming the Bury farm, Mortimer's, Fuller's and the Rectory land. In the previous harvest (he died in December 1675) he had garnered:

83 qrs Barley Thresht and Unthresht	(£75)
Barley in the Reekes (ricks)	(£63)
Pease and Lentells	(£12)
60 qrs barley thresht & unthresht	(£54)
Wheate and Rye	(£60)
35 qrs of Barley in the Straw	(£66)
16 qrs Wheate and Rye	(£19)
10 qrs Oats	(£5)

(There appear to be several discrepancies there, but we cannot judge the corn at this distance.) He had sown 55 acres of wheat and rye (£80), had 64 acres of Tilth unsown (£48) and 140 acres of stubble (£46). His 72 cattle and 163 sheep would need about another hundred acres. He was farming nearly 400 acres with the following equipment: 10 horses, 2 tumbrels, 2 waggons, 1 long cart, 5 ploughs and 3 harrows. So even he, by far the best-equipped farmer in the village, was by no means over-equipped.

Now let us take a look at a complete inventory, that of John Rayner (John Rayner the Seventh, I think, though I cannot be certain. There are another five John Rayners to come yet, at least. This, I know, is the John Rayner whose holding of land I summarized earlier in this chapter.)

A trew invatory of the goods and Chattels of John Raynor Sen of Foxton in the County of Cambridge yeoman, paysed by us wch have here unto set our hands the 18 Daye of April in the yeare of our lord 1689.

Inprimas his waring aparrel and money in his purse	04 15 00
In the parler	
Item a joynd bedsted with the beding and all things belongeing unto it, a preas Coberd wth other things in that Rome	03 15 06

In the hall

Item a longe table and six stools wth other things in that Rome	02 01 07

In the Chamber over the parler

Item Two bedsteds wth the beading and other things in that rome	05 02 06

In the Chamber over the hall

Item one bedsted wth the beading and other things in that rome	02 01 00

In the Chamber

Item a table wth other things in that rome	01 03 04
Item all the bras	03 06 08
Item all the peuter	02 0 06
Item all the lening	04 03 04
Item Safforn in the house	07 10 00
Item in biles and bonds	180 00 00
Item five lead vesel wth Tobs and other things *in the kechen and drinkhouse*	02 13 04
Item a quarne	00 07 06
Item the mault in the garner	40 10 00
Item barly	19 00 00
Item the wheat and Ry in the barne	01 16 00
Item the wheat and Ry in the feld	03 03 06

In the yard

Item Cows and hefers	13 15 00
Item the sheep and lam	02 15 00
Item Two shoots (young pigs)	01 01 00
Item wood in the yard	02 06 08
The pouleri in the yard	00 09 00
a longe Cart and a Tombrel	03 10 00
the straw	01 06 08
The donge in the yard	01 05 00
one Cart shed	01 06 06
	316 01 07

Edward Chapman
Thomas Wallis

The house there referred to is No. 1, The Green (No. 6 on my list). The rooms are still identifiable, but it is a pity that Chapman and Wallis skimped their task and failed to list the 'other things in that rome'. I selected this as showing the substance of one of the richest men in the village (after the Singletons and Welbores), and you can see that it does not amount to a great deal. The absence of horses from the list is explainable, I think, by the fact that they have been 'borrowed' by John Rayner's sons. Old John had finished with farming anyway – I mean, finished before he died. It rather looks as though he had been in business as a moneylender for the last few years.

What was a 'labourer' worth? The majority were too poor to leave a will, or indeed to leave anything. One man classed as 'labourer', William Pink (1669), had a house consisting of hall, chamber and buttery; he had a yard and barn and was farming, or had farmed, nine acres. His clothes and money were valued at £1 10s 0d; he had corn to the value of £1 6s 0d; a cow worth £1; pulses and saffron worth £2 14s 0d. The rest of his belongings were valued at just over £2 the lot.

How did the elderly widow fare when 'valued' by her neighbours? Here is an example:

Foxton. Cambridge. Shier   Aprill the 16 Anno Dom 1695
A tru invetory of all the goods and Chattell of Elizabeth Dunnidge late desased.

Imps. Hur warring aparrell and muney in hur pours	0	15	0
Itm in hur Chamber one beed-sted one ould fether beed one boulster one pellow two blanketes a cuerled a set of curtns	2	12	4
Itm two ould Chestes two boxes two Chayers one ould Cuperd	0	8	2
Itm in Linning	1	6	8
Itm in Bras	0	6	4
Itm in Putter	0	2	6
Itm in Debts and desprete debtes	31	4	2
Itm one stoul with sum other lumber	0	1	6
Sum	36	16	8

Prysed by us
Nathanaell Singleton sener
John Rayner sener his marke

That old lady was seventy-two years old when she died. For more than fifty years she had been a servant in the Singleton household. Her savings had been lent, with no hope of repayment. She ended her days in a single room, not neglected, not even lonely, for her family lived just across the road. She had her own brand of religion; she was a 'Muggletonian'.

Finally, this:

Aug. ye 10, 1713
An Inventory of all ye Goods & Chattells of Edmund Osler lately decd in Foxton & apprised & Valued the day & year above said by those whose names are under written.

Imprs His wearing apparell & money in his pourse	2	10	0
Item *In the Room where he lay* one Bedstead one feather Bed & Curtains & Valance and a pair Sheets, 2 Blanketts, one Hutch, one Table & three Chairs	2	07	6
Item one old Horse	1	04	0
Item Two Collars, one pair of Iron Trace, and two pair of plow trace, & one Cart Saddle		11	6
Item one Cart and Wheeles	2	05	0
Item ffour Acres of Rye	7	04	0
Item Three Acres of Wheat	4	10	0
Item six Acres of Barley in the Tilth ffield	9	15	0
Item Three Acres of Pease	3	00	0
Item ffive Acres of Oats & Lentills	3	12	6

| Item Thirteen Acres of Land fallowed | 2 | 03 | 4 |
| Item Twenty Load of Dung in the Yard | 1 | 06 | 8 |

| | Sum is | 46 | 04 | 6 |

Nath. Singleton
James Rayner

There you have a picture of an old man, with no family, living in one half of a two-roomed cottage. In the other half lives another similar old man. Between them, with the aid of an old horse, they have been farming thirty-six acres of land. There was a time when that much land would have supported two families in comparative comfort, but there is not much sign of comfort here, apart from the feather bed. The bare state of the cottage may be due in part to the absence of womenfolk. The poverty of the farm is certainly due in no small measure to the lack of wives and children to provide unpaid labour in the fields and look after the poultry, pigs and cow. Notice that there are no pigs, no poultry, no cow.

If the picture is true, as I believe it is, the life of that old man for the last ten or fifteen years has consisted in working, eating and sleeping. Just that. Working for what? In order to eat and sleep, to stay alive. Stay alive to go on working. Working the same old land in the same old way for an ever-diminishing return. One third of the land, you will notice, is producing nothing and worth virtually nothing to Ostler and his partner. The value of the crops which they are growing – and how will they be harvested in this year of 1713, with one of the partners dead at the beginning of harvest? – has not increased in the last fifty years. The yields, already pathetically low (even allowing for undervaluation), will get lower yet. The land has been cropped for a thousand years. The life has gone out of it. The life of this old man has gone into it, but the hungry soil needs more than sweat and toil. And thirty-five acres of land need more than twenty load of dung. One acre could consume that much in one year and then cry out for more. This document is not just a pathetic memorial to Edmund Ostler. It is a portent of the doom of the small farmer. One by one the Edmund Ostlers of England are going to give up the hopeless struggle. By the end of the century there will be few of them left. The one-time yeomen's houses will be labourers' cottages. The gap between rich and poor will be ever widened. Within fifty years the entire village, as near as does not matter, will be owned by two men and farmed by about ten. And the rest of the men? Labourers at seven shillings a week – or 'on the parish'.

Now you know what sort of a picture to expect in the next chapter.

Nominally, as I have said, the affairs of the parish were under the control of the Vestry. In practice all the work was done by a mere handful of men, answerable to the Vestry for some of their actions, to the Justices of the Peace and Chief Constable for the rest. These parish officials did not make the laws; they simply carried them out, but in such circumstances that it often appeared to the villagers that they *were* the Law. When one considers that a good deal of what nowadays is done by Parish Councils, Rural District Councils, County Councils and Government Departments was in the eighteenth century done by a few unpaid local officials in every parish, one cannot escape the thought that those officials must have been men of outstanding qualities. And I believe they were. They were honest, public-spirited, thrifty, hard-working, hard-headed, hard-hearted or compassionate as the circumstances demanded, conscientious, shrewd, good fellows. Not all of them, all the time, but most of them, most of the time. They were not necessarily men of education. So long as two of their number in any one parish could read and write and do simple arithmetic on paper, then they could manage the clerical side of their business and do it with an economy of paper-work which modern administrators and executives might well envy or emulate.

Their paper in fact consisted of one single book, in which they wrote their accounts from time to time, page by page until the book was filled. One such volume, only one, of the Overseers and Churchwardens Accounts for Foxton has survived. It covers the period from 1770 to 1795, and from it practically all the material of this chapter is taken. Since the entries consist entirely of statements of money spent and received, my extracts will be brief and often cryptic, and we shall need to do a lot of reading between the lines. But when we have finished I think you will have in your mind as clear a picture of eighteenth-century rural England as it is possible to have. Note that I say 'rural'. There were at this period two other Englands – as indeed there are now. There was the England of industrial towns which were well on the way to becoming the blight on the landscape that they have increasingly been ever since. And there was the England of gracious living in the stately mansions and parks and elegant town-houses from which the non-gracious were rigorously excluded, or, if admitted, kept below the stairs or in the attic. That is the 'Georgian England' of books and art-galleries. You will see nothing whatever of those other Englands in these pages. Nor am I going to get myself involved in an argument as to which of the three was the most important, for that would involve a discussion as to the relative merits of people, pounds and prestige. My theme is people.

About this handful of men, then. They were six in number – two overseers, two churchwardens and two constables. Theoretically, that is. In practice their number was often reduced to five or even four, for one of them nearly always served in two capacities. It would seem that the main qualification for office was not so much the possession of any or all of the attributes listed above as willingness to do the job. Committee members of modern village organizations will see in this a striking parallel with conditions of today. Here, to make my point, is the nominal roll of officers for a consecutive period of years:

Year	Overseers		Churchwardens		Constables	
1771	Hurrell	Whenham	Hurrell	Wakefield	Barron	Bateson
1772	Barron	Thornton	Hurrell	Wakefield	James	Bateson
1773	Hurrell	Wakefield	Hurrell	Wakefield	Rayner	Bateson
1774	Hurrell	Salmon	Hurrell	Wakefield	Rayner	Williamson
1775	Hurrell	Salmon	Hurrell	Wakefield	Rayner	Williamson
1776	Hurrell	Wakefield	Hurrell	Wakefield	Spring	Ellis
1777	Hurrell	Knights	Hurrell	Wakefield	Spring	Bateson
1778	Hurrell	Knights	Hurrell	Wakefield	Spring	Bateson
1779	Hurrell	Knights	Hurrell	Wakefield	Spring	Bateson
1780	Spring	James	Whenham	Wakefield	Whenham	Bateson
1781	Spring	Hurrell	Whenham	Hurrell	Whenham	Pink
1782	Spring	Hurrell	Whenham	Hurrell	Whenham	Pink
1783	James	Hurrell	Godfrey	Hurrell	Wright	Pink

And so it goes on. This was democracy – the people met once a year to have their say, if any, and for the other 364 days the willing horses did the work. They got no pay. They got no thanks. What satisfaction they got from it I do not know for certain, but I have a feeling that it was simply the satisfaction of serving the community.

The Vestry met annually, at Easter, to elect officials and approve the accounts, which then had to be officially approved by two Justices of the

Peace. Originally the Vestry had met in the church, when it played a role similar to that of the Parochial Church Council of today, but now it met in the Town House, a move necessitated by the wider scope of its business and no doubt influenced by the fact that two thirds of the people in the parish were Dissenters and Methodists. There is nothing to indicate how many attended the Vestry meeting, whether there was any degree of compulsion to attend, or whether any qualifications were needed. I have a strong suspicion that only the ratepayers attended, for the only item of interest on the agenda was the disclosure of how much money had been received and how much had been paid out, the bulk of the money coming from a rate levied on property. There were nominally two rates, a Poor Rate and a Church Rate, but it is evident that they had become merged, for the accounts of all three sets of officials are merged, and their duties overlap at many points.

Let us take a look at the money coming in:

1771	Cash received by rates at Michaelmas	33	19	3
	Cash received by rates at Lady Day	33	18	3
1780	Recd. by Rate at 1s 6d	75	6	0
1781	Recd. by 2 Rates at 1s in the Pound each	99	0	0
1783	Recd. by rates at 1s in the pound	48	13	0
	do. at 9d in the pound	37	2	1½
	do. at 6d in the pound	24	4	9
	do. at 6d in the pound	24	7	6

The amount rose steadily year by year. In twelve years the rate had risen from 1s in the pound to 2s 9d. Twenty years later it reached 5s in the pound, and the total collected amounted to £166. In some parishes almost the whole of the rate contribution was coming from one or two men; in others almost the whole of the population was on parish relief. Neither of those extremes operated in Foxton, but William Hurrell, farming over eight hundred acres of land, must have contributed a major part of the rates. He could doubtless afford it. Several of the small farmers, however, were finding the rates a crippling burden, and yet only one instance is recorded of refusal to pay.

1781 J. Sallmon, W. Loughts and J. Young have refused to pay the rate as agreed on at a vestry.
   Lost by bad rates   18s 7d.

It does not appear that any further action was taken, though obviously payment was enforceable by law. Salmon, be it noted, was one of the overseers a few years before, and again a few years later, which suggests not so much refusal as inability to pay, small though his contribution was.

Another steady source of income was the letting of the meadows which had once been common property; indeed they still were common property, but conditions had changed so much that the community no longer had any use for them. It was the same with the right to graze the balks in the arable fields.

1790	Balks to J. Bateson		15	6
	Town Meadow Havens	2	5	6
	Town Meadow – Barron	7	10	0
	Tressock	1	14	0
	Gossham	3	7	0

This needs to be borne in mind when considering – as we shall later – the effects of Enclosure upon the cottagers, labourers and smallholders. It is obvious that the need for common grazing-ground, common meadows, 'commons' in general, had long since declined, and would not be revived until games and recreation became part of everyday life. The villagers, as distinct from the farmers, no longer had any animals to graze. With a few exceptions, this had been the case for many years; the exceptions being the one or two who still had a close of an acre or so attached to their cottage in which they kept a cow. Two hundred years previously everybody with any land kept a cow or a few sheep; now hardly anybody did.

This change in the pattern of life is not easy to trace or explain. The reason might well be a blend of a new attitude, in which laziness plays a part, and a new scale of values. Keeping a cow was – and still is – a seven-day-a-week occupation; it involved a lot of effort, taking the animal to the pasture, minding it, bringing it back again, fencing, tethering, doctoring, milking, etc. It provided sustenance, but it did not provide much money. The milk was only worth a penny a pint and the cow itself was only worth a pound. In the old days of independence a man was prepared to go to a great deal of trouble to make a few shillings, and even more so to avoid owing a few shillings. Not any longer. Well, whatever the reason, the Town Meadows had been abandoned long ago, in about 1640 as near as I can judge. They had been let to individuals, originally to provide funds for the upkeep of the church, administered by a Trust, which was reformed in 1708, and the money received was now being used to supplement the rates. It seems that the officials themselves frequently rented the meadows, but they were not getting them cheaply.

There were three other minor sources of revenue:

1771	By Willows		3	6
1781	By Willows sold	4	3	6
	By Mud sold		12	6
1790	Willows	4	13	4
	Moules	2	3	9

One can easily understand the willows having a value. Willows grew relatively quickly and were planted along all the brooks and beside the river. They are still a feature of the landscape, though fast disappearing in recent years. They constituted a valuable crop, providing the material used in making baskets, hurdles, fencing, etc., in addition to the bark, which was essential in the process of tanning leather. But that is the first, and last, time I ever heard of anyone buying or selling mud. It obviously came from the scouring of the ditches, our Brook in particular, and it could only have been used to spread on the land as a sort of manure. I should think it was an experiment on the part of Mr Hurrell, and one not likely to be repeated when he saw the crop of weeds which it produced. My previous observation about the loss of fertility in the soil would seem to be supported by this little item. As for the 'moules', they needed no cultivation and were a profitable crop over a long period, with wide fluctuations in the yield, of course. The churchwardens, within whose province by some sound if unexpected process of logic, the destruction of vermin had always come, paid for the moles at the rate of $1\frac{1}{2}d$ each, and sold the skins to furriers and hatters at about double that price. In the year 1771 there were 131 moles caught, for which 16s $4\frac{1}{2}d$ was paid; the next year yielded 154 moles, for which 19s 3d was paid. After that the little gentlemen in velvet were left in peace for ten years; or else the mole-catchers had realized that they could make more money by selling the skins direct to the furriers. I should be interested to know whether the churchwardens had to do the actual skinning and curing, and whether they wore moleskin waistcoats. But those are among the many things which the book does *not* tell us.

So much for the getting of the money. It is the spending of it which tells us most about life and conditions in the village. First call upon the Poor Rate was, naturally, the relief of the poor. That was the reason for its existence. It had at last been realized that one could not abolish poverty by whipping people who were poor and that one could not compel those who were not poor to be charitable. Old prejudices die hard, however, and the practice of whipping underwent a series of modifications before it was finally abolished. First, the whipping of pregnant women was stopped, then the whipping of any female. By the time of which I am now writing the only ones to be whipped were sturdy beggars from other parishes who refused to accept work offered to them, and they were few and far between. The Stocks were still there on the Green for use if required:

1777 To fixing the Stocks up 7 6

but I have found no evidence, other than that, of their being used. The most usual method of dealing with vagrants was, as it had been from time out of memory and as it continued to be until very recently, to hustle them out of the parish as quickly as possible and thrust the nuisance on to somebody else. Part of the constables' duty was to ensure that there were no vagrants from outside lurking in the village, where they might steal something or, which was even worse, might die and have to be buried at the expense of the parish.

1775 To Searching the Town twice 1 0
1776 To serching the Town twice for vagrants 1 0

Some of these vagrants were on their way to their own parish, and were equipped with a 'pass' certifying the fact and stating to which village they were going, in which case it was the constables' duty to assist them on their way:

1771 Paid to a Woman 6*d*
1776 To money gave to Traveller 6*d*
1777 To a Man & Woman with a Pass 3*d*

When the vagrant had no pass – as some obviously had not, because they had no idea where they were born, or when – then a humane constable would take him in and keep an eye on him for the night, doubtless providing some sort of refreshment, at the ratepayers' expense:

1772 To Cash for sitting up with a Traveller 1 0

Which was far better than leaving the poor fellow in the Stocks.

The real problem of poverty, however, was not in dealing with vagrants, but with the people of the village itself. As already stated, the majority of the men in the village were labourers, with a weekly wage of seven shillings. It may sound incredible, but it is nevertheless a fact that a man could live reasonably well on that wage, provided he earned it *every* week. Not only live, but marry and raise a family. It is clear that it could be done, because it *was* done by countless thousands. Much depends, of course, on what one means by living reasonably well. Comparison with working-class life of today is barely feasible because so many expensive necessities of modern life were non-existent in the eighteenth century. Sanitation and hygiene, for instance, cost the eighteenth-century working-man nothing, except the trouble of getting a bucket of water. Travel cost him nothing – he walked. He spent nothing on newspapers, sport, entertainment. And there was at least one feature which was to his advantage – he paid either no rent at all for his house or, at the most, a few pence per week. His 'house' in most cases was one half, or even one third, of what had been a yeoman's house – those houses about which I wrote in preceding chapters – some of which were becoming rather dilapidated. Two rooms, one up and one down, was normal accommodation for a labourer and his family. There was nearly always a garden – and even when it was only half a garden it was still a fair amount of ground – in which he could grow vegetables, keep a few hens and perhaps a pig, though the latter practice was not encouraged by the farmers because it often meant stealing food for the animal.

The staple diet of these men was bread, cheese, milk, eggs and beer. Meat, apart from that of their own pig, was out of the question, even at sixpence per pound (it could sometimes be bought for 4d); so were tea, sugar and any form of sweets other than those which could be picked from the hedgerows. Soup made from vegetables and bones would often constitute a main meal, reinforced by a hunk of bread. It is obvious that a man nurtured on such a diet was not physically capable of a vast amount of work, though he might spend a vast amount of time 'working'. For that reason the average farmer was prompt to dispense with the services of his men when they were not essential to the running of the farm. Moreover, there was always a slack period after harvest and hay-time, when many workers were laid off, even the good workers. So serious did this aspect become that an Act of 1781 gave able-bodied men entitlement to parish relief for the first time, and we find their names regularly on the list after that date.

The main recipients of relief, as one would expect, were widows, orphans and the aged. Their names and the weekly amounts of money they received fill most of the pages of this account-book, and they make pathetic reading, yet so dully prosaic that one is in danger of losing all sense of their significance. It is not easy to imagine the degradation of these wretched people as they trudged along to the overseer's house each week to collect the pittance on which they had to survive until the same time the following week. It is not easy to imagine the humiliation caused by the scorn on the faces half-hidden by curtains in the windows past which they had to walk. It is not easy to imagine the despair at the sight of hungry children on their return to their wretched hovels. It is not easy and, if one succeeds, it is painful. That is why I will spare you all but a mere selection, just enough to illustrate the growing nature of the problem.

1771 Henry Cooper 3s. Wm. Rayner 2s, Judes children 3s, Ruth Gregory 1s 6d, Ann Richardson 1s, Mary Chapman 1s, Widdow Gentle 2s 6d, Eliz. Smith 1s, J. Carter 2s.

1776 Total spent on poor £52 8s 6d.

1782 The underwritten are the Paupers which are by agreement at the vestry to receive weekly collection,
Ann Beamont 3s, Susan Scot 3s, Eliz. Rayner 3s, E. Pink 1s, Ann Buxton 1s, T. Whiston for child 2s 3d, L. Wallis 1s, Thos. Godfrey 1s.

1784 Mary Thornton 3s, T. Wheston 2s 3d, Mrs Moss 6s, Wid. Pink 1s 6d, Wid. Scot 2s, Wid. Jeaves 2s, Wid. Beamont 4s, Wid. Buxton 1s, Wid. Rayner 2s, Jas. Worland 1s, Wid. Empey 1s 6d, T. Beamont 6d.

1787 Widow Thornton 3s, Wid. Pink 2s, Veals children 6s, Wid. Ford 4s, Wid. Beamont 4s, Wid. Buxton 1s 6d, Mary Buxton 1s 6d, Wid. Rayner 3s 6d, Eliz. Rayner 2s 6d, Selby for Wallis 1s 6d, Wallis's boy 2s, Scott 1s, Worland 1s, Impey 1s, Evans 2s, J. Beamont 1s, T. Beamont 4d.

The weekly payments had risen from 17s to 37s 10d in sixteen years, and they were to rise higher yet.

The amounts mentioned above were intended for the provision of food. How an old man could stay alive on one or two shillings' worth of food a week is beyond my comprehension, but evidently many of them did, for several years at least. They must have received, in addition to their pittance, frequent meals or morsels from compassionate neighbours. But food was not their only requirement. They needed clothes and fuel:

1771 Bought a pair of Breeches and Stockings	4	6
Rutter – two Shirts	2	10
Rutter – Shirts Makeing & Buttons		10½
Ann Buxton three bushel of coals	3	0
1772 paid for a pair of shoes for Thos. Blacktop	3	0
Bought Blacktop a Coat and Wastcoat & pair of Breeches	9	4
paid for a pair of Breeches for Rutter	2	6
a pair of shoes for Rutter	3	0
1773 To pr of shoes for Grigory's girl	3	6
To pr of shoes for Jude's boy	3	6
1777 To Mary Ward a Gown	6	4
1782 Bill for Cloths	1 4	2
1788 To 175 Bus Couls & Carring [Bushels of Coals]	8 15	0½

There is only one instance recorded of a pauper being assisted to earn a little money by her own efforts:

1772 Bought a wheel for Ruth Gregory   1   6

That was in all probability the last spinning-wheel to be used in Foxton. Home-spun yarn and hand-made cloth were already things of the past. The mills and factories of industrial England were already clothing the millions.

Medical attention was a costly item, but at least it was available now, and a good deal more effective than it would have been a century earlier.

1777 Jorney to Cambridge for the Doctor   2   6
1780 Paid Doctor Bond   21   0   0

How many years of attendance that sum represents, I do not know. This entry looks as though it could be for a single visit:

1783 paid M. Caldecoat for Doctrine   1   0   0

I am quite sure that Mr Caldecoat was a medical practitioner, not a Methodist preacher! Sometimes the medical attention was of a non-professional nature:

1777 To Mary for looking after Ellen Rayner   12   0
1778 To fetch the Midwife   2   6
1780 Paid Mary Green for Doctorering Rutter's leg   1   0

Epidemics, of frequent occurrence, found the poor an easy target:

1778 Paid to the Small pox   4   0
1788 keeping Ford's family the time of small pox   2   9   6

Mercifully, perhaps, many of the paupers did not live long. I hope that I shall not be misjudged or misunderstood in saying that. They had so little to live for; nothing but hardship, pain, misery and degradation. They were the helpless victims of a social system in which there was no place for them. Blame society if you will, but do not blame those few men who were doing what they could to lighten the load of misery borne by those poor wretches. It might be said that William Hurrell could have sold half of his land and houses and given the proceeds to the poor. So could all the other well-to-do people in England. Meanwhile, William Hurrell, and his son after him, did what he could within the bounds of reason and common humanity. He served as a parish official all his adult life; he employed half the men in the village and so kept them off parish relief; he provided four-fifths of the money doled out to the poor; he lent money free of interest to many old people. He probably did much more of which I know nothing. Other men in Hurrell's class were spending their time and money in trying to rise higher in the social scale for the gratification of their own vanity and ambition, to achieve which they had to migrate to such places as London, Bath, Cheltenham and Harrogate. He saw fit to stay in, and serve, his own village. Many, very many men in England had less justification for a clear conscience than William Hurrell of Foxton.

In an ideal society, it might be supposed that everybody felt so sorry for these poor people when alive, or so glad to see the last of them when they died, that the carpenter would make the coffin for nothing, the grave-digger would dig the grave free, the parson would charge no burial-fee, and so on. Not a bit of it. The coffin was a plain one, to be sure; there was no carved headstone, no funeral oration; but, poor or not, these people were buried decently, and everything was paid for – out of the rates.

1771	for burying of Buxton		19	3
1772	paid Rose Bentley for sitting up and laying out W. Rayner		3	3
1778	Moveing Hitch		1	0
	Laying out Hitch		2	0
	Burying fees for Ward and Hitch		8	0
	Carring Hitch and Ward		4	0
	Bt Nan Ward Shift & makeing		4	1½
	To Carrieing Ann Ward to Cambridge		3	0
1780	For Buring Ann Richerson	1	1	9
1788	Paid for Shifting Clorth Ann Wallis		3	0
	For Elling Rayner Berial		4	3

Mary Green had spent the last years of her life looking after the aged poor, of whom she was one. We do not know who looked after her when the time came, but the story of her last few days is poignantly told in the brief entries on one page of the book, here quoted entire:

1791–92.	Disbursements of Jos. Salmon, Overseer.			
Nov.	Paid the Poor. Set of Mary Green 2 shillings		16	4
Oct. 31	Paid Mary Green		1	6
Nov. 7	For 2 Bushels of Coals for Green		2	1
Nov. 14	For Mooving Green Bed			6
	Paid for Nusing Green		3	0
	Paid one bushel of Coal do.		1	0½
	For Removing the Goods & Selling them		1	6
	For Laing out Green & a pound Wool and Vittils & Drink		4	10
	For Carring Mary Green to Church		1	0
	For Washing the Surples		2	6
	For the Buril of Green		4	3
Ap. 9	Paid Jams Pink for Mending the Bells and Mary Green Corfing	1	14	6

I am sure that the observant reader will have noticed that 'Vittils & Drink'. It is not the only such entry:

1772 for Vitals an Drink had of me	13	2
1786 Paid Wm. Dunn for beer at Ann Evans Burying	1	0

No one who attended a funeral fifty years ago in a rural area will be the least bit surprised by that. Funerals were sad occasions, but they were events after all, and an event could not be permitted to happen without refreshments. It was unthinkable that beer should not be drunk at a funeral. Had it not been provided at the funeral of Ann Evans there would have been mutterings of righteous indignation on the part of everybody concerned. Except Ann Evans.

While the overseers and churchwardens were busy looking after the poor, the constables had just as much work to do, or even more. They were expected to tackle any of the wide variety of situations which might arise, and must have spent a lot of time chasing around trying to find men to do jobs which had once been the responsibility of individual landholders and which now had to be done 'on the parish'. That is to say that the jobs were done by whoever could be persuaded to do them for the miserable rate of pay offered, often, no doubt, as an alternative to the workhouse. When no such men could be found, the constable did the job himself and paid himself 2d a day extra, thereby showing a most commendable restraint, in my opinion. Foremost among these jobs was ditching:

1771 For cutting of Harridge and Elbor pool		
For cutting the river at Barrington foot Bridge	7	6
For cutting of Ham River Twice	1	0
For Cutting Orslock Brook from Barrington foot-bridge up to Pitles 9 days work	8	0
1772 ditching in Harston Meadows 95 pole at 4d a pole	9	0
paid for ditching at Mill Ditch 10 score 12 pole at 2d a pole	1 11	0
1775 To Cutting Auslock Brook my self 3 days	1 15	0
My Man half day Ditching	3	6
		6

'Harridge' is what used to be 'Hayditch'. This is the period during which the most baffling corruption of names took place, and many of the corruptions have survived into modern times. 'Auslock Brook', incidentally, is the original Brook with which my story began. It was still flowing apparently; rather sluggish, no doubt, and somewhat choked with reeds but, thanks to a resourceful constable, still flowing.

One of the constables was specially designated as Surveyor of Highways. The main road running through the parish from Cambridge to

Royston and London had by this time become a Turnpike road. That relieved the constable and the parish of what had been a major problem for a long time, though the maintenance of the other local roads was as big a problem as ever, and it was being solved, or rather tackled, in the same haphazard fashion as it had always been. Never very good, the condition of the village street seems to have been exceptionally bad in the winter of 1772. The method of dealing with it was equally exceptional, as the following extract shows, again quoting one entire page of the book:

The Disbursements of William James Surveyor of the Highway from 2 Dec. 1772 to April 9, 1773.

Dec. 7 Paid John Nott for 3 days Digging of Gravel	3	0
Paid the Widdow Cowper 10 Load of Stones	15	0
Paid the Widdow Gregory for 4 load of Stones	6	0
Dec. 12 Paid the Widdow Buxton 3 load ½ of Stones	5	3
21 Paid the Widdow Gregory for 5 load of Stones	7	6
paid Stephen Ogle for 6 days Digging of Gravel	6	0
Dec. 23 paid the Widdow Buxton for 4 load of Stones	6	0
for 1 Days Work My Man in the Highway	1	0
24 Paid to Widdow Cowper 10 load of Stones	15	0
28 Paid for 11 days Work and half to Stephen Ogle for Diging of Gravel	11	6
Jan. 25 paid Stephen Ogle for 6 days work	6	0
Apr. 10 paid the Widdow Cowper for gathering 7 load of Stones	10	6

I suggest that you read that again, for I doubt whether the full implication of it has struck home at one cursory reading. William James's handwriting is not such as to fire the imagination; cold print even less so. Now, can you picture to yourself those poor, half-starved old women trudging about the muddy fields in the depth of winter, stooping down, picking up ice-cold stones with frozen fingers, dropping them into a sack which gets heavier with every step, dragging them to a waiting cart, tipping them out of the sack into the cart, then starting all over again – and again – and again? How many stones to the bag? How many bags to the load? How many loads to the grave? Stephen Ogle's job was easy by comparison; all he had to do was to dig down to the gravel, then shovel it into a cart. But you cannot pick up stones with a shovel, and stones are not found in heaps. Old Widow Cowper, *with her hands*, picked twenty-seven cart-loads of stones that winter. If she had been on parish relief she would have received £2 10s 0d. By doing this work she earned £2 0s 6d, and her name did not appear on the paupers' list. If you know of an instance of courage, stoical pride and endurance which can surpass that, I would like to hear of it.

Old women were never again used as stone-pickers. The technique of road-mending, however, continued unchanged:

1786	Jas. Impey for Digging in Jankins land	1	2	0
	Scott for 2 loads of Stones		3	0
	Brand & Jude for Labor		13	0
1790	Digging gravel & c & in the streets	8	5	7½

That last item is rather confusing, due, I think, to the word 'carting' having been missed out. The gravel was certainly not dug in the streets, though, as you may remember, clunch had been dug there two centuries previously. One can still see clearly the hollows in the fields near the highways from which gravel was dug to make the roads. The Romans had used the same technique (but not, I think, using old women as labourers) some seventeen hundred years before; it had been rediscovered about two centuries before and was now at last being applied on a large scale. Even so, minor roads and village streets were tackled in such a piecemeal and penny-saving fashion that another hundred years were to elapse before anything like a satisfactory state was reached.

Bridges also, except those on main roads, were a parish responsibility. This might be a simple affair of a few rough planks:

1771	Laid down a Bridge at Paines, Bawlks and Spikes	1	0

Or it could be quite an elaborate undertaking:

1772	paid Mr Foster for 600 of Bricks	15	0
	and for fetching of them	7	0
	paid for bricklayers Work for doing a bridge in Drainer	6	4½
	paid for 20 Bushel of Lime	10	0
1773	paid for making an Arch at paretree Brook	7	1
	paid for 400½ of Brick	11	3
	and for fech of them	5	0
	for fechting of sand and lime to the Two Bridges	18	9

The bridge 'in Drainer' (where the farm-road from Mortimer's crosses Hoffer Brook, on what was once the road from Foxton to Newton) was still there until 1920, when it was demolished by the passage of a steam-engine used for ploughing. The engine, weighing some ten tons, actually managed to get across the bridge, which says a great deal for the workmanship of that bricklayer of 1772 – at just over a shilling a day. The other bridge I cannot identify with certainty, but I think it must have been where the Town Brook was taken underneath the road opposite the Bury.

Then there were the scores of odd jobs to be done about the place:

		£	s	d
1771	To Wm. Dunn for the Town Plough		13	0
	for 2 plates for the Town Plough		4	0
	for laying the share & sharpening two Counters			10
	for lyning a bolt, 4 Keys, 1 Cotterill		1	6
	for a staple for the Town Gate			2
1773	for wood to mend the Bars at the Sheard		2	6
	To one pound Nails & mending a Ketch			9
1776	Blacksmith's Bill for Nails & Iron, Town Gates		1	6
	Carpenter's Bill for Town Gates	1	2	2
	To wood used for Gates		6	8
1777	To fetching 2 loads Clay for the Town House		2	0
	To Straw		1	6
	To Splents		1	3
1783	paid to Jas. Pink for makeing & mending fieldgates and stiles as per Bill	3	2	10

William Dunn was the publican of the 'Blackamoor's Head', where the town plough was evidently housed, but just what the town plough was used for I am not sure. It could have been for loan to the labourers with allotments (though there is no record of allotments at this date, or of the receipt of rents for them), or it could have been part of the road-maintenance equipment. The various gates referred to were gates across the roads to prevent the straying of animals from the open fields. The Town House, of course, was the Village Hall of those times, which seems to have undergone major repairs in the seventies of that century. 'Counters' were obviously coulters; a 'ketch' was for fastening a gate; a cotterill or 'cotterel' was a pin for securing a bolt.

The protection of the crops against the depredations of birds had been a major problem since the earliest times. For centuries it had been the recognized prerogative of boys armed with stones, slings, rattles and loud voices. And I have no doubt that they continued to function, for the sake of something to do, for the few pence which they could earn thereby, and for the sheer fun of it. But it seems that the problem was now so acute that it provided a full-time occupation, during the critical part of the season, for a man armed with a gun.

		£	s	d
1777	paid for cleaning a Gun for W. Chapman		1	0
1783	paid Mrs Whittingstall for powder and shot		2	4	5
	Page field keeping	1	12	0
	W. Chapman eight days		8	0
1788	Paid Wm. Chapman 1 Weak		6	0
	Powder & shot for field keeping		10	5

Did Mrs Whittingstall actually manufacture the powder and shot, I wonder? William Chapman's gun was probably made by his father, who was a blacksmith, and it seems to have had a short life:

1789 To a gun for the parish   6 0

As William Chapman also disappears from the records at the same time,
I fear that his life may have been cut short too by a nasty accident. However, the new gun, cheap as it was, seemed to function well enough, and
the birds were presumably frightened if not seriously hurt.

1790 Powder & shot for field keeping   1   7   2½
      Cooper 9 weeks field keeping   3 15   0

I wonder whether the thousands of pigeons kept in the various dove-
houses in the village were legitimate targets for the fieldkeeper? They
were the worst of the culprits, and always had been. They now no longer
enjoyed manorial protection as they once did, and it seems likely that the
keeping of pigeons declined rapidly from about this time. The Rev.
Gooch, writing in 1804, said of this area: 'Almost every farm has a
pigeon-house. Many would not keep them but for their muck. They
destroy thatch and oblige to sow more seeds than would be necessary.' It
might be thought that the following entry referred to Will Chapman's
activity:

1773 To Stopping Gulls at Flagpicle   2 0

But they were not sea-gulls. They were gullies, or drainage-channels.
When the boggy bit of ground along the Brook at the western foot of West
Hill had been drained it was necessary to block up the gullies, otherwise
the land would have been flooded again the next time the brook was in
spate.

One of the regular tasks of the constables was to keep a list of men
eligible for service in the Militia, to present the list to the Chief Constable
every quarter, and to pay the statutory levy. This latter was a special tax
evied on landowners in lieu of service. Five hundred years previously it
would have been called 'scutage', and would have been levied only on
those holding the rank of knight. Now it was called 'quarterage', and
every able-bodied man had the privilege of fighting for king and country.
In fact few of the men who were liable for service actually did serve. The
ones who did were those who had been unlucky in the ballot or 'draw',
and for them the only escape from three years' service was to pay £10 for
a substitute to replace them.

1771 A Journey to Burnbridge paying the Bills and Quarteridge and Straw
      Money   1   1   6
      My Journey to Arrington Tyger to carry in the names of the Militia   2   6
1778 Jorney to Arrington for Drawing the Militia   2   6

1780 Paid the Quarterage to the High Constable	2	8	0
A Journey to Bournbridge to have the Book Signd		2	6
1783 paid the Militia Quarterage	1	16	0

Bourn Bridge is on the Icknield Way (A505) where it joins the Roman road (A11) from Gt. Chesterford to Newmarket. Arrington is on the Ermine Street (A14). It is interesting to note that the Chief Constable travelled only along main roads, and that the rendezvous for this military business were just where they would have been in the days of the Roman Empire. The following letter might also be of interest, as showing that old soldiers did not necessarily just fade away in the thoughts of their fellow men:

13 April 1766.
J. Cowper, vicar, and Edward Rayner & Henry Howard, churchwardens, petition on behalf of Thomas Wenham, who first served 3 years and 4 months in the Regulars, was discharged in the year '44 in Flanders & afterwards served in the Militia for the County of Norfolk one year & 9 months under your Lordship. By an unfortunate accident which he met with in his march to Hilsey Barracks he has been rendered incapable ever since of getting his livelyhood and is at present no inconsiderable Burthen to the Parish. He has a wife and two Children, which, added to other circumstances of distress, has induced him to apply for the Chelsea Pension of seven pounds 12 shillings per annum.

We have been informed that your Lordship can easily procure it for him, and, being truly sensible of your Lordship's Humanity and Benevolence, have the confidence to hope that his being in every respect a worthy object will be more than a sufficient Recommendation in his favour.

The old soldier *did* get his pension, and showed his gratitude by serving as parish officer, whilst practising the trade of 'cordwainer' (cobbler) to the end of his days.

On the happily rare occasions when crime was committed, involving a trial at the Assizes, the cost fell heavily on the parish and the constables were put to a good deal of trouble.

1777 To 3 Journeys to Cambridge with Betty Ivons with Warrant & Charges		8	6
To Jorney to London – Warrant & Charges at London	6	18	5
1782 Mr Motts Bill for trial of Day & removal	11	17	1

That is a good example of what I meant by saying that the entries are 'cryptic'. Does the word 'removal' mean the removal of the convicted Day to gaol? Or does it mean the removal of the poor man's corpse after he had been hanged? And if so, for what was he hanged? It need not have been a very serious crime, by modern standards. Being found in possession of a single forged bank note would have been sufficient to hang him, as it did William Wright of Foxton in 1802.

It must have occurred to the reader to wonder whether these important officials wore any sort of a badge or uniform, I regret that I cannot supply much enlightenment on that point. This entry attracted my attention and curiosity:

1770 Paid for thing for a cockade   1 0

If I have deciphered the writing correctly, and interpreted it rightly, then the constables in that year *did* wear a badge of office, and the 'thing' was a means of attaching it to their coat or hat. They did not know the correct name of the 'thing', and neither do I. Anyway, the Vestry was not prepared to tolerate this display of ceremonial pomp, and made it quite clear at the next meeting:

1771 No Cockade to be paid for by the Poor Rates.

So, any subsequent constables who wanted to dress up for the part would do so at their own expense.

The duties and expenses of the churchwardens, as church officials rather than officers serving the whole parish, were by comparison quite light.

1772 paid to Wm. Barron for the Church Book	4	0
1787 Cowling ½ a year winding of the Clock	10	0
Bread & Wine for the Communion 5 times at 3s	15	0
1790 Washing the Surplus twice	5	0

That last item must refer to the vicar's surplice. Robed choirs were not yet in vogue in village churches, I am told. The charge seems excessive; probably a special perquisite of the churchwarden's wife. The only other item occurring regularly in the churchwarden's accounts is this:

1787 To Sparrows as per Account	1	2	8½
1791 Sparrows		10	7
1794 Sparrows		9	6

Any reader who has a garden and lives in a thatched cottage can hardly fail to experience a momentary regret at the passing of the ancient custom which those brief entries illustrate. Sparrows, God's creatures though they may be, were recognized as a serious pest and treated as such with no sentimental nonsense. They were caught by whatever means human ingenuity could devise, decapitated, and their heads taken along to the churchwardens, who paid a bounty of one halfpenny per head. There was no risk of anyone breeding sparrows for a living, and no likelihood of the sparrow population ever being wiped out, though a bag of 545 in one year must have thinned it out appreciably. Any reader who feels sorry for the sparrows may be consoled by the thought of the number of happy cats there must have been. And sparrow-pie was quite a treat.

There are many more interesting items, usually occurring once only, of which I will quote only a few.

1776 pd Mrs. Whittingstall for keeping a Town Boy   13 0

Do not imagine that that refers to a sickly boy from the town sent to recuperate in the country air at public expense. The 'Town' was the village of Foxton, and the 'Boy' was an orphan. This is the only instance known to me of official fostering, though it must have been common enough. The boy would not be a charge on the rates for long; he would soon learn to earn his keep.

1782 Beamont's rate & window tax   3 6

That is unique in two respects. Firstly in that a man was chargeable with rates and in receipt of relief at one and the same time; to have one's rates paid out of the rates seems a good idea. Secondly, it is the only reference I have found to window-tax in such a context. The window-tax was in force from 1695 to 1851. The sight of windows bricked up in large houses to minimize payment is familiar enough, but I would not have expected Beamont's house to be subject to it.

1789 To the informer for hedge-breakers   10 6

The magnitude of the reward indicates the seriousness of the offence. Presumably a corresponding sum was extracted from the offender by way of fine.

1790 Beamont, a tin kettle   4 6

Oh that it should come to this – a tin kettle – after all those great pans of brass and copper and pewter about which we were reading some little while back! What happened to them all, I wonder? Tin kettles are with us yet.

That is all as regards the Accounts, but there is one event which occurred during that period which, though it does not figure in the Accounts in any way, must figure in my story. There are few villages in this part of the country in whose annals a similar event does not occur at least once, and few events more frightening when they did occur. Fire! It was in the east end of the village, on the afternoon of 1 April 1788, that the tragedy happened. Let the reporter of the *Cambridge Chronicle and Journal* of 5 April give his account:

On Tuesday last, about 3 o'clock in the afternoon, a fire broke out in a wheatcase belonging to Mr William Hurrell, of Foxton in this county, which raged with irresistable fury till past midnight, and destroyed seventeen dwelling houses, a malting office containing a considerable quantity of malt, a great number of barns, outhouses, stacks, etc. A man who had been confined for 20 years as a lunatic perished in the flames, notwithstanding every endeavour was used to save him. Several pigs, calves and sheep were burnt. It is supposed the premises were maliciously set on fire. We are sorry to add that a very considerable part of the property was not insured.

The Parish Register records the burial on 6 April 1788 of Philip Bateson, aged 38, 'burnt to death in a sudden fire'. It seems almost certain that Bateson himself was responsible for the fire, for it could only have been the work of a lunatic. The risk of fire was so constant and so frightening an element of village life that no child, however mischievously inclined, would ever dare to put himself in a situation in which it might occur. Sheer malice, a desire to be avenged on William Hurrell for some imaginary wrong, can be ruled out as a motive. Even the most stupid or aggrieved incendiary would have known that his action would hurt a number of poor people much more than it would harm Hurrell. How many poor people it did in fact hurt it is difficult to say. The reporter was certainly exaggerating when he wrote of 'seventeen dwelling houses' being destroyed. The area affected contained three farms and five houses, all of which were totally destroyed. Those five houses were each housing two families, and some of the 'families' consisted of one old person only. I think the truth probably is that seventeen persons were rendered homeless. That was bad enough, but it could have been much worse. If the wind had not dropped, or if it had been strong enough to carry the sparks across the gap created by the two closes which from medieval times had acted as a buffer between the east end and the rest of the village, then the whole village would have been destroyed. It would have been useless to try to remove the thatch from roofs with the large hooks kept for that purpose but hardly ever used because of their inefficiency. There was no other way of fighting a fire; no fire-engine, and our Brook would hardly have sufficed to quench half a dozen fires raging at the same time.

Before the report had appeared in the Press, the Senate of the University unanimously voted £50 'for the relief of the sufferers by a fire at Foxton'. That explains why there is no reference in the Overseers' Accounts to any relief being paid out of the rates. All the homeless were re-housed, and only one of the destroyed houses rebuilt.

11 Stagnation

The reader will find a marked difference between the material of these last two chapters of my book and that of the preceding chapters. The scope of my theme has widened, and for that reason I have omitted a good deal of what I might have been expected to include. With the beginning of the nineteenth century there dawns an era which might well be called, among other things, the age of statistics. The National Census from 1801 onwards gives, at ten-yearly intervals, nearly exact figures of population and houses. Land Tax Returns give almost exact details of property and its value. Gazetteers give summaries, often far from exact, of these official statistics. Newspapers provide detailed reports, often exaggerated, of local as well as national events. Parliamentary Reports, correspondence, diaries, memoirs, literature – there is no lack of documentation. The only trouble is that most of it is rather dull, and some of it indescribably dull, as reading matter. Perhaps that is mere personal prejudice on my part, arising from a lack of enthusiasm for this more recent stage of history. I do not seek to defend or justify my attitude, for I know that the history of the nineteenth century is every bit as important as that of any other age, perhaps a great deal more so, but the fact still remains that I do not much like the nineteenth century and all that was therein done in the name of progress. Avoiding as much as possible the great masses of statistics and the interpretation of them, I propose to discuss briefly a number of attitudes which in my view characterize the period, illustrating them in a more general manner than has so far been my practice.

Before embarking on that discussion, just a few words to illustrate the difference between the national and the parochial view of the same event. Every schoolboy knows that the great happening of the early nineteenth century was the Napoleonic Wars, and it is all too easy to form the impression that every village in England was wholeheartedly engaged in the conflict against 'Boneypart' and the French. One has visions of the village blacksmith hammering ploughshares into bayonets; farm-carts idle because horses have been requisitioned to draw munition-carts; musketry-drill on the village green; bird-scaring banned to save powder; constables manning the semaphore, ready to ring the bells to announce the coming of the invaders and summon the populace to the barricades. Search the records, and what do we find? That Colonel Stewart reviewed the Bassing-bourne Militia on Foxton Common one day in 1804, and that Mr Hurrell afterwards provided refreshments, a memorable occasion which was 'graced by the presence of a great part of the beauty of the district'. And that, so far as I can discover, was the only disturbance which the Napoleonic Wars inflicted on the tranquil life of the village.

It would not surprise me to learn that amongst my readers there are several students of history who, on seeing the title of this chapter, thought that I had a mistake in chronology and slipped back into the Middle Ages. Any normal history-book will tell you that the nineteenth century was the age of Political Reform, Great Statesmen, the British Empire, Expanding Commerce, Railways, Industry – in short, Progress. How can anyone call all that 'Stagnation'? My answer is that 'all that' is outside my theme. I might add a few pertinent queries as to the present whereabouts of the British Empire, the present state of Railways and the results of Political Reform, or ask the reader to take a more critical look at the benefits conferred upon mankind by Industry. But that, too, is not part of my theme, except in so far as it reflects in some measure the first of the attitudes with which I propose to deal, namely the attitude of the townsman towards the countryman and the countryside.

It is an attitude – I say it *is* because it still persists to some extent though happily much diminished – based on the belief that life in a town is civilized, refined, comfortable, fashionable, elegant, vastly different from and superior to life in the country; and that the townsman is clever, smart, progressive and educated in complete contrast with the 'yokels', 'country bumpkins' and 'rustics' who inhabit the countryside. The notion, fostered by literature current only or mainly in towns, had been slowly developing over the two centuries prior to about 1800, after which it seems to have intensified. Like most ideas affecting the attitudes and behaviour of masses of people, it originated in the upper strata of society and gradually seeped through to the lower layers. It would have been unthinkable in the thirteenth century, when nine-tenths of the population were countrymen, or in the sixteenth century, when monarchs and nobles spent as much time in the country as they did in the towns, which were even more filthy and pestilential than the villages, and when the difference between town and village was otherwise so slight (places such as London, York, Norwich, Bristol excepted) that the same word 'town' designated both. That it is merely a question of fashion, not based on any permanent truth but, like all fashions, subject to change and decay, is testified by the modern mania for a 'second home' in the country and the mad scramble to get away from towns at weekends or indeed at the end of every working day.

The idea reached its peak of intensity, I believe, in the latter half of the nineteenth century, and, in all fairness, it must be admitted that there was a good deal of apparent justification for it. On numerical grounds alone, the towns achieved superiority for the first time in history around the year 1850, and by the year 1900 the urban population was in many regions more than double the rural population. Progress did in fact affect the towns to a marked and lasting degree, whilst the villages remained almost unchanged throughout the century. Factories, mills, warehouses, banks, offices, shops, theatres, schools, libraries, public baths, main drains, street-lighting – these were all features of the expanding urban scene. The villages, by way of emulation, had each acquired a school and a chapel by the end of the 1880s, and little else, apart from perhaps another pub and another small shop.

Most villages, it is true, had also acquired a railway-station or were within easy reach of one, which theoretically brought the whole of the outside world within easy reach. Though it would be foolish to deny the effect of railways on suburban development and even more foolish to belittle their influence on the expansion of commerce, I think that their effect on village life has been somewhat exaggerated. Those intrepid souls, many of them from the villages of eastern England, who decided hope-fully or despairingly to seek a better life in Canada, Australia or New Zealand, undoubtedly found it much easier and cheaper to do so, and their going was undoubtedly to their own benefit and the benefit of the countries to which they emigrated. The villages which they left were no richer for their absence, and within a generation or so were to be drastically im-poverished by the importation of food from overseas to feed the industrial populations. This was the unkindest cut of all in the town-versus-country conflict. One further comment, albeit in a very minor key, on the influence of the railways is provided by the fact that the village 'carrier' with his cart, a vital link between the village and neighbouring towns, was just as active in 1901 as he had been in 1840.

As regards rural populations, they did in fact increase, in some cases double, during the first half of the century, after which they remained fairly static or even declined slightly. What about the quality of those rural populations; were they really stupid, backward and uncivilized? It all depends, surely, on what criteria you apply, what yardstick you use to measure by. It does not surprise me that, in reporting on Foxton school in 1886, the School Inspector said that 'the majority of the children in Standard One knew little or nothing'. He would, I do not doubt, have said the same of their parents. The children of Standard One could not read or write, evidently, could not say their nine times table or recite the list of the capes and bays of Scotland. But I am sure that they knew a good deal more than the Inspector thought they knew, and knew things which he did not know. They would not, for instance, play in a field of growing corn in spring thinking that it was 'only a grass field', or chase a herd of in-calf heifers 'for fun', both of which escapades are amongst the many lapses attributed in recent years to educated visitors from the town on a day out in the country. Their knowledge was of a different kind, one might say of a different world, from that of the townsmen in the banks, offices and shops. I do not accept that this made them inferior.

The next attitude of which I want to speak is one which more than any other emphasizes the continuity of history and shows how the present is firmly rooted in the past, namely the attitude of the employer towards the employed. It is a feature common to both town and country, and by no means peculiar to the nineteenth century, but, like the previous attitude discussed, it reached a peak of intensity and universality about the middle of that century, when the great majority of people were either employers of labour or 'labourers' of some kind, the only exceptions being the small shop-keepers and the few independent artisans still left. I will confine my observations to the country, and illustrate them with quotations from a book published in 1811 – *General View of the Agriculture of the County of Cambridge* by the Rev. W. Gooch. The author draws largely upon similar surveys made previously by Arthur Young and C. Vancouver, and his theme is the improvement of farming techniques. It is only by accident, as it were, that amongst the masses of details about crops and costs and yields there appears the occasional indication of what the farmer, and the author, thinks of the labourer.

Speaking of the recently introduced threshing-machines, worked by horses, Mr Gooch is not very enthusiastic, and concludes:

But perhaps the comparative expense between threshing by hand, and by a machine, is not the most weighty consideration, and though the latter be greater than the former, it may be preferable from the many attendant advantages; these no farmer wants to have pointed out; a material one is, that *it protects him from imposition of workmen*, where they are plentiful, and affords him a resource where they are not –

The italics are mine, as elsewhere throughout this chapter.

The right of the poor to go gleaning in the cornfields at harvest time, or immediately after, was a privilege dating from the earliest times. Evidently the privilege was being abused, as it always had been by some, especially under pressure of extreme poverty:

Gleaning is a general evil in this county, and is unlimited, extending to every grain and without any regulations, the gleaners going amongst the shocks of wheat and following the rakers of soft corn so closely and in so disorderly a manner as to cause perpetual dispute and complaint.

He was here echoing the sentiments of numerous farmers, one of whom suggested to the Board of Agriculture the following remedy:

Would it not be worthy of the Board to consider how the custom of gleaning might be so regulated as to protect the property of the farmer and to secure to the poor that portion of the grain necessarily left on the ground? A short act giving the magistrate a summary jurisdiction and prohibiting the poor to glean till the land was cleared, *under penalty of 10 shillings or one month's imprisonment* and prohibiting the farmer to turn any stock on the ground for so many days after it is cleared, under a penalty of £5 to be levied by distress, would I think answer the purpose.

Speaking of the cultivation of woad, a crop already scarce even in the Fens, where it was once grown extensively:

Culture while growing – Weeded twice by women *on their knees*.
Harvesting – Pull off the leaves – carried to mill – made into balls – dried – in winter they are taken to mill again and broken in pieces – are there watered and turned frequently, turned as muck is, which causes *a heat, stench, and smoke to such a degree that only persons who have been accustomed to it can bear it –*
– this seemed an irregular way of doing it, machines might be invented that *would neither be drunk nor careless*.

I offer the next few quotes without comment, apart from italics.

To clay our light silty lands would be the first and greatest improvement and this I fear must ever be retarded by the badness of the roads and the *dearness and scarcity of labourers*.

The fen farmers keep their horses at comparatively no expense. Mr Wedd thinks it so trifling that he keeps four to every plough he works, using two horses at a time for half the day, *the men going the whole day*.

I think where two horses are sufficient to work a plough, one horse is kept on an average to every 20 acres of ploughed land, and every horse will furnish employment (exclusive of harvest) *for half a man and a quarter of a boy.*

The farmers whose wives attend the dairy say nothing pays better than cows; but all agree they are unprofitable unless that is the case.

An intelligent and large farmer observed to me (and I am inclined to think justly) that fattening hogs pays a cottager, or anyone who himself attends them, as in that case *less is suffered by robbery,* less waste is made, and they are not kept a moment longer than is done for profit. They require, he observed, *more attention than servants will give them,* at any rate he said more economical management than they would exercise.

In this parish (Harston) an acre of land was allotted to each cottage, but as most of the cottages belonged to the owners of the large estates, they laid the land to them instead of attaching it to the cottages. Mr Leworthy does not think land that advantage to a cottager which it is generally supposed to be; *the farmer will not assist him with horses, etc.*; he therefore has ploughing etc. to pay for at the dearest rate, and few of them have proper buildings –.

The profit of cows is said to be much lessened by the increased price of cooperage, firing, etc. and fewer are kept owing to the difficulty of getting men to milk, *without extra wages.*

What were the wages of these drunken, careless, lazy, thieving labourers? There was no fixed scale; there were no regulations; and the only principle in operation was that the employer paid as little as he could, whilst expecting the maximum of work. Here is a brief summary of the situation in agriculture at the beginning of the century; it had not changed very much by the end of the century:

Shepherd   – up to £30 a year.
Dairy-maid   – £5 a year, plus keep.
Labourer   – from 9s to 15s a week.
Harvest wages – from 13s to 30s a week, varying according to meals supplied.
Reaping   – (per acre) oats 16s, beans 21s, wheat 7s to 21s.
Mowing   – (per acre) 2s 6d to 4s.
Turning muck   – one penny per load.

I might add that a 'week' was about seventy hours on average, sometimes much more; and that payment for holidays, which by modern standards were almost non-existent, was neither given nor expected.

Mr Darnton of Babraham, during the high prices of provisions, instead of advancing the wages of his labourers, allowed them in harvest six lbs. of pork, 2 lbs. of cheese, 4 lbs. of rice per man per week, at 4d per lb. each article. This plan *proved advantageous to himself* and was well received by the people. The farmers who advanced the wages have found it *difficult to reduce them.*

The farmers not only complain of the rapid advance of wages but of the difficulty of procuring *steady and deserving* labourers; they are much less industrious and *respectable* than in many counties. In the fens it is easily accounted for; they *never see the inside of a church*, or any one on a Sunday but the alehouse society or that of their neighbours met together to drink away the day.

At every parish is annually a 'feast', viz. a meeting of the *lower classes* for the *purposes of merriment* etc. etc.

That last quotation is literally all that the Rev. Gooch has to say on the subject of this survival of what were once the great religious festivals. I am grateful to him for providing evidence, however slight, that there was *some* merriment in the lives of the lower classes.

I think I have quoted enough to make my point about the attitude of employers towards the employed. There are masses of documentary evidence in support of the belief that it was even worse in the industrial regions, where conditions of work were frequently so appalling as to defy belief, and deservedly attracted the attention of social reformers to a greater extent when the social conscience was at last awakened. The farm-labourer did at least spend most of his working time in a healthy atmosphere, even if it was wet and cold at times, and there was one season of the year when even the labourer had a real sense of sharing in the bounty of the earth. No mill-worker or factory-hand, I imagine, ever had the good fortune to live on the following regime for six or seven weeks at harvest-time:

  6 a.m. – one pint of strong beer, bread and cheese.
  8 a.m. – breakfast of cold meat and beer.
11 a.m. – one pint of strong beer, bread and cheese.
  1 p.m. – Dinner. One day roast beef or mutton (pork will not do) and plain pudding, next day boiled beef or mutton and plum pudding.
  4 p.m. – one pint of strong beer, bread and cheese.
  7 p.m. – hot mash or mutton pies.

On Saturday night an addition of good seed-cake of one lb. covered with sugar, and a quart of strong beer poured over it.

  Hence each man has daily
      Nine pints of beer (strong)
      Three times bread and cheese
      Three times meat.

The *expense of these will be found great* at the present prices of the several articles.

The prices of the several articles were:
beef 8*d* a lb., veal 7½*d*, mutton 7*d*, pork 5*d*, cheese 4*d* to 7*d*.

    Unfortunately the price of bread and beer is not given, but the liberality with which they were doled out suggests that they were relatively cheap.

The harvest-ration routine quoted above was by no means a general practice. It applied only to harvest-workers 'living-in' and employed by a particularly generous and humane farmer. It was a 'gentleman at Wimpole' who supplied the information. I have good reason to believe that Mr William Hurrell of Foxton treated his men in similar fashion. In some other places things were different, for example: 'At Wisbech, harvest men are hired every morning at four o'clock on the bridge there, *for the day only*, or for two days at the most.'

It all sounds, I must admit, rather like something from the Middle Ages, and the reader may need a reminder that what I am writing about is the early part of the nineteenth century, the century in which many people still alive were born. This attitude, the preoccupation of the employer with his profits and the concern of the clergyman for respectability, to the virtual exclusion of all else, was to persist right through that century and well into the present. It goes a long way towards explaining the present acute troubles in labour relations, which neither political changes nor economic reform seem able to eradicate. For people have long memories. Superficially they forget a great deal, and only remember what they want to remember. But instinctively they remember much that they do not wholly comprehend.

I do not know whether there is any law or convention which decrees that a chronicler, as distinct from a propagandist, should be strictly impartial. If there is, I have probably infringed it a dozen times already, so there is little point in apologizing for doing it again. I cannot honestly regard these attitudes which I am discussing with impartiality and I deplore the next one as much as any. That is, the attitude of the property-owner towards his property. Had it taken the form of a justifiable pride of possession, a determination to take care of what one owned coupled with a willingness to share it, or part of it, with others willing to show the same care and respect, then it need not have become a cause of social discontent and class antagonism. But it went far beyond that, and took the form of rigid and absolute exclusiveness. It was not new. The upper classes had practised it for centuries, with their massive gates, water-filled moats and miles of expensive brick walls round their parks. The middle classes had likewise practised enclosure whenever and wherever possible, sometimes resulting in the disappearance or removal of whole villages. Now it was the turn of the common man, or, to be more precise, the more energetic, resourceful and wealthy of the common men.

As regards agricultural enclosure – usually given a capital to denote its social status, and often written 'Inclosure' – there was a sound practical justification for it. The crops and cultivation of the late eighteenth and early nineteenth centuries differed but little from those of preceding centuries. Over vast areas of England wheat, rye and beans were sown in the autumn; barley, oats and peas or lentils in the spring; and roughly one third of the land left fallow every year. Clover, cole, rape, rye-grass, lucerne, sanfoin, turnips were known, tested and found advantageous half a century earlier, or even earlier than that. They were in fact being grown in small acreages in many areas, but the great mass of farmers were slow to adopt new crops or new systems, if for no other reason than that they were new. There was, however, another reason for the failure to change, namely that these new crops could not be cultivated on any worthwhile scale so long as the thousand-year-old system of open fields remained in operation, for some of the new crops had to occupy the same ground for up to five years in succession, and all of them would have fallen easy victims of 'common' grazing of livestock. The abolition of the old system involved prolonged and often bitter controversy and hundreds of separate Acts of Parliament (one for each parish, starting in 1770 and finishing about a hundred years later, with the bulk of them between 1795 and 1850) before Enclosure was complete and almost universal. I am going to alter my perspective here for the time being to give a close-up and hence clearer view of Enclosure in one parish. What happened in Foxton is typical of what happened in a hundred other parishes.

The chief instigators of the Parliamentary Bill for the Enclosure of the Common Fields of Foxton were, naturally enough, William Hurrell and John Bendysh, Esq., who between them owned three-quarters of the land in the parish. A meeting of those interested was held in the Eagle Inn, Cambridge; a notice was fixed on the outer door of Foxton church on 23 June 1826; announcements were printed in the *Chronicle*, and the campaign was launched. There was no opposition – there were none to oppose; few who would wish to, and fewer still with the vocal and financial resources needed. The Bill was passed. Commissioners were appointed; surveyors, engineer, solicitors engaged, and the work began. Exactly four years after the start of the campaign, on 13 June 1830, the Award was proclaimed in the parish church. It had cost over £3000. What had it achieved?

Ham Field, Hopper Field, Chardwell Field, Hill Field existed no longer. The shotts, lands, balks, pightles, gores, doles – all gone. The parish boundaries were defined in detail for the first time in a thousand years and, with minor divergences, were declared to be what they had in fact been for a thousand years, and what they are still. The roads were defined and delimited – 40 feet wide, most of them, but Barrington Road only 30 feet, and the Turnpike Road 60 feet. Seventeen ancient lanes and paths were abolished, leaving only three. No longer were areas 'by estimation' or 'more or less', but a precise statement of acres, roods and perches. This must have provided some shocks for many who all their lives had been measuring by foot and eye. The parish was found to contain 1726 acres – nearly three hundred acres less than had been thought – of which 34 acres were roads, drains and brooks. The land was re-allotted on the basis of previous ownership, rights of common and various other interests being taken into consideration with scrupulous thoroughness. Exchanges were made in order to bring farmsteads and land into proximity, but, inevitably, some farmsteads were still separated from some of their land by distances of anything up to a mile. The result was the pattern of fields large and small which we know today. The size of the allocation to Bendysh (800 acres) and Hurrell (400 acres) meant that three of the former open fields were left almost intact; only Hill Field and a corner of Hopper Field were parcelled into small lots. The distinction between freehold and copyhold remained, and manorial rights were preserved – for what they were worth. Actually they might have been worth a great deal if the geology of the region had been different; if, for instance, coal or iron-ore had lain beneath it. Those who owned houses and closes ('ancient inclosures') invariably kept them or exchanged them for equivalent holdings. There would be little point in my giving here all the details of allocation – any one who wishes to know them will find the information readily available at the County Record Office, written in beautiful script in an enormous bound volume. Here is the information reduced to its very simplest form, exclusive of the two major allocations mentioned above:

50 acres approx.	–	Banks, Salmon, Trinity College.
25 ,, ,,	–	Elborne, Palmer, Whittingstall, Pearce, Tuck.
9 ,, ,,	–	Eversden, Faircloth, Hitch, Miller, Wilshire.
5 ,, ,,	–	Barron, St John's College.
2 ,, ,,	–	Brock, Brand, Rectory, Cooper, Tuck, Wright, Rayner, Scott.
1 acre or less	–	Clare College, Caldecoat, Kimpton, Rayner, Steward.

That list makes it immediately obvious that there was not, in this as in any other Enclosure Award – and at this point we can revert once more to our broader view – the least desire or attempt to secure an equitable distribution of the land in the sense of giving everybody a fair share. That was not the object of the exercise. It was, however, perfectly equitable in that, when the change had been made, everybody owned exactly as much, or as near exactly as possible, as he or she had owned before. The great difference, apart from the compactness of the holdings and the proximity of most of them, was that now nobody owned any land, or had the use of any land, in common with anybody else, or everybody else. There were no more 'commons' and no more 'common rights'. Even the one solitary allocation of $6\frac{1}{4}$ acres made in a manner of speaking to the whole village was not 'common', but placed under the authority of the Overseers and Churchwardens to administer as they saw fit. This land being situated in a remote corner of the parish, a good mile and a half from the nearest cottage, they saw fit to let it to the cottagers as allotments at an annual rent of five shillings, and no doubt felt aggrieved at the lack of gratitude on the part of the cottagers who had to walk three miles to fetch some potatoes for dinner.

There had always been, from earliest times, closes attached to the houses of which it could be said that they were private property, or 'several'. Now, every acre or group of acres in the parish was private property, to be enclosed by a hedge or fence, and somebody could say of it: 'This is mine, and mine alone – Keep Out!' From this phase of our history dates one of the most provocative features of the countryside in the eyes of the visitor from the town; notices saying 'Private Property', 'Trespassers will be Prosecuted', and so on. In some villages and towns (for towns, too, had their Enclosure Awards) some 'commons' were preserved. They were intended to serve as they always had served, for the pasturage of animals, and many of them still do serve in that capacity, but the instigators of the allocation can have had no idea of the immense value of their action for future generations.

Was this, then, what all that money had been expended to achieve (incidentally, the cost already quoted did not include the cost of fences, hedges and ditches; the landholder still had to face that) – the right to exclude all and sundry from private property? No, I do not suggest for one moment that that was the main objective. But it would be idle to deny that what facilitated the achievement more than anything else *was* the general desire, on the part of those who had property, that it should be private property. The main objective was that henceforth a farmer should be free to cultivate his own land in his own way, and it was hoped that he would at once put into practice the improved farming techniques, resulting in better stock-breeding, a fuller range of cropping, higher productivity and, of course, cheaper food for the towns.

That objective was in fact achieved, eventually, and to some extent; though when the plentiful supply of cheap food for the towns – and for the country as well – was at last achieved, it had nothing at all to do with Enclosure, and not much to do with English farming. The big landowners and their tenants, already pioneers in the new farming techniques, went ahead unhampered and raised the general level of productivity and their own prosperity. Those with viable holdings of about fifty acres followed suit to the best of their ability – in the end. They did not change their ways overnight. The older men went on farming in the old way because they were older men and knew no other way. Some of them even found difficulty in getting used to the privacy of their land, and anything up to fifty years elapsed before the hedges were planted. Many of the hedges in this locality were planted by the grandfather and father of a man still living in the village; they kept turkeys, fed them on hips and haws, and used the droppings to make the hedgerows. Many of the hedges which ought to have been made never were in fact made, and much of the southern part of the county has never lost the appearance which it had as open fields. Those hedges and fences which *were* promptly made were the ones alongside the roads and the few public footpaths which remained. The trees which grew up with them, mostly ash and elm, still survive in places, though nearing the end of their natural life.

As for the score or so of landholders in the parish who had less than ten acres allotted to them, they all within a short space of time abandoned any pretence of 'farming'. Some joined the already swollen ranks of the labourers; some went into other occupations. Twenty years after Enclosure there were only eleven farmers left in Foxton. Ten years later there were only eight, and that is how the situation remained until today. The pattern of social stratification was set for the rest of the century and beyond – fewer employers, more employed – and the relationship between them was likewise firmly established for a long time.

I promised in the previous chapter to say something about the effect of Enclosure upon the poorer people of the village, a matter which cannot be lightly cast aside, though all I intend to do is refute the main argument advanced by the opponents of Enclosure. This was a vehement assertion of the injustice of depriving poor people of their common rights which they had had for centuries. In principle, as a matter of social theory, I think most people would support the contention. But in actual practice it is found to be of purely academic interest. Moreover, the motives of those who claimed to support the idea were often suspect. They maintained that if the poor were able to keep a cow or a few sheep they would be less poor – 'less dependent upon the rates' was what they meant and what some of them actually said. Practical and theoretical champions of the poor alike overlooked one fact which could easily have been learned by visiting the villages and asking the poor or seeing for themselves. (The Rev. Gooch, in making his survey, never once quotes the views of labourers or cottagers.) They would have learned that the poor, even when they still possessed common rights, had given up keeping cows and sheep many years before, and that they had no intention of starting to do so again. The reasons for this were, I believe, in the main that the poor did not want the trouble and could not afford the expense of keeping animals. I only know of one instance where, by the terms of the Enclosure Award, the poor were actually forbidden to keep livestock; that was the prohibition on keeping geese on the Green at Barrington, which in any case was ignored by all and sundry.

The root of the matter lies in simple economics – never quite as simple as it seems. It ought, theoretically, to be possible to live on 'two acres and a cow', I suppose – at any rate the theory died hard, and still had some notable advocates in the early days of the present century. It *ought* to be possible, but it is not possible, and has not been so since somewhere around the year 1600. The reason is a highly complex combination of human attitudes, values, time and circumstances. Especially time and circumstances – and the odd twist which Fate gives to our affairs from time to time. Let us suppose, for instance, that those many recipients of small allocations of land had somehow managed to hang on to them and hand them on to their descendants, and that those descendants had been able to put them on to the market in the last few years – quite a lot of them would have made fortunes of anything up to £100,000. Unfortunately for those descendants, their ancestors did not foresee this; they sold their allocations as quickly as they could, for about £10 an acre, to those who already had larger allocations.

The overall effects of Enclosure on the rural population at large are difficult to assess. The proportion of poor people increased; the proportion of labourers to employers increased; the total numbers living in villages increased – and none of these things can be directly attributed to Enclosure, for exactly the same things were happening in the towns. It is not even certain to what extent the period of prosperity enjoyed by agriculture from about 1850 to about 1880 was due to Enclosure. '*Post hoc ergo propter hoc*' is convenient but unsound reasoning. So let us leave it, and pass on to a brief mention of a feature of working-class life which during the latter half of the nineteenth century attained a level of social significance very hard to realize today, namely the practice of girls going into 'service'. It had been current in the towns for a long time; now it spread to the country; girls from the country were in great demand in the towns, and the farmers, or their wives, considered at least one girl essential to the maintenance of their improving status. Even though these girls earned the derogatory title of 'skivvy' or 'slavey' in some quarters, there was frequently a sort of social prestige attached to the office, despite the low wages and long hours of work. Many a farmer's wife of the early twentieth century began her career in service in a farmhouse of the late nineteenth century, and many a working-class family was bettered, both socially and financially, as a result of this practice.

Once a writer has embarked on a discussion of human attitudes he soon finds his horizon widening in an alarming manner, for human activity in all ages and of all classes is so essentially a matter of attitude. I will deliberately set a limit to my horizon by omitting consideration of the attitude of the employed to the employer, that of all classes to religion and politics, that of the white-collar worker to the no-collar worker, that of all classes to morals, and a good many other attitudes. One, however, I cannot omit, for it is an attitude which possibly more than any other has earned for nineteenth-century progress the wholesale condemnation of the present generation. That is the attitude towards the land and its riches, the exploitation for commercial gain of natural resources in disregard of natural beauty and amenity. To see the results at their worst one must visit a district where coal-mining, quarrying for mineral ores, chemical manufacture or brick-making was carried on. In such areas the accepted justification was, until quite recent times: 'Where there's muck there's money.' No such ugly squalor, I am glad to say, was inflicted upon the truly agricultural areas of the countryside, though the present-day hunger for cement and gravel is going to leave scars on the landscape which will cause future generations to wince. That is, unless Time – which works more wonders than most other remedies – heals them as effectively as it has healed the major wound inflicted on the valley of the Cam in the latter half of the last century.

The episode – it cannot be rated more than an episode in the great mobile pattern of Progress – besides furnishing an example of ruthless exploitation, is also a good illustration of the interplay of commerce, economics, agriculture, and science, with a moral thrown in for good measure. In the 1860s farming was thriving but farm-wages were low, still only twelve shillings a week or less. Farmers could not afford higher wages because their costs were rising. The prices of their products were falling because cheap supplies of food were coming into the country from overseas, since mechanization and transportation improvements and low labour costs were enabling this to be done more cheaply, etc. The only way to offset falling prices was to increase productivity. The best way to do that was to increase fertility. This had been known and practised in a haphazard fashion for centuries. We have seen how 'cumpas' was prized in the sixteenth and seventeenth centuries; how 'donge' was counted among a man's possessions to be valued at his death; how even river-mud was a commodity of price. Now Science was coming into its own (the only good mark which I have so far been able to award to the nineteenth century), especially the geologists and the chemists. It had at last been discovered what it was in the soil that really made things grow, and, by an odd freak of circumstance, one of the substances most needed to restore fertility was right here on the spot, underneath the land which needed it so badly on the surface.

How the discovery of the 'coprolites' came to be made I do not know; I have a vague idea that it was accidental. The so-called coprolites were not in fact the fossilized droppings of prehistoric animals, though the search for them did bring to light the remains of some fantastic creatures now to be seen at the Sedgwick Museum and elsewhere. They were nodules of almost pure phosphate of calcium which had been deposited – no one knows just how or when – in a rich intermittent seam along the valleys of the Cam and Rhee and around the edges of the Fens, particularly concentrated in the stretch from Grantchester to Meldreth. Treatment with sulphuric acid produced a 'superphosphate' of immense value as artificial fertilizer, selling at £3 a ton. One acre of land would yield as much as three hundred tons, which made it an irresistible field for exploitation. Contractors paid £150 per acre for a three-year lease on the land, with the obligation to level it and replace the top-soil at the end of the operation, an obligation which was not always scrupulously fulfilled. In places the earth was dug out to a depth of twenty feet, though usually much less, sometimes as little as three feet. The seam of phosphates varied in thickness from a few inches to two feet. It is perhaps just as well that the width of the seam did not exceed half a mile in any one place, otherwise half the county might have been turned upside down.

This was a windfall for the relatively few landowners concerned. It was even more of a windfall for the labourers, very much more numerous. All the work had to be done with picks, shovels and barrows; fortunately for the men, Science had not yet invented the mechanical excavator. All the men were employed on a piece-work basis, at so much per cubic yard of earth and mineral removed. A good worker – that is a member of a gang all of whom were as strong as horses and had skins as tough as leather, and there were plenty of that breed – could earn £2 and more in a week. Even an ordinary worker, leaning on his shovel half the time – and there were some of *that* breed, then as now – could earn £1 a week. The local farmers, far from seeing prosperity coming their way, saw ruin staring them in the face, for they could not compete with wages such as that. But they were forced to compete, or see their harvest rotting in the fields, and agricultural wages 'leapt' to 24s a week. How edifying it would be to record that the thrifty workmen, overbrimming with gratitude for this unexpected bounty, put aside their earnings to provide security for themselves and their families when lean times should return once more. That is how middle-class Victorian morality would have had it. Alas for middle-class morality – and this is the moral of my tale. The truth is – I report this on good authority at first hand – that the extra money so earned was spent largely on beer. Of course there were some men who did save something, whose families did benefit as they ought to have done. But few can have benefited as much as the enterprising man who set up a beer-house on the site, open all day and every day. Exactly the same feature accompanied the construction of the railways a generation earlier. I am sure that the same thing happened when the canals were dug in the preceding century, and I cannot help wondering whether the construction of those massive Cambridgeshire Dykes, referred to in an earlier chapter, was achieved by the simple expedient of providing unlimited free beer.

A profitable subsidiary activity for the workmen, especially the men engaged on the removal of the topsoil, was the discovery and disposal of objects of archaeological and antiquarian interest. There has never been, before or since, an excavation in England on such a scale or in such rich soil, archaeologically speaking. Hundreds of brooches, coins, weapons, tools, vases, etc., were unearthed, many of which eventually found their way into museums, many more of which went astray. I know of one instance where £5 was paid by the Rev. Conybeare for a large amphora, and every penny of that £5 was spent on beer. The greatest loss to archaeology lay in the fact that there was little or no recording of the finds; in the circumstances it was not possible.

At the height of the boom, around 1884, something like 55,000 tons of fertilizer were extracted from the Cambridgeshire beds in one year. Then came the decline. The seam of phosphates was exhausted or too thin to be worth exploitation. Similar deposits were discovered in America, on the surface and therefore cheaper to exploit. Other forms of artificial and natural fertilizer became available. British farming was entering upon the greatest depression of all time, and farmers could not afford the high prices demanded for the substances which alone could increase their yields. By 1893 it was over. There was an attempt to revive the industry during the First World War, but it met with little success, simply because the mineral wealth had gone.

And the net result of it all? The beer-sellers and the fertilizer merchants were wealthy men. Several hundred thousand acres of English soil were enriched for a few years. The show-cases of several museums were filled. Several hundreds of acres of land along the river were lowered by several feet and were subject to annual flooding until the recent dredging and deepening of the river. The farmers reverted in the majority of cases to the old system of 'muck and muddle', if they had the muck. The farmworkers went back to the farms on a wage of 14s a week, and continued to be the lowest-paid manual workers for the next sixty years.

A comparison between the Cambridge of 1801 and 1901 would produce two pictures startling in their difference. Similar comparisons in respect of Birmingham, Leeds, Liverpool, Middlesbrough and a hundred other towns and cities would provide a contrast truly astounding. Take two pictures of Foxton, or any of a thousand other villages, with the same hundred-year interval, and the effect is again startling, but this time it is not the contrast but the similarity which surprises. The outward appearance of the village had changed little in the intervening century. Several of the old houses had fallen down or been demolished. Some of the farmbuildings had gone. Foxton House (1828) was the only new building with the slightest claim to 'character' or attractiveness. Foxton Hall, two outlying farms, a pub and three houses near the station, a new vicarage, a chapel, a school, and half a dozen houses rebuilt on old sites constituted the difference. Only the church would have presented the visitor, returning after long absence, with a pleasant surprise. Almost in ruins, it had undergone a restoration which amounted to an exterior reconstruction in 1876–81. The work cost over £3000, largely contributed by three wealthy people.

The villagers, too, of 1901 would have looked remarkably like those of a century earlier. Their occupations were almost exactly the same as they had been in 1851, and could not have differed much from those of 1801 – vicar, carrier, shopkeeper, blacksmith, bricklayer, carpenter, publican; all the rest farmers or farm-labourers. The only additions in the list of 1901 are schoolmistress, coal-dealer, threshing-machine proprietor and Parish Clerk. A stroll along the village street would still have meant getting plastered with mud in winter and covered with dust in summer, whilst only the most intrepid or ill-intentioned would have faced Station Lane on a dark night. One innovation in the rural scene was the bicycle, a wonderful invention for those on pleasure bent, but its utility was somewhat diminished by the general state of the roads. Moreover, though it was ideal for getting to the pub on time, it was not much use for the homeward journey; nor was it ideal for going to or from the allotments. The latter, incidentally, were now much more extensive, having been increased to about thirty-five acres, a good deal nearer to the houses than the original allotments had been. That feature, and the provision of four alms-houses in the churchyard, was the sum of the betterment of the poor in the nineteenth century. The much-vaunted Progress which had transformed the towns was not much in evidence in the villages at the beginning of this present century, or indeed for the first quarter of it.

Farming, despite the steady advance of mechanization, was in the doldrums. Britain's hungry millions were being fed from the other side of the Atlantic, or the other side of the globe. It was cheaper to rear a sheep in New Zealand and carry its frozen carcass twelve thousand miles than it was to rear it in Suffolk and carry it ten miles. The loaves of bread eaten in an English village were made from wheat grown in Canada. It was cheaper that way, therefore it was better. Better for the farmers of Canada and New Zealand, that is, many of whom had emigrated there from the villages of England. Better for the millers and merchants and shippers. Better for the millions of industrial workers in English towns. *Why* it was more economic to produce food several thousands of miles away from where it was consumed I do not understand. Nor, I imagine, did the English farmers. All they knew was that it was difficult, if not impossible, to make farming pay, and if they could have got out of farming they would have done so. Many were in fact forced out of it by bankruptcy, but for most of them farming was a way of life, and a way of life is something not to be abandoned lightly, even for people less traditionally conservative than farmers. So they stayed on, and stagnated. And the farm-workers stayed on, or most of them did, and they too stagnated. Stagnation – there is no other single word which can describe village-life in rural England in the century prior to 1914. Unless it were decay.

And there is no other feature which symbolizes that stagnation and decay more aptly than our Brook in the same period. Its doom was foreshadowed in the late eighteenth century when, all control and restriction having at last been abandoned, every farmer dug a pond on his holding for the watering of his animals. These ponds were all fed by the Brook, and some were capable of quenching the thirst of eight horses at a time. Some were still traceable a few years ago, but now all have disappeared, for tractors do not drink from ponds. The conditions of the Brook got steadily worse as a human drinking-water supply, and people no longer brewed their own beer. Wells dug in back-yards and gardens met the need for a time, but the water from such a source must have been unsavoury, little better than that drawn from the muddied Brook, or that used for washing, which was collected in butts from the roofs of the tiled or slated buildings. Between 1830 and 1870 bores were sunk and pumps installed at every farmhouse, a costly business which ensured that at last, after a lapse of several centuries, pure water was once again available in the village. Available to some people in the village, that is. There were still a lot of people who did not have access to a pump and who, rather than risk a snub by asking if they might use the pump at a neighbouring farm, drew their drinking-water from the Brook.

That state of affairs might have continued until well on into the present century – I know of several villages where it did – had not Canon Selwyn, then living in retirement at Foxton House, come to the rescue in 1873. He was 'well endowed with worldly means, and used them in a liberal and Christian spirit; was a great scholar, and well-loved'. His practical benevolence had a greater effect on the life of the village than any other single action since the digging of the Brook, the fate of which, incidentally, it sealed for ever. At his own expense he caused deep bores to be sunk into the lower greensand (reached at a depth of 254 feet, I am reliably informed), one on the Green, one at the end of Mortimer's Lane, and pumps to be installed for the use of all and sundry. They were so efficient,

The Village Pump in Mortimer's Lane

so dependable – they never dried up, whatever the season – and the water was of such excellent quality that they were used by everybody, even by those who had their own wells and pumps. For nearly ninety years the sight and sound of the villagers trundling their water-carts to one or other of the pumps was the most noticeable feature of the village. The pumps became social centres, where one could be sure of meeting certain people at regular times – just as the church-porch used to be, just as the pub still is. Parish-pump politics and parish-pump philosophy flourished – to say nothing of parish gossip.

The Brook, now utterly neglected, slowly filled with soil from the burrowing of rabbits in its upper reaches by the Connigree, and on its course through the village it became a convenient place for dumping rubbish. No 'sweet rill of water' any longer flowed along its bed; soon it had no water at all other than the surface-water which drained into it and lay in stagnant pools, becoming ever shallower as the weeds and nettles took control. Now and then, especially in a rainy spring, it gave as it were a dying convulsive kick in protest at the strangulation of a living, life-giving thing, and flooded parts of the village street with water which it would once have carried laughingly on its way to the river. It could no longer carry anything anywhere, for it was going nowhere. It must be all of seventy years since any water flowed along it from the chalk hills with their bounteous springs. For the past fifteen years it has been an underground drain, and many who tread the footpath above it today do not even suspect its existence. Thus easily are a thousand years of history forgotten.

When I was a boy I read and heard about the Agrarian Revolution as something which had happened in the past, in the eighteenth and nineteenth centuries, and learned that it was due to men with such improbable-sounding names as Coke of Holkham, Turnip Townshend and Jethro Tull. I saw with my own eyes the reaper-binder at work, drawn by a team of three splendid horses; delighted in its rhythmical clatter and chased the startled rabbits which scampered from the rapidly diminishing patch of standing corn. I saw, and later helped to build, the massive corn-stacks in the yards, and learned to appreciate them as much for their beauty, when trimmed and thatched, as for the wealth and work which they embodied. Threshing-days, with the humming and throbbing of the machine, the rustle and the bustle with no time for idle chatter, the dusty smell of chaff and straw, the never-ending stream of golden grain that poured into the gaping sacks, the wild excitement of the last half-hour when rats and mice were forced to make a despairing bid for freedom, made upon my young mind an impression which time has not yet effaced. On occasions all too rare I saw and marvelled at those gigantic steam ploughs which, I was told, turned over in one day as much earth as would have kept five plough-teams busy for a week, and broke up clay which no horse-drawn plough had ever touched.

I also saw the conditions in which the farm-workers lived, knew what they earned, saw their household belongings and families piled upon the farm waggons when they arrived or departed – 'flitted' as we used to say – at Lady Day. I sometimes joined them in the annual ritual of gleaning; I often wondered why such honest hard-working people should be so poor. The scythe was still an essential farming tool, used to open up a passage for the reaper-binder round the edges of a crop. I never mastered its use, despite many a clumsy attempt, but I did learn how to make bands of twisted straw to bind the corn in sheaves, woefully unkempt compared with those which the binder threw out, and knew that I was doing something which had been done like that, or better than that, for hundreds of years. More than once I saw in action a 'sail reaper', which cut the corn but could not bind it into sheaves. Frequently I saw, hanging from a rusty nail or a beam in the barn, a flail, a dibber, or a wicker basket used for sowing seed broadcast, and there was always somewhere at hand an oldish man who had actually used such things and was pleased and proud to demonstrate their use to ignorant boys. Though I sometimes had the feeling, much more vivid today in hindsight, that this 'revolution' in agriculture was taking a long time to happen, at any rate in north Lincoln-shire, it never once occurred to me that the real Agrarian Revolution, far from having happened, was in fact just about to begin. For vision is given to few ordinary men, still less to ordinary boys.

Even twenty years later, just after the Second World War when, for the sake of healthy exercise and also as a means of keeping alive boyhood memories, I took an active part in the harvesting operations, this time in my adopted county of Cambridgeshire, I had little sense of momentous change. Horses were as much in evidence as tractors, and started much more easily. Sheaves and shocks and stacks of corn were still essential elements in the pattern, as were gangs of men, some of whom, though not many and not often, could still be seen wielding a scythe, and all of whom wielded pitchforks.

Now that I am a man getting on in years, still capable of lifting one of those heavy sheaves of corn if one existed anywhere other than in my nostalgic imagination, I realize that the revolution *has* happened. I am not at all clear in my mind as to just when, how or why, and my vision of the future is certainly no clearer than it ever was. Being unable either to explain or foretell, I will be content to record, and once again I will revert to the technique of illustrating something of enormous size and importance by giving microscopic examples, leaving the reader to do the enlarging and multiplying. Only in that way can I guarantee the accuracy of the picture which I draw, and leave the reader free to see in it what he will. Here, then, are two pictures of events which occurred in the same place, eighty-five years apart in time.

Walter Stock's father described to him when he, Walter, was a boy – he is now well past eighty – how, going to Cambridge along the main road one day in August 1885, he saw a field of barley being mown by men with scythes. The field was on the right, between the road and the railway, half a mile from Foxton station. He stopped to count the mowers, for there was something about this otherwise commonplace scene that made it an event to be remembered. There were twenty-four mowers. The leading mower was at the far end of the field when the last man in line was just setting in at the near end. They finished the field that day, as was obviously intended, for the whole labour force of the two Gifford farms was concentrated on that one field. At the end of the day some thirty acres of barley lay in swathes. Later it would be turned, raked, heaped, carted, stacked in the barn, threshed, dressed and stored for eventual delivery to the maltster. I cannot say with certainty how many man-hours of labour all that involved, but I will risk an estimate of about five hundred and sixty, and leave my farmer friends to argue it out for themselves. Likewise as to the yield one cannot be sure, for it would depend so much on the season, as always; but if we assume that the season was good or average, then the yield can safely be put at about fifteen tons.

Now the other picture, eighty-five years later. In August 1970, in that same field, virtually on that same ground, Mr Derek Stevens and two men, using a combine-harvester and two tractors and trailers, harvested 30 acres of barley *in one day*. At the end of their day, which was not nearly so long as the day of those 24 mowers of 1885, the field contained only swathes of straw. In the barn were 60 *tons* of malting barley, ready for collection when it suited the maltster. The total of man-hours involved was not much over thirty. The relative costs of the two operations, however vital they may have been to the farmers concerned, are not relevant to my theme, and would not, I think, materially affect the significance of the contrast.

Incidentally, it was that same Mr Gifford who, a few years after the episode quoted above, introduced the first self-binding reaper ('binder' as it was to be called) to be seen in the village, and was heard to comment: 'A wonderful invention is the knotter!' What would he have said if he could have seen the successor to that wonderful invention? I regret that I cannot present an intermediate picture of say, forty years ago. The best that I can do is to make an estimate, based on my experiences as a boy, and hope that my farmer friends will not disagree too violently with it. I would say that, in 1930, the reaping, setting-up, carting, stacking and threshing of 30 acres of barley would have required about 330 man-hours, and that a fair crop would have yielded 30 tons. Derek Stevens assures me that 'the yield has doubled in my time'.

So much for one aspect of the revolution. Now for another, in which the social and agrarian changes are illustrated simultaneously. Much as I dislike statistics, a statistical table seems the shortest and clearest way of stating what I have to say. Most of the figures are factual, taken direct from official census returns, or actual counts; the rest are estimates resulting from the searching of several long memories, longer than mine. There may well be errors, but if there are they cannot be of such a magnitude as seriously to affect the overall significance of the picture. Nor, I think would a parallel picture relating to another village in any way alter that significance. Here is the picture:

Year	Population	Houses	Farmers	Farm-workers	Horses	Tractors	'Combines'
1901	426	72	8	45	35	0	0
1911	481	94	8	35	32	0	0
1921	480	98	8	34	32	1	0
1931	469	122	8	31	29	7	0
1941	490	123	7	30	25	18	0
1951	567	131	7	29	7	18	0
1961	680	181	7	20	1	19	5
1971	950	281	6	6	0	19	5
1974	1200	380	6	6	0	19	6

The figures relating to farming in 1971 have had to be adjusted in view of the fact that two of the biggest farms, totalling some six hundred acres, were being farmed from outside the village. Those for 1974 are all estimates, the accuracy of which depends on how things develop during the year; at the time of writing it does not appear that they will need much modification.

The story illustrated by those figures is, I think, clear enough; a story repeated in village after village, sometimes much more emphatically than here, sometimes much less so. There may be, in the remoter corners of England, villages where these changes have not occurred, but I do not know of one. The population, having doubled in thirty years, looks like trebling in a few more years. Planning authorities have set limits to the growth of villages, but the latest pronouncement from one of their spokesmen is that they 'may have to modify their plans or scrap them altogether'. The reasons for this increase are many and complex. Chief amongst them is that the population of the whole country has increased, and that the towns are already full, resulting in an overspill which is now filling the villages and creating new towns. By an ironic twist of circumstance the one-time supposed 'superiority' of the town has been reversed, and many people now prefer to live in the country. It is cheaper, healthier, quieter, cleaner and more pleasant. It is all that, but the real reason, of course, is that, thanks to the motor-car and the bus, one can now live in the country and work in the town, so having the best of both worlds. The one dominant factor in both the agrarian and social revolution – the *deus ex machina*, and surely never was metaphor more apt – is the internal combustion engine which powers cars and combines. Someone is sure to interrupt at this point with the remark that some of them use a compression-ignition engine. Let us say, then, that the Great God Oil is responsible for it all. What will happen when Oil is no longer on the list of deities – a spectre which even as I write is beginning to show rather more than the tip of an ear – I cannot imagine. But that is another story.

Just what proportion of the present population works or goes to school outside the village I can only guess; it varies from month to month in any case, but it cannot be less than about one third at any one time. The proportion of elderly people living in retirement is likewise vague but undoubtedly high and steadily increasing, for retirement to 'a cottage in the country' is one of the many indications of the wisdom which comes with advancing years. The proportion getting a living by agriculture calls for no guessing; it is less than three per cent now, including farmers and their families, and will undoubtedly diminish. A hundred years ago it was 90 per cent; fifty years ago it was about 45 per cent. This is one of the most startling changes of all, yet it has been so gradual and predictable that it has resulted in no crisis of unemployment, or none to speak of. Foxton and neighbouring villages have perhaps been exceptionally fortunate in this respect. The University Tutorial Press since 1908 and the Barrington cement-works since about 1914 are but two of the easily accessible providers of alternative employment. The drift away from the land had in fact begun long before mechanization made it compulsory. There was never anything catastrophic about it, such as has occurred elsewhere from, for instance, the closing of a factory or coal-mine. Even the horses were phased out gradually; they were not replaced by tractors overnight. Both were in use during the Second World War in about equal numbers. Some of the horses surviving into the fifties were on the retired list, and the last to go had only been kept for reasons of sentiment – a sentiment which most of us, I think, understand and share.

The full story of agricultural mechanization belongs to a history of farming proper, tracing the advent, development and impact of each machine. In this brief survey I will mention only three. The 'binder' made the first real impact on the number of man-hours needed for the harvest. The tractor did not, odd though it may seem, greatly affect the number of men employed full-time, but it did vastly increase the amount of work which the same number of men could do, and vastly shorten the time in which they could do it. That is to say that the tractor opened up the way to a shorter working week, and thereby earned more gratitude than any of its mechanical predecessors – though I have never heard any-one address a tractor with terms of endearment such as the horses evoked. The real break-through – the term reminds me that we have witnessed a linguistic revolution also – was made by the combined thresher-harvester, 'combine' as it was immediately and universally called, whose entry on the scene was delayed for about ten years by the war. It did more than revolutionize the labour situation. No other machine ever invented has done more, or indeed one hundredth as much, to alter the pattern and tempo of work, or the appearance of fields and farmyards throughout the land. Since its full-scale adoption there are no more fields full of shocks (stooks or stowks, according to the district), no more yards full of stacks (or ricks – I record these words on their way to obsolescence), no hedges or gates between fields, no more animated harvest scenes, no more 'harvest home', no more threshing-days. The partridges are rapidly disappearing from the stubbles; the last one may well have to seek refuge in that mythical pear-tree, for there are virtually no stubbles left. The traditional Harvest Festival is still bravely kept up in many village churches, and the fruits of the earth are mostly displayed in cans, packages and plastic bags. Oh, for the sight of a sheaf of golden corn! What symbolism *is* there in a can of beans?

The non-farming element of the village – that is to say nearly all of it – would hardly know that there was a harvest, were it not for the occasional hold-up of their cars as the mechanical monster trundles down the street, or the dense clouds of smoke rising from the burning straw like some gigantic holocaust. Even so, I wonder how many of those fuming motor-ists realize what is going on. The same generation which thinks that water always came from a tap probably thinks that bread originates in the factory where it is made and wrapped, or that beer is a by-product of industry. They may be right. But those sixteen hundred acres are still there, more cultivated than ever before in their long history. There is more farming done in the parish than ever there was; twice as much barley being grown; three times as much wheat; twenty times as much sugar-beet; four times as much pork and bacon being produced as forty or fifty years ago. Those figures are of necessity somewhat figurative, for the ratio varies from year to year. And all this is being done by a mere handful of men and a few machines. True, there is almost no beef, no milk, no butter, no cheese and no wool being produced, but those commodities are produced elsewhere in similarly increased proportions. The Agrarian Revolution really *has* taken place.

What about the village? What about the common stream of humanity whose course we have followed through the ages? Has it, like the common Brook, been enveloped in a straitjacket of plastic and concrete, filled in and forgotten? Is there still a village community conscious of its identity? Or is the village just another place like any other place?

Well, Progress has brought us electricity with all its attendant appliances, gas from the North Sea, mains water-supply, main drainage, good roads with pavements and well lighted, an adequate bus service, television for all who want it, newspapers at breakfast-time, telephones for many and in reach of all, plastic bags for weekly disposal of garbage, etc. So that, as regards the amenities considered essential to life in a civilized locality, life in the village *is* like life anywhere else. It has an added advantage, that the streets are not choked with traffic and there is not noise all day and all night. It really is quiet. I rate this an advantage of the first order, as do many others. Some of my younger friends however take the opposite view and complain that it is 'too quiet', though they are not necessarily thinking of noise. They complain that there is 'no life' in the village; there is 'nothing to do'; 'nothing ever happens'. Their complaint is not, I believe, a condemnation of the village so much as a reflection of the malaise of modern society.

Life is too easy in this day and age, especially for the young. They do not have to go to work, as would have been the case a mere sixty years ago; indeed they are forbidden by law to work at an age when many of them would like to. They do have to go to school, and most of them enjoy it, but it involves the minimum of effort on their part. They live in the country but they are not *of* the country. The countryside is there all around them, but it has not for them the lure which it had for me when I was a boy. It is perhaps too tamed, too civilized or too enveloped in barbed wire to invite exploration. A favoured few do explore it on the backs of their ponies, but the rest, with rare exceptions, seem never to have learned to use their legs except to kick a football or straddle their mopeds. This is one of the outstanding social problems of the day, one to which I do not know the answer. It does solve itself, of course, for each succeeding generation, by the simple process of growing up. Many grown-ups, it is true, also complain of boredom, but for my part I do not take them seriously. So long as there are books to be read, gardens to be tended, families to be looked after, cars to be tinkered with, houses to be decorated, neighbours to visit – to say nothing of the television, that great filler-in of wasted time – surely having 'nothing to do' is a reflection on the individual rather than on life. As a collection of individuals, the village population never before had such an easy comfortable life.

And as a community? Well, the opportunities are there. There is no lack of organizations whose professed objective is the encouragement of 'togetherness'. The church may no longer be the focal point of village life that it was throughout the Middle Ages and up to the Reformation, but it is still there and still exerting an influence far beyond the limits of the relatively small circle of regular worshippers. The chapel, a relative new-comer to the scene, from being a rival and antagonist of the church has changed to a collaborator, and the actual union of the two may not be far distant. The village hall has proved itself a worthy successor in the line of descent through manorial hall, Town House and Parish Room, playing a role greater and wider than that of its predecessors, serving as it does the Women's Institute, Parish Council, Gardens Association, Youth Club and various other organizations from time to time. There is still there-fore a village-centre, a magnetic core, and it is where it ought to be, where it always was, at the centre.

Close at hand is the recreation-ground, in the very spot where once the air resounded with the twang of bowstrings and the thud of arrows hitting their target, and later the clunk of wood on wood as the bowlers indulged in their illicit pastime. For almost three centuries nothing more exciting than the cawing of rooks or the lowing of cows disturbed the peace of this central part of the village – save on Sundays, of course, when the church-bells sent out their summons as they do yet. Now once a week the air vibrates with the leathery thud of boot on ball and anguished shouts pro-claim that village loyalty is not dead. No longer do the young men of Foxton seek occasion to assert their superiority by 'bashing one of the Barrington chaps' – for which activity old Joe Loker's father, so Joe told me, was sent to gaol some eighty-five years ago. That, as far as I know, was the last episode of the inter-village feud which had been waged inter-mittently for nigh on two thousand years. Its modern counterpart is fought out on the football-field, and 'fought' is not always the meta-phorical term which it ought to be.

Yes, the opportunities for 'getting together' are there, and a lot of people do get together for an hour or two from time to time to meet their fellow villagers and share an activity or interest. There is undoubtedly a 'social spirit' alive in the village, though perhaps less alive than it was in the days when everybody knew everybody else, and when one of the chief social pleasures lay in knowing and discussing everybody else's business, not necessarily in an uncharitable spirit. With the newcomers now far outnumbering the 'natives', this traditional feature of village life has gone, perhaps for ever, and it is only natural that the natives should feel a certain resentment at being deprived of what had seemed an established right. To offset this, however, there is the recognition that it is the newcomers who as often as not supply the driving-force in the village organizations. Not everybody is able, not everybody wants to take part in the activities of all or any of these organizations. Indeed the majority of people today seem just to want freedom to live their own lives in their own way, freedom to opt out if they choose to do so, freedom to join in if they feel like it, and the village is the ideal place for that. There is no longer any compulsion or restriction. True, our lives are subjected to more compulsions and restrictions than ever before – taxation, insurance, rates, regulations, stamps, forms, quotas, permits, etc., etc. – but they are all at national or regional level. I cannot think of one at village level.

For that reason alone I have doubts about the existence of a community spirit. It is an elusive and complicated thing. The more one thinks about it, the more elusive and complicated it seems, though I am fairly clear in my mind on two points: firstly that a community spirit cannot exist without real community of interest; secondly that it cannot manifest itself except under compulsion. There was, I am sure, a community spirit in the sixth century, or whenever it was, when the village was newly and permanently established by the digging of the Town Brook; when any potential breakaway minority group would be rapidly converted to the majority view by sheer necessity and the prospect of starvation or slavery. There must have been a community spirit when the threat of Mercian cattle-raiders or Danish pillagers rendered the life of all precarious and the death of stray individuals certain. There was a community spirit in the thirteenth century, imposed by the manorial system which kept, or tried fairly successfully to keep, Foxtonians in Foxton and all outsiders out. It was a community akin to a prison. There was a community spirit in the later sixteenth century, when everyone in the village was striving to better himself and his family by his own efforts, and thereby bettered the whole village; but again it was subject to restrictions and prohibitions at village level which forced the individual to conform to a pattern. There was a community spirit right through the eighteenth and nineteenth centuries, with the compulsive element steadily diminishing but the common interest as strong as ever, for every person in the village looked to the land for his livelihood; the same situation still holds in many a Welsh mining village.

One of the risks inherent in this discussion is that of confusing 'community' with 'equality'. There has never, so far as I can judge, been anything like equality of wealth, status or condition in the community. The nearest approach to it was probably in the earliest phase of all, and each succeeding phase has seen an ever-widening gap. Another risk is the confusion of community with harmony. When I recently asked one of the older inhabitants whether he considered that a community spirit still existed in the village he replied without hesitation: 'No I don't. People aren't as friendly as they used to be. I remember the time when everybody went for a stroll on a Sunday afternoon and inspected the gardens and allotments and crops, and talked with everybody about how things were doing.' When I pressed him more closely, however, he admitted that there were frequent quarrels, backbitings and jealousies even in those happy days. Of course there were. And of course there always will be. If the day ever comes when nobody has anybody to quarrel with, nothing to quarrel about or complain about, people will be as miserable as sin.

Though I am not really sure about this community spirit, I suspect that it may well be there all the time, lying dormant like an instinctive memory of the past, a potential force that could emerge if circumstances favoured or compelled its emergence. If, for instance, 'they' planned to drive a motorway through the middle of the village, 'we' should all rise up in arms and confront the plan with concerted opposition. And in the foremost ranks of militant villagers would be found the newcomers to the village. No one uses the term 'outsiders' now – I have not heard it for more than twenty years – and all would agree that it is the flood of newcomers that has hastened and completed the revival of the village, just as a flood of newcomers revitalized and rebuilt it four hundred years ago. For revival it certainly is. The young people who talk of the village as being 'dead' are talking utter nonsense, as in their hearts they must surely know.

No, the village is not dead. There is more life in it now than there ever was. But, paradoxically, 'village life' is dead. Gone for ever. It did not die suddenly. These things never do happen suddenly. It began to decline about a hundred years ago, when many girls left home to go into service in towns many miles away, and men likewise left home in increasing numbers in search of work, and home was where work was. I have been told that the advent of the Tutorial Press in 1908 upset the established order of things by introducing an industrial element into the village, though I would have thought that in the main that was advantageous. There are still a number of people alive today who can remember what 'village life' meant in the early years of the present century. It meant knowing and being known by everybody else in the village. It meant finding your entertainment, such as it was, in the village or within walking distance of it. One of my inform-ants sometimes went to London and back in a day on his bicycle, but he was a rather exceptional young man. To go anywhere at all was for most country people a treat; for many children the one and only treat was the annual Sunday School outing. I can remember one such outing which involved a three-mile ride on a horse-drawn dray, precariously balanced on a wooden form, one hand clutching the side of the dray, the other clutching warm pennies which were intended to be exchanged for sticks of rock if we ever got to the seaside – which we did, via the nearest railway station.

It meant housewives tied to the home all day and every day, their monotony relieved by a regular succession of 'packmen', 'tally men', itinerant traders calling at the kitchen door with groceries, hats, crockery, brushes, underwear, ribbons, etc. Nobody bought or sold fruit, flowers, vegetables, plants – one exchanged, bartered, begged or gave them away. The same with pig 'fry'. The same with sittings of eggs. It meant speaking the local dialect, and distrusting or despising anyone who did not – except the parson and the schoolmaster. It meant 'going to the toilet' – a phrase we never used – in a dark and draughty privy at the bottom of the garden or at the back of the house. It meant going to bed early to economize in lamp-oil and coal; washing in cold water from pump or well; eating cold fat bacon for breakfast or going without. It meant finding your way across fields and along deserted lanes in the dark, and enjoying it, especially if you were courting. All that, and very much more, is what 'village life' used to mean.

Then came the First World War. It took for a time all the able-bodied men out of the village and killed fifteen of them, but it was not so much their loss that affected village life as what the experiences of the war did to those who came back. New ideas, new attitudes, new horizons, new trades and occupations were revealed to them. The long-established order of society was no longer taken for granted. Jack was as good as his master, or better. The motor-bike had been invented. Young men could go to work or go courting into the next county if that was where their fancy took them. Village halls and Women's Institutes halted the process of disintegration for a time, but electricity and the motor-car were steadily operating to make 'village life' and 'town life' indistinguishable. World War Two actually brought about a revival of village life for a period of some seven years. There was less gadding about among those who stayed in the village, and they once again had to seek such entertainment as there was in their own community or their own homes. The village saw itself as a unit, albeit only a tiny unit in the great national entity, with its own Home Guard, its own contingent of W.V.S., its own 'Dig for Victory' campaign, to say nothing of its own share of danger in the form of a stick of German bombs which straddled the village, luckily without serious damage. Everybody in the village did his or her bit for victory, everybody shared the hardships, the rationing, the disappointments, the elation – and everybody in a strange way enjoyed it, despite the sad loss of six more young men.

Then, gradually at first but with ever-increasing momentum, came the social avalanche which swept away the last traces of 'village life' and transformed life for everybody, everywhere. For the first time in this book I am able to give credit to politicians and planners, and I do it unreservedly – for the 1944 Education Act and subsequent legislation which has brought about a huge expansion in secondary and higher education; for the Social Security plan which did more to abolish poverty in ten years than Poor Laws had done in four hundred years; for Town and Country Planning, Housing Authorities, Health Services, etc. All this, in conjunction with paid holidays, higher wages, cheaper travel, cars by the million, air-travel, television and a host of electrical gadgets in the home, this is what I mean by the avalanche that swept away 'village life'. There is no point whatever in talking any longer about 'village life' and 'town life'. It is just life. And life – though I say it with just a slight shade of misgiving as regards those cars by the million – is better.

Are people better? Others may tackle that question if they will. I shall content myself with a brief statistical survey of village people today, leaving aside all consideration of their qualities, good or bad. I have already shown that there is only a small part of the old village left, and that it constitutes only a small fraction of the modern village. What about the village people? What do we mean by 'village people'? A hundred years ago the answer would have been: people who were born in the village, lived all their lives there, and died there. In many cases it would have meant people who lived in the same house as their father, grandfather and great-grandfather had lived in. The main emphasis was on the 'born'; if you were born in the village you belonged to the village. It is a survival of the medieval attitude, and we ought not to apply it to modern considerations. But we will, for want of a better criterion.

Today, there is just *one* person, and she an elderly spinster, who lives in the house where three generations of her forebears lived. There is *one* family living in the village whose ancestry in the village goes back four generations. There are *six* people – I have counted only those who are approaching middle age or who are well past it – living in the houses in which they were born. But when we come to consider the number of village people who were born here and are still living here, in a different house – still middle-aged or over – we get a mild surprise. They number not less than sixty-four, and I may have missed one or two in counting. That is roughly what the number would have been if a similar count had been made a hundred years ago; hence the surprise. 'Village people', contrary to expectation perhaps, have not disappeared. When, however, we consider them as a percentage of the people in the village – adding wives and children for this purpose – we find that 'village people' amount to less than 25 per cent of the village population. That, and the fact that one third of my starting total of sixty-four are over seventy years old, amply explains, I think, the increasing take-over of village affairs by the newcomers. The process, I imagine, will go on.

Finally – and here I dare to speak of quality – if we have any doubts about the future, or about the many changes which we have seen in our lives, we have only to look in at the school playground any mid-morning, or see the children as they walk homeward in little groups. These children are healthier, better fed, better clothed, better educated, better behaved, prettier and – did they but know it – happier than any generation of children that ever before walked the village street. For us of the older generation the past is past, and we do not regret it. For them – the future.

Envoi

I chatter, chatter, as I flow
To join the brimming river,
For men may come and men may go,
But I go on for ever.

(The Brook – Alfred Lord Tennyson)

The poet was wrong, as poets sometimes are. The brooks and streams do not go on for ever. They, like every other feature of the environment, are subject to the changes wrought by time and circumstance, and particularly to the modifications wrought by Man. Men may come and men may go. Yes, but Man goes on for ever. The common stream of humanity flows on. Its course is seldom straight for very long. Its water is not always bright and pure, for many a 'noysome sinke' and much 'puggell water' drains into it from time to time; the casting and the scouring is a tiresome business too often and too long neglected, and many a stagnant weed-choked pool retards its flow. But, for all that, it flows.

To what brimming river – or to what bright sea – who knows?

Glossary

Note on Currency

Bibliography

Glossary

ACOLYTE: lowest of the four orders of priesthood; a boy who had taken the 'first tonsure', with a view to becoming sub-deacon, then deacon, then priest.

ALMERYE: cupboard.

AMPHORA: large earthenware vessel, very thick and heavy, used for storage and carriage of oil and wine.

ANDIRONS: pair of iron bars with hooked brackets for supporting roasting spit.

ARRETINE: name given to a type of fine pottery made at Arrezzo in Italy in first centuries BC and AD; of pinkish clay coated with dark red slip; made in a mould and decorated in low relief.

AUNGELL: angel, gold coin worth about 10s; bore the image of St Michael.

BAYLE: a ladle for beer.

BENCHBORDE: a plank placed on two trestles to make a seat.

BERE: pillow-bere, a pillow-case.

BORDAR: Villager; differing from the villein in that the latter held little land, the bordar still less. It would be convenient if one could say that the villein farmed 30 acres and the bordar 15, or 18 acres and 9 acres respectively, but it just does not work out like that. At a later date it does become clear that 9, 18 and 36 acres were standard holdings.

BROCKFIELD: the field which was ploughed in the spring, having been left fallow all the previous year.

BUHRSILVER: medieval tax on whole village for upkeep of manorial hall or 'bury'.

BUSHEL: measure of volume of corn; 8 gallons; $\frac{1}{4}$ of a coomb.

BUTTERY: room where ale was brewed and kept.

CAPON: castrated cockerel intended for eating.

CAWDERN: cauldron, large vessel for heating water, same as 'copper'.

CHAFER: dish with a lid, for keeping food hot.

CHALDRON: measure of volume of coal; equal to 52 cwt.

CHARGER: large flat dish for serving meat.

CLUNCH: chalk, usually soft chalk for making floors.

COBIRONS: pair of iron supports for roasting-spit, simpler than andirons.

COLEFAYER DAY: either (a) a certain day on which coal-fires started for the winter, probably Michaelmas, or (b) 'coal-fair', at which coal was bought from itinerant merchants, in which case it would be in August.

COMBE: corn measure; four bushels; one sack. The weight of a coomb or sack varied according to variety of corn; oats 12 stone; barley 16 stone; wheat 18 stone; beans, peas, tares 19 stone.

COPPER: large cauldron.

COUTTOLYNE: covering for a bed.

COVERLEAD: coverlet, cover for a bed. French 'couvre-lit'.

CUMPAS: compost, manure.

CURTAIN: hanging round a bed; not used for windows until eighteenth century.

DAUBING: mixture of clay or clunch, cow-hair and lime to make walls.

DEMESNE: that part of manor not held by tenants, but kept for use and profit of the lord of the manor; later farmed out to one man.

DIAP: linen with diamond pattern.

DIGHTE: prepared, 'dressed'; i.e. husks, chaff and rubbish removed.

DISTRAINT: seizure of goods or animals for debt or other reason.

DOUBLET: sort of sleeveless jacket.

DOWNECKE: fine down from neck and breast of goose.

DRYPING PAN: placed beneath roasting meat on spit, to catch the fat.

ESSOINED: excused absence from manor court, being represented by another.

EXECUTOR: person charged with duty of carrying out the terms of a will.

FARM: block letting for fixed payment for a number of years; applied not only to land, but to tithes, rents, fines, etc. First used in connection with the manorial demesne let to a 'farmer'.

FEALTY: loyalty: the tenant on taking a holding had to swear an oath of fealty, i.e. promise to conform to the customary practice of services and payments; continued in use long after the feudal system dissolved.

FEE: the area of jurisdiction of a lord of a manor.

FIFTEENTH: occasional tax levied by sovereign for special purpose, e.g. waging war, or royal marriage; one fifteenth of annual income.

FINE: sum of money payable on admission to a holding; so called because it was 'final', only had to be paid once by that person.

FLAXEN: made of flax; linen.

FLITCH: one side of a pig, when killed, minus legs, thighs and ribs; i.e. bacon.

FLOCK BED: bed stuffed with wool, bits of cloth, etc.

FURNITURE: the various items needed to go with a bed; mattress, bolster, pillows, sheets, blankets, coverlet.

FUSTIAN: thick coarse woollen cloth dyed dark.

GARNER: small barn for storing corn.

GARNESS: set of pewter dishes, plates, bowls, etc.

GELDING: castrated horse.

GERSUMA: fee paid on inheritance of freehold land by daughter.

GIRDLE: chain worn round the waist, knotted or buckled, with the ends left hanging almost to the ground; often very elaborate and decorated; mostly with links of precious metal.

GRIDIRON: grid placed on or near the fire, suspended on andirons or supported on legs, for roasting and toasting.

HECKFERTH: heifer; cow before it has first calf.

HERIOT: payment made when a holding was inherited on death of previous holder; usually the best animal, later such things as a feather bed, a silver cup, etc.; usually bought back by the inheritor, for cash.

HEYWARD: one of the constables with special responsibility for boundaries and encroachment. (Nothing to do with hay.)

HIDE: measure of land; varied according to region; here 120 acres. Used for purposes of taxation only.

HOGGE: pig.

HOGGET: one-year-old sheep.

HOGGSHEAD: medium-sized barrel holding 54 gallons of ale.

HOLDING: a tenant did not own land, he 'held' it.

HOMAGE: the jury at the manor court, usually twelve tenants who were sworn.

HOSE (HUSSEN): long stockings, thigh length, usually of wool, worn by men.

HUE AND CRY: when it was 'raised' by the constable or injured party, it was the duty of everyone to help catch the offender. The actual cry was probably 'Hue! Hue!' – hence modern 'hoot' and 'hooray!'

HUTCH: a large wooden box with a lid, for storing clothes, or anything.

IMPRIMIS: firstly, in the first place. Latin.

JOINED: made by a 'joiner'; used of a table, stool or bedstead with legs joined to the top, not trestles.

KERCHER: square scarf worn over the head, with or without a hat. French 'couvre-chef'. Survives in modern 'handkerchief'.

KETTLE: deep vessel for cooking food.

KING'S EVIL: scrofula; glandular swellings; until about 1700, thought to be cured by the touch of the monarch.

KIRTELL: short gown or petticoat.

KYMNELL: wooden trough for kneading dough before baking.

LATTEN: yellow metal like brass; mostly copper mixed with zinc. French 'laiton'.

LAVER: bowl for washing.

LIENTALL: number of masses said or sung for the soul of the departed; I think it is fifty.

LIVERY CUBORD: cupboard for keeping clothes.

LUMBER: odds and ends; discarded things.

LYNTELLES: lentils; like peas, only smaller and yellow.

MASLIN: mixed corn, usually wheat and rye.

MESSUAGE: a house with land attached.

MORTUARY: payment to the priest on death; usually the second-best animal; often not made because there was no second animal.

NOBLE: gold coin worth 6s 8d.

NUNCUPATIVE: used of a will not written but spoken.

OBIT: service of remembrance for one dead, usually kept annually, sometimes monthly. Also called a 'yeremind'.

OFFAL: bran or mixed corn, undressed.

PAINTED CLOTHS: sheets of canvas with pictures painted on them; hung on walls as decoration.

PECK: a $\frac{1}{4}$ of a bushel; 2 gallons.

PINNER: the constable with special duty of impounding stray animals.

PIPE: large barrel holding 126 gallons of wine or ale.

PORINGER: porridge-bowl.

POSNET: small iron pot for use inside larger vessel, e.g. for cooking porridge.

POT-HOOKS: hooks for suspending pots over the fire, variable in length.

POTYNGER: (1) porringer, porridge-bowl.
         (2) pot-hanger.

POUND: small fenced enclosure for keeping animals found straying.

PRESS CUBORD: cupboard with shelves, for clothes generally.

QUARTER: two coombs; two sacks; eight bushels; five quarters made a 'load', i.e. a ton, more or less.

QUERN: two circular stones, one rotated on top of the other, for grinding corn.

REEKE: rick, stack of corn in sheaves.

RELIEF: payment by freeholder on inheritance of land; usually one year's rent; corresponded to heriot paid by copyholder.

ROOD: (1) one quarter of an acre.
      (2) cross of Christ, or crucifix.

ROOD-LOFT: gallery on top of rood-screen, accessible by stairs at one side.

ROOD-SCREEN: screen of open woodwork or stone dividing chancel from nave in a church; the rood was fixed on top of it.

SALLE: salt-container, often of silver.

SCUMER: skimmer, for removing cream from the top of milk in a shallow pan.

SEISIN: possession; the right to hold.

SESTERNE: cistern, pond.

SEVERAL: private, not held in common; applied especially to pasture.

SHOTT: (1) part of an open field, usually about 30 acres, with all strips or lands going the same way, and a headland at each end.
       (2) a young pig.

SKELLET: small iron cooking-pot with handle and legs, placed at front of hearth.

SOLLER: originally 'solar', a room where a lady could be alone; later simply an upstairs room.

SPIT: iron contraption to hold meat, game, poultry, etc., in front of fire for roasting; turned by hand, or by a dog in a wheel-cage, or mechanically.

SPLENTING: thin strips of wood nailed across upright beams to form base on which plaster or daubing could be spread.

STOCK: (1) bees in a hive or skepp.
       (2) animal kept for breeding.

STRYNER: strainer; flat ladle with fine holes in it, for removing scum from beer.

TALLAGE: tax levied annually by manor court on all the tenants, for no specific reason, except that they were there.

TAPER: rush or string dipped in wax, to give light in houses, and used in churches as part of ritual.

TENEMENT: a holding, consisting of house and land.

TILTH: land which had been ploughed in previous autumn and was ready for sowing in early spring.

TITHE: one tenth of all produce payable to the Church. The great tithes of corn, wool and hay were due to the Rector. The small tithes of fruit, eggs, honey, saffron, etc., were due to the vicar.

TITHING: originally a group of ten men all mutually responsible for the good behaviour of the group.

TITHINGMAN: a member of the group. A boy had to join the tithing at the age of twelve. Obsolete by sixteenth century, but pretence still kept up.

TORCHES: skeins of rope dipped in pitch, etc., carried at funerals as part of ritual. The dead person made provision in his will for the torches at his own funeral.

TOWE: hemp fibre, much coarser than flax; used for canvas and rope, also sheets.

TUMBRELL: two-wheeled cart, which could be tipped backwards to empty load.

VALLENCE: curtain round a bed, completely enclosing the bed; later, simply a curtain round the bottom of the bed.

VILL: village or town.

VILLEIN: Villager, see Bordar.
VIRGINTALL: twenty masses said or sung for the soul of a dead person.

WAINSCOTT: panelled oak boards lining the walls of a room, usually very decorated.
WARMING-PAN: pan of brass or copper, with lid and long handle, for inserting between the sheets to warm a bed. (It was removed when the occupant got in.)
WETHER: one–year–old castrated ram sheep.

YEOMAN: name given to farmer in fifteenth, sixteenth and seventeenth centuries. Origin not known.
YIELDING TUB: wooden trough for brewing beer. Lead was also used.

Note on Currency

I have used the old style of £ – s – d – pounds, shillings and pence – throughout the book for reasons which, I hope, are obvious. To have converted shillings and pence to New Pence would have been not only difficult but silly. However, it occurs to me that there may be, amongst future readers, some who have never heard of 'shillings' and 'pence'. For their benefit, then, there were twelve pence to the shilling, and twenty shillings to the pound. It also occurs to me that some readers may be curious to know what a shilling or a penny was worth at a given time, in terms of modern currency. That is a very difficult question indeed, and any answer I give now may be hopelessly wrong in, say, ten years from now. As a very rough guide, I would say that the 'penny' of the mid-thirteenth century was about equivalent in purchasing power to the pound of today, i.e. multiply by about 200; a penny of the mid sixteenth century was equivalent to the modern 40p, i.e. multiply by about 100; and the penny of the mid nineteenth century was equivalent to 20p, i.e. multiply by about 50. But it all depends what service or commodity you are considering – and it depends on a good many other things besides.

Bibliography

The full list of works which might usefully be consulted on a subject such as this is almost endless. Here I have listed only those which I have specifically used, though to a widely varied extent.

(A) GENERAL

Barley, M. W., *The English Farmhouse and Cottage* (Routledge & Kegan Paul, 1961).

Coulton, G. G., *Medieval Village, Manor and Monastery* (Harper & Row, 1925, reissued 1960).

Elton, G. R., *England under the Tudors* (Methuen, 1955).

Ernle, Lord, *English Farming Past and Present* (Heinemann, reissued 1961).

Frere, S. S., *Britannia* (Routledge & Kegan Paul, 1967).

Maitland, F. W., *Domesday Book and Beyond* (1897, reissued Fontana, 1960).

Tate, W. E., *The Parish Chest* (Cambridge, 1946).

West, J., *Village Records* (Macmillan, 1962).

(B) LOCAL

Cambridge Antiquarian Society Proceedings – in particular 1852, 1886, 1906, 1908, 1917, 1922 and 1935.

Cambridge Chronicle for 5 April 1788, 5 March 1802 and 2 July 1881.

Conybeare, E., *History of Cambridgeshire*, 1897.

Farrer, W., *Feudal Cambridgeshire* (Cambridge, 1920).

Fox, C., *Archaeology of the Cambridge Region* (Cambridge, 1948, out of print).

Gooch, W., *General View of the Agriculture of Cambs.*, 1811.

Hill, A. G., *Architectural and Historical Notices of the Churches of Cambs.*, 1880.

Lysons, D. and S., *Magna Britannia – Cambridgeshire*, 1808.

Palmer, W. M., *Cambs. in the XVIth Century*, 1935.
  John Layer, Historian of Shepreth, 1930.
  Monumental Inscriptions & Coats of Arms from Cambs., 1932.
Reaney, P. H., *Place-Names of Cambridgeshire* (Cambridge, 1943).
Victoria County History of Cambridgeshire.

(C) MANUSCRIPTS PRINTED AND PUBLISHED
In the County Record Office, County Library and University Library.
'Domesday Survey'.
'Inquisitio Comitatus Cantabrigiensis'.
'Rotuli Hundredorum'.
'Vetus Liber Archidiaconi Eliensis'.

(D) MANUSCRIPT SOURCES
In the County Record Office:
  Manor court rolls re Foxton Bury, Wimbish & Chatteris, 1492–1820.
  Terriers and Deeds re same.
  Rolls and Deeds re Docwra's and Tyrrell's manors.
  Enclosure Award and Map, 1830.
  Land Tax Returns.
  Bendysh Papers.
  Microfilms of Cole, Add. MSS 5803, 5819 and 5823.
In the University Library:
  Archdeacon's Visitation Records.
  Bishops' Registers.
  Overseers' and Churchwardens' Accounts, 1771–1795 (Add. MS 3297).
In the British Museum:
  Chatteris Cartulary (Cotton Jul. A.I.VI).
In the keeping of Trinity College, Cambridge:
  Manor court rolls re Foxton, Barrington and Shepreth, 1292–1327.
  Terriers re Michaelhouse lands in Foxton and elsewhere.
In the Principal Probate Registry:
  Welbore wills.

Index

Abbess of Chatteris 55, 57, 58, 64, 68, 74, 99, 113
acolytes 77
Alan, Count 58
Alanson 94, 116, 120
ale 60, 71, 83, 207
ale-houses 101, 104, 105, 172, 175
ale-tasters 71, 104, 159
Alfred, King 51
Alfwen 55, 60
allotments 211, 218
Amys 102, 117, 129
Andrews 66
Anglesey 34, 35
appropriation 85
archdeacon 154
Archford 81, 82
Arretine bowl 24
Arrington 195
Asgar 56, 58
Attleborough 64
Aunger 124, 135
Ayler 136
Ayre 126, 136

Babraham 160, 206
bailiff 60, 67, 69, 109
Balsham 49
balks 78, 133, 158, 163, 184
Bancs 64, 66, 70
Barley 16, 55, 63, 70, 77, 86
Barret 102, 121
Barrington 41, 42, 45, 50, 52, 55, 56, 57, 58, 63, 69, 72, 74, 81, 103, 104, 105, 111, 153, 213
Barron 182, 197, 210
Barton 64
Bateson 182, 199
Beaumont 122, 126, 144, 188, 198
Bendysh 104, 160, 161, 209

bird-scaring 194
Birkenhead 114
Black Boy 19, 106, 175, 194
Blyton 96, 97
Boston 160
Boudicca 33, 34, 35
Bournbridge 196
Bran Ditch 48, 49
Brestbone 122, 125, 154
brewing 147, 175
bridges 193
Brightwell 126, 129
Burwell 63
Bury, The 19, 60, 111, 124, 131, 158, 160, 161, 171
butts 109
Buxton 188, 190, 192

Caesar 25
Cam 41, 214, 215
Cambridge 18, 24, 34, 69, 75, 104, 144, 155, 189, 191, 196, 209, 223
Cambridge, John of 69
Campion 98, 122, 124, 134, 140, 147, 154, 163
Caratacus 26
Cassivelaunus 25
Catuvellauni 25
Chapman 167, 171, 178, 194
Chardwell 62, 79, 133, 163, 209
Charles, King 152, 153
Chatteris manor 60, 63, 65, 69, 91, 99
Chatteris nunnery 55, 69, 100
Chichely 134, 145
Chishill 16
Christianity 43, 51, 54
church 51, 60, 64, 85, 93, 157, 217
churchwardens 148, 151, 153, 155, 182, 185, 197, 211
Civil War 152

249

Social History in Paladin Books

The Common Stream   £1.95 □
Rowland Parker
The history of a Cambridgeshire village from the first traces of human
settlement to the present day, and the common stream of ordinary
men and women who have lived and died there. 'Beautifully written,
imaginative and truthful.' **Ronald Blythe**

Men of Dunwich   £1.95 □
Rowland Parker
An imaginative reconstruction of the life of an ancient community
in East Anglia, which, over the centuries, took its living from the
sea, until finally the sea assailed, eroded and then engulfed the
community. Illustrated.

American Dreams: Lost and Found   £2.95 □
Studs Terkel
From Miss USA to an unknown New York cab driver – these frank
confessions, woven together by a master craftsman, represent the
authentic voice of America. A rum and original piece of social history
that will surprise, shock and move you.

To order direct from the publisher just tick the titles you want
and fill in the order form.   PAL7382

History in Paladin Books

Africa in History   £2.95 ☐
Basil Davidson
Revised edition of 'one of the most durable and most literate guides to
contemporary knowledge of Africa' *Tribune*

A Higher Form of Killing   £2.50 ☐
Robert Harris and Jeremy Paxman
The escalating nuclear capabilities of the superpowers have been
extensively publicized. Less well documented has been the revival of
interest in chemical and biological weaponry. Drawing extensively
on international sources, this book chronicles for the first time the
secret history of chemical and germ warfare. Illustrated.

Decisive Battles of the Western World (Vols 1 & 2)   £3.95 ☐
J F C Fuller   each
The most original and influential military thinker Britain has ever
produced: his major work.

The Paladin History of England – the first three titles of the series are

The Formation of England   £2.95 ☐
H P R Finberg
This volume deals with Britain in the Dark Ages between Roman and
Norman conquests.

The Crisis of Imperialism   £3.95 ☐
Richard Shannon
England in the realm of Victoria. A time of development, expansion,
colonisation, enormous social upheavals and reform.

Peace, Print and Protestantism   £3.95 ☐
C S L Davies
C S L Davies' book deals with the period 1450–1558 encompassing
the reign of the Tudors and the breakaway from the Church of Rome.

To order direct from the publisher just tick the titles you want
and fill in the order form.
                                                        PAL7082

Anthropology in Paladin Books

Humankind £2.95 ☐
Peter Farb
A history of the development of man. It provides a comprehensive picture of how we evolved to reach our present state, and analyses the remarkable diversity of human beings.

Shabono £2.95 ☐
Florinda Donner
'A masterpiece . . . It is superb social science because in describing her experiences among the Indians of the Venezuelan jungle Florinda Donner plummets the reader into an unknown but very real world' *Carlos Casteneda*

The Mountain People £2.50 ☐
Colin Turnbull
A remarkable and gripping account of two separate periods in which Turnbull lived with a declining African tribe, the Ik, in a mountain area on the borders of Uganda and Kenya.

The Forest People £2.50 ☐
Colin Turnbull
A fascinating study of the Pygmies of the Ituri Forest – a vast expanse of dense, damp and inhospitable forest in the heart of Stanley's 'Dark Continent'.

Lucy: The Beginnings of Humankind £2.95 ☐
Donald C Johanson and Maitland A Edey
'A riveting book that is at once a carefully documented report, an exciting adventure story, and a candid memoir of a brash young palaeoanthropologist . . . What Lucy suggests about our forebears will keep palaeoanthropologists arguing for years' *Publishers Weekly*. Illustrated

To order direct from the publisher just tick the titles you want and fill in the order form.

All these books are available at your local bookshop or newsagent, or can be ordered direct from the publisher.

To order direct from the publishers just tick the titles you want and fill in the form below.

Name _____

Address _____

_____

Send to:
Paladin Cash Sales
PO Box 11, Falmouth, Cornwall TR10 9EN.

Please enclose remittance to the value of the cover price plus:

UK 45p for the first book, 20p for the second book plus 14p per copy for each additional book ordered to a maximum charge of £1.63.

BFPO and Eire 45p for the first book, 20p for the second book plus 14p per copy for the next 7 books, thereafter 8p per book.

Overseas 75p for the first book and 21p for each additional book.

Paladin Books reserve the right to show new retail prices on covers, which may differ from those previously advertised in the text or elsewhere.